First World War
and Army of Occupation
War Diary
France, Belgium and Germany

56 DIVISION
169 Infantry Brigade
London Regiment 16th (County of London) Battalion
(Queen's Westminster Rifles)
1 February 1916 - 24 April 1919

WO95/2963/2

The Naval & Military Press Ltd
www.nmarchive.com
Published in association with The National Archives

Published by

The Naval & Military Press Ltd
Unit 10 Ridgewood Industrial Park,
Uckfield, East Sussex,
TN22 5QE England
Tel: +44 (0) 1825 749494

www.naval-military-press.com
www.nmarchive.com

This diary has been reprinted in facsimile from the original. Any imperfections are inevitably reproduced and the quality may fall short of modern type and cartographic standards.

© **Crown Copyright**
Images reproduced by permission of The National Archives, London, England, 2015.

Contents

Document type	Place/Title	Date From	Date To
Heading	WO95/2963/2 1916 Feb-1919 May 1/16 Battalion London Regiment (Queen's Westminsters)		
Heading	56th Division 169th Infy Bde 1-16th Bn London Regt Feb 1916-1919 May		
Heading	War Diary Of The 1/Queen's Westminster Rifles 1/16 Bn London Regt. T.F Vol XV		
War Diary		01/02/1916	31/05/1916
Miscellaneous	War Diary		
War Diary		01/06/1916	30/06/1916
Miscellaneous	H.Q. 169th I.B	27/06/1916	27/06/1916
Miscellaneous	Not To Be Taken Beyond Bn. H.Q. In Y Sector	27/06/1916	27/06/1916
Miscellaneous	Stores to be Carried in Assault		
Map	Assembly Formations		
Map	Map		
Heading	169th Brigade 56th Division 1/16th Battalion The London Regiment July 1916		
Heading	1st Queens Westminster Rifles (16th London Regt) War Diary July 1916		
War Diary		01/07/1916	31/07/1916
War Diary	Hebuterne	01/07/1916	01/07/1916
War Diary	J.S. Engall	01/07/1916	01/07/1916
War Diary	Hebuterne	01/07/1916	01/07/1916
War Diary	E.H. Bovill	01/07/1916	01/07/1916
War Diary	Hebuterne	01/07/1916	01/07/1916
Miscellaneous	Attack On Gommecourt	01/07/1916	01/07/1916
Heading	169th Brigade 56th Division 1/16th Battalion London Regiment (Queens Westminster R) August 1916		
War Diary		01/08/1916	31/08/1916
Heading	169th Brigade 56th Division 1/16th Battalion London Regiment September 1916		
War Diary		01/09/1916	30/09/1916
Diagram etc	Diagram		
Miscellaneous	56th Division	27/10/1916	27/10/1916
War Diary		01/10/1916	30/04/1917
Operation(al) Order(s)	1st Battn Queens Westminster Rifles Operation Orders No.85		
Miscellaneous	Administrative Instructions With Reference To Operation Orders No.85	06/04/1917	06/04/1917
War Diary		01/05/1917	31/07/1917
Heading	War Diary Of 1/16th Battn The London Regt. (Queens Westminster Rifles) From 1st August 1917 To 31st August 1917 Vol 33		
War Diary		01/08/1917	31/08/1917
Heading	War Diary Of 1/16th Bn The London Regt. From 1st September 1917 To 30th September 1917 Vol 34		
War Diary		01/09/1917	30/09/1917
Heading	War Diary Of 1/16th Bn The London Regt. From 1st October 1917 To 31st October 1917 Vol 35		
War Diary		01/10/1917	31/10/1917

Heading	War Diary 1/16th London Regt. November 1917 Vol 36		
Miscellaneous	Cover For Documents. Nature Of Enclosures.		
Miscellaneous	56th Div.	11/12/1917	11/12/1917
War Diary		01/11/1917	30/11/1917
Miscellaneous	Amendment To War Diary For Month Of November 1917	22/11/1917	22/11/1917
Heading	War Diary 1/16th London Regt. (QWR) December 1917 Vol 37		
War Diary		01/12/1917	31/12/1917
Heading	War Diary Of 1/16th Bn The London Regt. For Month Of January 1918 Vol 38		
War Diary		01/01/1918	31/01/1918
Heading	War Diary 16th London Regiment (Q.W.R.) February 1918 Vol 39		
War Diary	In The Field	01/02/1918	28/02/1918
Operation(al) Order(s)	1st Battn Queens Westminster Rifles. Operation Order No. G.13	07/02/1918	07/02/1918
Heading	16th Battn. The London Regiment (1st Queen's Westminster Rifles) March 1918		
War Diary	In The Field	01/03/1918	31/03/1918
Miscellaneous	HQ 169 IB	01/04/1918	01/04/1918
Miscellaneous	Narrative Of Operations	28/03/1918	28/03/1918
Heading	169th Brigade 56th Division (Queen's Westminsters) 1/16th Battalion The London Regiment April 1918		
War Diary	In The Field	01/04/1918	30/04/1918
Heading	War Diary 1/16th London Regt. (Q.W.R.) May 1918 Vol 42		
War Diary	In The Field	01/05/1918	31/05/1918
Heading	War Diary 16th London Regiment (Q.W.R.) June 1918 Vol 43		
War Diary	In The Field	01/06/1918	30/06/1918
Heading	War Diary 1/16th London Regt (Q.W.R.) For Month Of July 1918 Vol 44		
War Diary	In The Field	01/07/1918	31/07/1918
Miscellaneous	Report On Raid		
Heading	War Diary 1/16th London Regt. (Q.W.R.) For Month Of August 1918 Vol 45		
War Diary	In The Field	01/08/1918	31/08/1918
Map	Map		
Heading	War Diary 1/16th London Regiment (QWR) For Month Of September 1918 Vol 46		
War Diary	In The Field	01/09/1918	30/09/1918
Operation(al) Order(s)	1st Queens Westminster Rifles Order No. 73	24/09/1918	24/09/1918
Miscellaneous	Instructions No.1	25/09/1918	25/09/1918
Operation(al) Order(s)	1st Queens Westminster Rifles Order No. 73	26/09/1918	26/09/1918
Miscellaneous	Instructions No.2	26/09/1918	26/09/1918
Miscellaneous	Instructions No.3	26/09/1918	26/09/1918
Miscellaneous	Addition To Instructions No.3	26/09/1918	26/09/1918
Heading	War Diary 1/16th London Regiment (Q.W.R.) For Month Of October 1918 Vol 47		
War Diary	In The Field	01/10/1918	31/10/1918
Heading	War Diary Queens Westminster Rifles 1/16 London Rgt Vol 48		
War Diary	In The Field	01/11/1918	30/11/1918

Heading	War Diary December 1918 1/16th London Regiment Vol 49		
War Diary	In The Field	01/12/1918	31/12/1918
Miscellaneous	Appendix A Monsieur le Commandant, Messieurs les Officers, Messieurs,		
War Diary	In The Field	01/01/1919	31/01/1919
War Diary	Genly Belgium	01/02/1919	24/03/1919
War Diary	Quaregnon Belgium	25/03/1919	24/04/1919
Miscellaneous	Nominal Roll		

WO/95/2063/2

1916 Feb - 1919 May

1/16 Battalion London Regiment
(Queen's Westminsters)

56TH DIVISION
159TH INFY BDE

1-16TH BN LONDON REGT

FEB 1916 - JAN 1916
1919 MAY

FROM 6 DIV 18 BDE

WAR DIARY.

of the

1/Queens Westminster Rifles

1/16 B⁰ London Regt T.F.

1-2-1916 — 29-2-1916

Vol. ~~X~~ XV

N/wounded 2ⁿᵈ Lt Comm'd

169ᵗʰ Bde.

WAR DIARY or INTELLIGENCE SUMMARY

Army Form C. 2118

Place	Date	Hour	Summary of Events and Information	Remarks and references to Appendices
	1/2/16		Nothing to report, visible S.E wind: POTIJZE shelled in afternoon and C/Lt.M. Adkins, his batman, and Rifleman Wingfield who had gone to look after Adkins, all sheltered in H.Q. R.E. Officer (& Clerk & Signaller) who motored up to Potijze Cross Roads, stayed there 5 mins. and then away again - damn him. Can have nothing except stray fire on the Influence inhabitants. We moved out of the front line altogether but left one company in Brigade Labialis - Lieut O.R. 2. Reinforcements O.R. 2. Officer cause. A.A. S. Officer Base. "B" Company report Company relief at night into Potijze taking "B" Company back to CANAL BANK. "S" Company to POTIJZE "S" Company back to POPERINGHE.	
	2/2/16		Casualties - Wounded 3 O.R. Sick 3 O.R. Other causes 2 to command 1 to discharge Reinforcements 2 O.R. Nothing to report, went back same as times S.W. Casualties - Sick 6 O.R. Reinforcements 2 O.R.	
	3/2/16		"B" Company withdrawn from POTIJZE back to CANAL BANK in anticipation of the move away from Brigade area. Division situation to-night "B" & "C" Companies in POPERINGHE "B" & "C" Companies on CANAL BANK. Casualties - Sick 4 O.R. Other causes 1 officer 3 O.R. (Officer and 1 O.R. Reinforcements 6 O.R.	

WAR DIARY or INTELLIGENCE SUMMARY

(Erase heading not required.)

Army Form C. 2118

Place	Date	Hour	Summary of Events and Information	Remarks and references to Appendices
	5/2/16		"B" & "C" Companies withdrawn to POPERINGHE. Headquarters remained at CANAL BANK. A fine bright day and a fair amount of aeroplane & artillery activity in consequence. Casualties - Nil. 3 O.R. Other ranks 2 O.R.(common) Reinforcements 4 O.R.	
	6/2/16		Headquarters moved to POPERINGHE. Casualties - Sick 1 O.R. Reinforcements 1 O.R.	
	7/2/16		Central refitting of companies in POPERINGHE. Reinforcements 1 O.R. Casualties - Sick 1 O.R.	
	8/2/16		General Plumer - 2nd Army Commander inspected the Battalion and wished us good-bye. Casualties - Sick 1 O.R.	
	9/2/16		Brigadier General (Brigadier 18th Infantry Brigade) came round from Canal Bank to visit us & bid us farewell. Battalion entrained at POPERINGHE at 9.30 p.m. Casualties - 3 O.R. to common Reinforcements 2 O.R.	
	10/2/16		Battalion detrained at PONT REMY about 11 a.m. marched about 7 miles to a small village named HUPPY where we were billeted in barns and stables. Casualties - 1 O.R. (Employed men) Reinforcements 2 O.R.	
	11/2/16		General rest and concerted effort to improve billet accommodation for officers and men. Casualties - nil.	
	12/2/16		Training by Companies. Casualties - nil	
	13/2/16		Voluntary Church Service. Casualties - Sick 2 O.R. Reinforcements 2 Officers Captain Savill & Lieut Bull and 32 O.R.	

WAR DIARY
or
INTELLIGENCE SUMMARY

(Erase heading not required.)

Army Form C. 2118

Instructions regarding War Diaries and Intelligence Summaries are contained in F.S. Regs., Part II. and the Staff Manual respectively. Title Pages will be prepared in manuscript.

Place	Date	Hour	Summary of Events and Information	Remarks and references to Appendices
	14/2/16		Brigadier General took of the 169th Infantry Bde. inspected the Battalion in the morning and the transport in the afternoon. Casualties:- Sick 2 O.R. to Brigade 1. to commission 1. to discharge 1.	
	15/2/16		Training - Reinforcements 1 O.R.	
	16/2/16		Training. Casualties, Sick 1 O.R.	
	17/2/16		Training.	
	18/2/16		Training.	
	19/2/16		Training. Reinforcements 1 O.R.	
	20/2/16		Church Parade	
	21/2/16		Training. Reinforcements 1 O.R.	
	22/2/16		Training. Casualties- Sick 4 O.R.	
	23/2/16		200 men sent a trench digging fatigue of 3 hours for Brigade purposes. Casualties - Reinforcements 3 O.R.	
	24/2/16		Training - Casualties 1 O.R. Reinforcement 1 O.R.	
	25/2/16		Training in morning. Fatigue party in afternoon to fill in trenches dug on 23rd. Heavy snow fall all day. Casualties - Reinforcement 1 O.R.	
	26/2/16		Fatigue party clearing roads of snow. Casualties Sick 7 O.R. Reinforcements 1 O.R.	

WAR DIARY
or
INTELLIGENCE SUMMARY
(Erase heading not required.)

Army Form C. 2118

Place	Date	Hour	Summary of Events and Information	Remarks and references to Appendices
	27/2/16		169 Infantry Brigade marched to AILLY a distance of about 12 miles. Though the roads were snow-covered and the weather bad, the Battalion arrived in splendid condition, the men were billeted in barns and 1 Company in the billets. Casualties Sick 13. O.R. Reinforcements 14 O.R.	
	28/2/16		The Brigade remained in the same area. Casualties Sick 5 O.R.	
	29/2/16		1 Officer & Officers' Ranks training.	

Strength on 1/2/16   Officers   O.R.
                            25   638

Less Officers   O.R.
                  3
Wounded Officers   55
Sick   1   33
Odds cases   1

                         Officers   O.R.   Total
                            23   547   570

                          2   91   93
                         25   624   649

Wound
Lieut Colonel
Commdg. 1/ Queens' Westminster Rifles

WAR DIARY
or
INTELLIGENCE SUMMARY
(Erase heading not required.)

Army Form C. 2118

Instructions regarding War Diaries and Intelligence Summaries are contained in F. S. Regs., Part II. and the Staff Manual respectively. Title Pages will be prepared in manuscript.

Place	Date	Hour	Summary of Events and Information	Remarks and references to Appendices
	1/3/16		Training. Casualties sick 1 Officer (Lieut Wiano) 3 O.R. To commission 1 Reinforcements 2 O.R.	
	2/3/16		Battalion route march in morning. Reinforcements 5 O.R.	
	3/3/16		One Company shot a short course on an excellent miniature range. Casualties sick 1 O.R. To commission 2 Reinforcements 1 O.R.	
	4/3/16		Training. Reinforcements 2.	
	5/3/16		Voluntary Church Parade. Casualties sick 10 O.R. To commission 1 O.R.	
	6/3/16		Training. Casualties sick 5 O.R. Reinforcements 1 O.R.	
	7/3/16		Training. Casualties sick 1 O.R. Reinforcements 1 O.R.	
	8/3/16		Training. Reinforcements 2 O.R.	
	9/3/16		Training. Casualties sick 4 O.R. Reinforcements 2 Officers (Capt Whitmore, 2/Lieut Cooke P.E.) 5 O.R.	
	10/3/16		Training. Casualties sick 2 O.R. Reinforcements 4 O.R.	
	11/3/16		Training. Casualties sick 9 O.R.	
GEZAINCOURT	12/3/16		Brigade moved on. The Battalion tickled from AILLY to GEZAINCOURT a distance of about 17 miles. The nature	

R Harding
Captain
Commndg. 1/ Queens Westminster Rifles

Army Form C. 2118

WAR DIARY
or
INTELLIGENCE SUMMARY
(Erase heading not required.)

Place	Date	Hour	Summary of Events and Information	Remarks and references to Appendices
	13/3/16.		Battalion marched in - an excellent performance. The men were fairly comfortably billetted in Barns - Officers accommodation was very poor. Casualties sick 2 O.R. To commission 1. To discharge 1 O.R. Reinforcement 1 Officer (Lieut. Bovill.)	
	14/3/16.		A day of rest. Casualties sick 13 O.R. Reinforcements 10 O.R.	
	15/3/16.		Training by Companies. Casualties sick 3 O.R. To commission 1. Reinforcements 2 O.R.	
	16/3/16.		Training. Reinforcements 1 Officer 2nd Lieut Say. Brigade moved on. The Battalion trekked from GEZAINCOURT to MONCHEAUX about 17½ miles took on this move and on that of the 12th we set Ham the longest trek in the Brigade. The Battalion again marching very well. Casualties sick 21 O.R. Discharged 2 O.R. Reinforcement 2 Officers (2nd Lieut Iveson & Yates) 64 O.R.	
	17/3/16.		Rest. Casualties 8 O.R. Reinforcements 12 O.R.	

P Stawling Capt
Commdg 1/5 [illegible] W[est] Riding Regt

Army Form C. 2118

WAR DIARY
or
INTELLIGENCE SUMMARY
(Erase heading not required.)

Instructions regarding War Diaries and Intelligence Summaries are contained in F.S. Regs., Part II. and the Staff Manual respectively. Title Pages will be prepared in manuscript.

Place	Date	Hour	Summary of Events and Information	Remarks and references to Appendices
	18/3/16		Training. Casualties:- Sick 2 O.R. Reinforcements 12 O.R.	
	19/3/16		Church Parade. Casualties Sick 4 O.R. to hospital 2	
	20/3/16		Training. Casualties Sick 1 O.R. Lieuts Hijson and Young. to rejoin their Unit.	
	21/3/16		Training. Casualties Sick 5 O.R. Reinforcements 3. O.R.	
	22/3/16		Training. Casualties Sick 1 O.R. Reinforcements 1 O.R.	
	23/3/16		Training. Reinforcements 2 O.R.	
	24/3/16		Training. Casualties Sick 3 O.R. Reinforcements 2 O.R.	
	25/3/16		Training. Casualties Sick 4 O.R. Reinforcements 2 Officers (Capt Babel and 2nd Lieut Bryan) and 3 O.R.	
	26/3/16		Voluntary Church Parade. Casualties Sick 3 O.R. Reinforcements 1 Officer (2nd Lieut Bryan) 1 O.R.	
	27/3/16		Training. Casualties Sick 2 O.R. Reinforcements 27 O.R.	
	28/3/16		Training. Casualties Sick 1 O.R. Reinforcements 1 O.R.	
	29/3/16		Training. Casualties Sick 3 O.R. Reinforcements 5 O.R.	
	30/3/16		Training. Casualties Sick 8 O.R. Reinforcements 3 O.R.	

P.S. Harding Captain

Army Form C. 2118

WAR DIARY
or
INTELLIGENCE SUMMARY
(Erase heading not required.)

Instructions regarding War Diaries and Intelligence Summaries are contained in F. S. Regs., Part II. and the Staff Manual respectively. Title Pages will be prepared in manuscript.

Place	Date	Hour	Summary of Events and Information	Remarks and references to Appendices
	31/3/16		Training. Casualties list I.O.R. Reinforcements I.O.R.	

Strength on 1/3/16

	Officers	O.R.	Total
	25	624	649

	Officers	O.R.
Kee		
Sick	1	108
Other causes	2	15
Att.		
Reinforcements	3	123
	22	501	523
	9	178	187

Strength on 31/3/16

| | 31 | 679 | 710 |

B.N. Harding
Captain.
Commanding. 1/16th London Regiment
(1st Queens Westminsters Rifles)

Army Form C. 2118

WAR DIARY
or
INTELLIGENCE SUMMARY
(Erase heading not required.)

Instructions regarding War Diaries and Intelligence Summaries are contained in F.S. Regs., Part II. and the Staff Manual respectively. Title Pages will be prepared in manuscript.

Place	Date	Hour	Summary of Events and Information	Remarks and references to Appendices
	1/4/16		Training. Casualties sick 2. O.R., to R.F.C. 1. O.R. Reinforcements 3. O.R.	
	2/4/16		Church Parade. Casualties sick 1. O.R. Reinforcements 1. O.R.	
	3/4/16		Training. Casualties sick 1. O.R., to discharge 1. O.R. Reinforcements 5. O.R.	
	4/4/16		Battalion Day. - Advance guard scheme. Casualties sick 5. O.R.	
	5/4/16		Casualties to commission 1. O.R. Reinforcements 3. O.R.	
	6/4/16		Training. Casualties sick 1. O.R. Reinforcements 2. O.R.	
	7/4/16		Battalion Day. rear-guard scheme. Casualties sick 3. O.R.	
	8/4/16		Training. Casualties sick 2. O.R. Reinforcements 1 Officer (Capt. Penrose) 26. O.R. (17 from England).	
	9/4/16		Battalion paraded to watch exhibition of a Flammenwerfer which was captured by the 6th Division at Froge. Casualties sick 2. O.R.	
	10/4/16		Battalion Day. rear guard scheme. Casualties sick 8. O.R. 2 Officers (1 Lieut. Engall & Compton) to 169 Brigade Machine Gun Company. Reinforcements 2. O.R.	
	11/4/16		Company Training. Casualties sick 3. O.R. to commission 1. O.R. Reinforcements (1 Officer (Lieut. Bazell) 1. O.R.	

Whroturd
Lieut Colonel
Commdg. 1/ Queens' Westminster Rifles

Army Form C. 2118

WAR DIARY
or
INTELLIGENCE SUMMARY
(Erase heading not required.)

Instructions regarding War Diaries and Intelligence Summaries are contained in F.S. Regs., Part II. and the Staff Manual respectively. Title Pages will be prepared in manuscript.

Place	Date	Hour	Summary of Events and Information	Remarks and references to Appendices
	12/4/16		Company Training. Casualties sick 3 O.R. Reinforcements 9 O.R.	
	13/4/16		Company Training. Casualties sick 1 O.R.	
	14/4/16		Company Training. Casualties sick 4 O.R. Reinforcements 3 O.R.	
	15/4/16		Company Training. Casualties sick 2 O.R. Reinforcements 3 O.R.	
	16/4/16		Church Parade. Casualties sick 3 O.R. Reinforcements 1 O.R.	
	17/4/16		Training. Casualties sick 2 O.R.	
	18/4/16		Training. Casualties sick 3 O.R. Reinforcements 1 O.R.	
	19/4/16		Battalion Day – Route March. Casualties sick 3 O.R. Reinforcements 1 O.R.	
	20/4/16		Company Training. Casualties sick 2 O.R. 1 Officer (Capt Baker) to hospl. Brigade Machine Gun Company. Reinforcements 3 O.R.	
	21/4/16		Training and Church Parade. Casualties sick 2 O.R. Reinforcements 3 O.R.	
	22/4/16		Company Training. Casualties sick 3 O.R. Reinforcements 11 O.R. (5. from England)	
	23/4/16		Church Parade. sick 2 O.R. Reinforcements 1 O.R.	

Whitehead
Lieut Colonel
Commdg. 1/ Queens' Westminster Rifles

WAR DIARY
or
INTELLIGENCE SUMMARY

Army Form C. 2118

Place	Date	Hour	Summary of Events and Information	Remarks and references to Appendices
	24/4/16		Company Training. Casualties. Sick 2. O.R. To commission 1. O.R.	
	25/4/16		Battalion Sports - Glorious weather - "B" Company won the Championship. Casualties 1 Officer (Lieut Horne) 2. O.R. Reinforcements 8 O.R.	
	26/4/16		Battalion Route March. Casualties Sick 4 O.R. To commission 6. O.R. Reinforcements 2. O.R.	
	27/4/16		Company Training. Reinforcements 1 O.R.	
	28/4/16		Company Training. Sick 2. O.R. From 169th Brigade 1. O.R. To 175th Brigade 1. O.R. Reinforcements 1. O.R.	
	29/4/16		Company Training. Casualties Sick 2. O.R. Reinforcements 1 O.R.	
	30/4/16		Church Parade. Casualties Sick 2. O.R. Reinforcements 1 Officer (2nd Lieut J. A. Horne) 9 I O.R.	

Strength on 1st/4/16.

	Officers	O.R.
Less: Sick	1	72
Other causes	3	12

| Add: Reinforcements | 3 | 89 |

	Officers	O.R.	Total
	31	679	710
	4	84	88
	27	595	622
	3	89	92
	30	684	714

M Shoolbred
Lieut Colonel
Commdg. 1/ Queens' Westminster Rifles

1st May 1916.

1/16 London Regt 56
Army Form C. 2118
Vol 18

WAR DIARY
or
INTELLIGENCE SUMMARY
(Erase heading not required.)

Instructions regarding War Diaries and Intelligence Summaries are contained in F. S. Regs., Part II. and the Staff Manual respectively. Title Pages will be prepared in manuscript.

Place	Date	Hour	Summary of Events and Information	Remarks and references to Appendices
	1/5/16		Company Training. Casualties:- 1 Officer (2/Lieut P. E. Coote) and 12 O.R. posted to 169/2 Trench Mortar Battery. Reinforcements 1 O.R.	
	2/5/16		Brigade Sports held at FREVENT. We entered about 50 competitors. Points were allowed for the principal events. We secured no less than 5 first places out of the 9 events which counted points. 100 yards. 1st place Lance Corporal McMillan } 8 points. 2nd " 2nd Lieut N. I. Thurston. 200 yards. 1st place Lance Corporal McMillan } 6 points 3rd " 2nd Lieut N. I. Thurston Relay Race. Won by about 200 yards from the L.R.B. The team was :- Lieut F. L. Boswell Corpl. Knudson A. J. } 5 points Sgt. Bueno G. Rfn. Bright J.	

Whinnel Lieut Colonel
Commdg. 1/ Queens' Westminster Rifles

WAR DIARY
or
INTELLIGENCE SUMMARY
(Erase heading not required.)

Army Form C. 2118

Place	Date	Hour	Summary of Events and Information	Remarks and references to Appendices

	2/5/16 (contd)		Hurdle Race. 1st place Rfn Ratcliffe } 6 points
			3rd " " Bowenham }
			
			Tug of War. We beat the L.R.B. by 2 pulls to 1 in the heats and easily pulled the Q.V.R. in the final - only two pulls being necessary. The team was excellently coached by the Sergt Major - 5 points
			
			We secured 6th place in the obstacle race and also in the ¼ mile through Lance Corporal Roper H.E. and Rfn Griffiths respectively. - 2 points
			
			    Our points totalled 32.
			    Q.V. R's 30.
			    L. R. B. 15.
			    2nd Londons 5.
			
			We were unplaced in the Cross country race, for which 10 and 5 points were given for 1st and 2nd respectively. We also	

Shoothed Lieut Colonel
Commdg. 1/ Queens' Westminster Rifles

WAR DIARY
or
INTELLIGENCE SUMMARY
(Erase heading not required.)

Army Form C. 2118

Place	Date	Hour	Summary of Events and Information	Remarks and references to Appendices
	2/5/16 (contd)		failed in the Grenade Throwing for which the points were 6 & 4. So that, considering the number of successes we got, our position as Brigade Champions was very seriously challenged by the Q.V.R. Casualties:- Sick 3 O.R. Reinforcements 2 O.R.	
	3/5/16		Practice attack on a trench by the whole Battalion. Casualties Sick 4 O.R. Reinforcements 3 O.R.	
	4/5/16		Company training. Casualties:- Sick 1 O.R. 2 Officers (Capt Henshaw and 2nd Lieut Berry transferred to England) Reinforcements 10 O.R.	
	5/5/16		Company training. Gas demonstration attended by those who were not with Battalion during German Gas attack on 19/12/15. Casualties Sick 4 O.R. (1 to discharge 1 O.R.) Reinforcements 4 O.R.	
	6/5/16		Company training. Casualties:- Sick 4 O.R. Reinforcements 1 O.R.	
	7/5/16		Battalion moved from MONCHEAUX to HALLOY. Casualties:- Sick 11 O.R.	

Whitwell Lieut Colonel
Commdg. 1/ Queens' Westminster Rifles

Army Form C. 2118

WAR DIARY
or
INTELLIGENCE SUMMARY
(Erase heading not required.)

Instructions regarding War Diaries and Intelligence Summaries are contained in F. S. Regs., Part II. and the Staff Manual respectively. Title Pages will be prepared in manuscript.

Place	Date	Hour	Summary of Events and Information	Remarks and references to Appendices
	8/5/16.		Rest. Casualties:- Sick 8. O.R. To Hospital off leave 1. O.R.	
	9/5/16.		Company Training. Casualties:- Sick 2 O.R. Reinforcements 1 O.R.	
	10/5/16.		Company Training. Major Harding appointed 2nd in command, Capt. Price appointed Adjutant. Casualties:- Reinforcements 2 O.R.	
	11/5/16.		Company Training. Casualties:- Reinforcements 1 Officer (2/Lieut Thomas) from Reserve Battn, 3 O.R.	
	12/5/16.		Company Training. Casualties:- Sick 3 O.R. Reinforcements 2 O.R.	
	13/5/16.		Company Training. Casualties:- Sick 1 O.R. Reinforcements 1 O.R.	
	14/5/16.		Company Training. Casualties:- 1 Officer (2/Lieut B. Spencer Smith) and 40 O.R. from Reserve Battalion.	
	15/5/16.		Company Training. Casualties:- Sick 1 O.R. Reinforcements 1 O.R.	
	16/5/16.		Company Training. Casualties:- Sick 2 O.R. Reinforcements 5. O.R.	
	17/5/16.		Company Training. Casualties:- Reinforcements 2 O.R.	
	18/5/16.		Company Training. Casualties:- Sick 4 O.R Reinforcements 2 O.R.	

Whitbread Lieut Colonel
Commdg. 1/ Queens' Westminster Rifles

Army Form C. 2118

WAR DIARY
or
INTELLIGENCE SUMMARY
(Erase heading not required.)

Instructions regarding War Diaries and Intelligence Summaries are contained in F. S. Regs., Part II. and the Staff Manual respectively. Title Pages will be prepared in manuscript.

Place	Date	Hour	Summary of Events and Information	Remarks and references to Appendices
	19/3/16		Company training. Casualties:- Reinforcements 4 O.R.	
	20/3/16		The whole Battalion on Corps work. 200 men felling trees for gun emplacements at PAS. 120 men at MONDICOURT station loading and unloading trains. Other fatigues amounting to 130 men on Corps work. Casualties:- Reinforcements 2 O.R.	
	21/3/16		"D" Company moved to MONDICOURT so that also "B" Company less 1 Officer and 40 O.R. Corps work. Casualties:- Sick 2 O.R. Reinforcements 2 O.R.	
	22/3/16		"B" Company returned to Halloy, as one of the working parties of "B" Company was taken over by the 48th Division. Corps work. Casualties:- Reinforcements 2 O.R.	
	23/3/16		Corps work. Casualties:- Sick 2 O.R. Reinforcements 13 O.R. (1 O.R. from England)	
	24/3/16		Corps work. A Reinforcement of 223 N.C.Os. and men arrived from the 2nd/2nd London Regiment. These men had seen service in the Gallipoli Peninsula. Casualties:- Sick 5 O.R. Reinforcements 225 O.R. (including 223 O.R. above mentioned.) Wwound

Lieut/Colonel
Commdg. 1/Queens' Westminster Rifles | |

WAR DIARY
or
INTELLIGENCE SUMMARY

Army Form C. 2118

(Erase heading not required.)

Instructions regarding War Diaries and Intelligence Summaries are contained in F.S. Regs., Part II. and the Staff Manual respectively. Title Pages will be prepared in manuscript.

Place	Date	Hour	Summary of Events and Information	Remarks and references to Appendices
	25/5/16		Corps work. Casualties:- Sick 4 O.R. To commission 2 O.R. Reinforcements 2 O.R.	
	26/5/16		Corps work. Casualties:- Sick 2 O.R. Reinforcements 2 O.R.	
	27/5/16		Corps work. Casualties:- Sick 5 O.R. Reinforcements 3 O.R.	
	28/5/16		Corps work. Casualties:- Sick 4 O.R. Reinforcements 3 O.R.	
	29/5/16		Corps work. Casualties:- Sick 3 O.R. Reinforcements 2 O.R.	
	30/5/16		Corps work. Casualties:- Sick 2 O.R. Reinforcements 1 O.R.	
	31/5/16		Corps work. Casualties:- Sick 6 O.R. Reinforcements 5 O.R.	

Strength on 1/5/16.
    Offrs. O.R.
    30   684

Less Sick   Offrs. O.R.
                    -    84
Other cause   3   16

	Offrs.	O.R.	Total
	30	684	714
	3	100	103
	27	584	611
Add Reinforcements	2	354	356
Total 31/5/16	29	938	967

Whereuntil
Lieut Colonel
Commdg. 1/ Queens' Westminster Rifles

SECRET.

SUBJECT:- War Diary.

The D.A.G.,
    3rd Echelon,
        B A S E.

      Herewith War Diary for the Battalion under my command covering the Month of June 1916.

R Shoolbred
              Lieut-Colonel.
Commanding 1/16th Bn. London Regiment.
    (1st Queens Westminster Rifles).

SECRET.

SUBJECT:- War Diary.

Army Form C. 2118.

1/16 London Regt
Vol 19

WAR DIARY
INTELLIGENCE SUMMARY
PAGE 1.

(Erase heading not required.)

Instructions regarding War Diaries and Intelligence Summaries are contained in F. S. Regs., Part II. and the Staff Manual respectively. Title Pages will be prepared in manuscript.

Place	Date	Hour	Summary of Events and Information	Remarks and references to Appendices
	1916 June 1st		Battalion still at Halloy. Both work during the day. Casualties:- Sick 6 O.R. Reinforcements 3 O.R.	
	" 2nd		Both Work. Casualties:- Sick 6 O.R. Reinforcements 4 O.R.	
	" 3rd		Battalion moved from Halloy to Bayencourt. Transport at Coigneux. Casualties:- Sick 4 O.R. Reinforcements 8 O.R.	
	" 4th		Was at Bayencourt resting. Casualties:- Reinforcements 2 O.R.	
	" 5th		Working parties of about 400 went up to trenches E of Hébuterne improving new fire trench. Casualties:- Wounded 3 O.R. Sick 3 O.R. Reinforcements 12 officers, 6 O.R.	
	" 6th		Battalion dug new fire trench Y/50 in front of S.W face of Gommecourt Park, very successful operation. No casualties. Casualties:- Sick 4 O.R. Reinforcements 69 O.R.	

Whoolrich
Lieut. Colonel
Commanding 1st Queen's Westminster Rifles

Army Form C. 2118.

WAR DIARY
or
INTELLIGENCE SUMMARY
(Erase heading not required.)

PAGE 2.

Place	Date	Hour	Summary of Events and Information	Remarks and references to Appendices
	1916 June 7th		Working parties sent up at night to HEBUTERNE improving new trenches. Casualties :- Wounded 1 O.R. Sick 4 O.R. Other causes 1 O.R. Reinforcement 3 O.R.	
	" 8th		Working parties at night in new trenches. Casualties :- Sick 8 O.R. Reinforcement 5 O.R.	
	" 9th		Battalion move to HEBUTERNE relieving 2nd LONDON Regt in Y Sector. A & B Coys in old front line trenches with Officers posts in new front line trench. C & D Coys in billets in HEBUTERNE in immediate support. Casualties :- Sick 5 O.R. Reinforcement 1 O.R.	
	" 10th		Position of Coys as yesterday. The whole battalion working in the new trenches at night & on the old trenches by day. Casualties :- Killed 1 O.R. Wounded 2 O.R. Sick 3 O.R. Reinforcement 3 O.R.	
	" 11th		As yesterday. Casualties :- Wounded 1 O.R. Sick 9 O.R. Reinforcement 2 O.R.	

Nwoodroff
Lieut-Colonel.
Commanding 1/16th London Regt.
(1st Queens Westminster Rifles)

Army Form C. 2118.

WAR DIARY
INTELLIGENCE SUMMARY
(Erase heading not required.)

PAGE 75.

Place	Date	Hour	Summary of Events and Information	Remarks and references to Appendices
	1916 June 12th		'C' + 'D' Coys relieved 'A' + 'B' Coys, weather becoming very bad and work greatly hindered by the wet. Three patrols went out to obtain samples of German wire and ascertain whether the sap running out from Gommecourt Park had a machine gun emplacement at its head. Personnel of Patrols as follows:— 1. 2/Lt. Webb. } D Co. Sgt. Dawn } 2. 2/Lt. Wagner (2/London a/ta Q.W.R) Cpl. Townsend. Rfm. Wernham. 3. Lt. Westmoreland. Lt. Page. (38th (Central India Horse) a/ta to Bn in Y Sector for instructional purposes. Each patrol brought in specimen of wire which wire (some was cut) but no trace of the sap could be found. The night was exceptionally dark & wet, & the patrols were worked to the utmost. Casualties:— Wounded 2 O.R. Sick 3 O.R. Reinforcements: 1 O.R. N.Woolnough Lieut: Colonel Commanding 1/16 London Regt. (1st Queen Westminster Rifles)	

Army Form C. 2118.

WAR DIARY
—of—
INTELLIGENCE SUMMARY
(Erase heading not required.)

PAGE 4

Instructions regarding War Diaries and Intelligence Summaries are contained in F. S. Regs., Part II. and the Staff Manual respectively. Title Pages will be prepared in manuscript.

Place	Date	Hour	Summary of Events and Information	Remarks and references to Appendices
	1916. June 13th		Everybody working hard on new trenches. Casualties:- Wounded 7 O.R.; Sick 7 O.R.; Other Ranks 2 O.R. Reinforcement 3 O.R.	
	" 14th		Everybody working hard on the new trenches. Casualties:- Killed 2 O.R.; Wounded 2 O.R.; Sick 20 O.R. Reinforcements 3 O.R.	
	" 15th		Weather improving & work rendered much less difficult. Casualties:- Killed 1 O.R.; Sick 18 O.R.; Other Ranks 2 O.R.	
	" 16th		Battalion relieved by L.R.B. & sent to BAYENCOURT in the afternoon. 100 then left behind on R.E. fatigue work. Casualties:- Wounded 1 O.R.; Sick 4 O.R. Reinforcements 3 O.R.	
	" 17th		Battalion at BAYENCOURT. Large working parties sent up to HEBUTERNE by day. Casualties:- Reinforcements 7 O.R.	

Whorwood Lieut-Colonel.
Commanding 1/16 London Regt.
(1st Queen's Westminster Rifles.)

WAR DIARY

INTELLIGENCE SUMMARY

(Erase heading not required.)

Army Form C. 2118.

PAGE. 5.

Place	Date	Hour	Summary of Events and Information	Remarks and references to Appendices
	1916. June 18th		Work as yesterday. Casualties:- Wounded 1 O.R. Other ranks 1 O.R. Reinforcements 1 Officer.	
	"19th"		Work as yesterday. Casualties:- Wounded 1 O.R. Sick 1 O.R. Reinforcements 1 O.R.	
	"20th"		Work as yesterday. Casualties:- Killed 1 O.R. Wounded 1 O.R. Sick 3 O.R. Reinforcements 6 O.R. Casualties:- Sick 3 O.R.	
	"21st"		Battalion moved back to HALLOY by companies in the afternoon.	
	"21st"		Battalion at HALLOY resting. 200 men on both fatigues. All ranks very dirty after the strenuous work and living in the wet trenches. Casualties:- Sick 1 O.R. Reinforcements 1 O.R.	

Ashmead
Lieut- Colonel
Commanding "A" London Regt
(1st Queen Westminster Rifles)

WAR DIARY
INTELLIGENCE SUMMARY

Place	Date	Hour	Summary of Events and Information	Remarks and references to Appendices
At MAILLY.	1916 June 23rd		Bernaville:- Sick 1 O.R. Reinforcements 10 O.R.	
	24th		Battalion practised the attack on dummy trenches - constructed to represent the enemy trenches were to be the objective of the Brigade attack. Bernaville:- Nil	
	25th		Attack practised as yesterday both in the morning & afternoon. Bernaville:- Sick 1 O.R. Reinforcements 1 O.R.	
	26th		Attack practice as yesterday, by whole Div. Smoke was used. Aeroplane up and armoured troops carried R.E. Stores with them. Army, Corps. and Div. commanders were present. Bernaville:- Reinforcement 1 Officer. Ashwood Slark - Colonel, Commanding 1/16th London Regt. (1st Queen's Westminster Rifles.)	

Army Form C. 2118.

WAR DIARY
or
INTELLIGENCE SUMMARY
(Erase heading not required.)

PAGE 7.

Place	Date	Hour	Summary of Events and Information	Remarks and references to Appendices
	1916 June 27th		Battalion moved to ST AMAND. Casualties. Sick 3 O.R. Reinforcements 1 Officer. 3 O.R.	
	28th		At ST AMAND. Casualties: Wounded 2 O.R. Sick. 2 O.R.	
	29th		At ST AMAND. Casualties: Reinforcement 2 O.R.	
	30th		Battalion moved up to trenches at HÉBUTERNE by platoon and took up their position in the Assembly trenches for the attack on GOMMECOURT.	Wounded Lieut-Colonel. Commanding Hon Jordan. Regt: (1st Queen Westminster Rifles)

Army Form C. 2118.

WAR DIARY
INTELLIGENCE SUMMARY

PAGE 8.

(Erase heading not required.)

Place	Date	Hour	Summary of Events and Information	Remarks and references to Appendices
			Strength on 31/5/16.	
				Officers.	O.R.	Total.
				29	938	967
			Less:- Officers. O.R.			
			Killed 1 4			
			Wounded 25			
			Sick 1 123			
			Other drawn - 6			
			___ ___			
			- 158	-	158	158
				29	780	809
			Add. Officers. O.R.			
			Reinforcements: 15 142	15	142	157
			___ ___			
			Strength on 30/6/16. 44 922	44	922	966
			Nivelles Lieut-Colonel			
			Commanding 1st London Regt.			
			(1st Queen Westminster Rifles)			

QWR

H.Q.
169th I.B.

I beg to forward copy of Batt'n orders for the attack.
I regret the irregular form they are set out in, but time prevents my having them re-done —

N Shoolbred
Lt Col
27/6/1916
Cmdg 1/Queen's Westminster Rifles

P.S. I assume I can draw on the Batt'n dumps at the top of YELLOW STREET for grenades - during Z day.
N Shoolbred

Queries: Where do our 20 men join the Sidron T.M.B.? Yankee St.

The Sidron T.M.B. attached to us is advancing behind my 3rd Coy. - do they assemble under in our trenches or in the top of Yankee St.

Copy No. 8

S E C R E T.

Not to be taken beyond Bn. H.Q. in Y Sector.

Reference Map.

1. The object of VII Corps attack is to establish itself in a line which runs approximately from our present front line 250 yds N.E. of the 16 Poplars - East of Nameless Farm - along ridge in K.5.a. & E.29.c. Little "Z" and thence back to our line.

2. The 46th Division attacks from the N.W. and the 56th from the S.W., the two Divisions meet about E.29.c.6.0.

3. The objective of the 168th Bde is to capture FAIR Trench about K.11.d.Q.E. along FARM, FAME, ELBE and FELON to a point in FELL 50 yards N.W. of trench junction in K.5.c.2. This Bde will establish a strong point at the cross trenches of FELL and FELON with EPTE.

K.11.d.1.3.

4. The task of the 169th Bde will be carried out in 4 Phases:-
<u>1st Phase</u>.
To capture from left of 168th Bde along FELL, FELLOW, FEUD - The Cemetery - ECK, MAZE, EEL and FIR and establish 3 strong Points
  (1) Near Cemetery.
  (2) At the MAZE.
  (3) At S.E. Corner of GOMMECOURT PARK.

<u>2nd Phase</u>.
(To take place immediately after 1st Phase.)
To capture EMS, ETCH and the QUADRILATERAL in K.5.a.

<u>3rd Phase</u>.
(To commence directly after 2nd Phase)
To secure the cross trenches at K.5.a.7.8. where INDUS crosses FILL and FILLET, to join hands with the 46th Division along FILL and to consolidate FILLET facing E.

<u>4th Phase</u>. 3 Hours after ZERO time - the clearing of GOMMECOURT VILLAGE and PARK.

5. OBJECTIVES (1ST PHASE).
Right Attack - Queen Victoria Rifles - FELL (exclusive of 168th Bde strong point) FELLOW - FEUD - EMS (Between FEUD and CEMETERY) and the CEMETERY.

Left Attack - London Rifle Brigade - ECK (exclusive of CEMETERY) the MAZE, EEL and FIR.

Centre Attack - Queens Westminster Rifles - to follow right attack from Y 47 and pass over FERN and FEED.

OBJECTIVES (2ND PHASE)
Right Attack - Victorias - (a) EMS to its junction with QUADRILATERAL and (b) consolidate strong points.

Left Attack - L.R.B. - Consolidate strong points.

Centre Attack - Westminsters - to pass over FELLOW capture ETCH and the QUADRILATERAL.

OBJECTIVES (3RD PHASE)
Centre Attack - Westminsters - Secure cross trenches at K.5.a.7.8. join hands with 46th Division along FILL and consolidate FILLET facing E.

OBJECTIVE (4TH PHASE).
The clearing of GOMMECOURT VILLAGE and PARK by troops detailed later.

6. DISPOSITIONS.

The disposition of Units before 1st Phase - The 169th Bde will be assembled before the attack in the Y 47 and Y 48 areas -

  2 Coys of the Victorias in Y 47 and Boyau
  2 " " " L.R.B. " Y 48 " "

Q.W.R. "A" Coy in Y 47 S (R)
  "B" " " Y 47 J
  "C" ½ " Y 47 K (R)
  ½ " Y 47 S (L)
H.Q. Bombers in Y 47-S (L)

Attached to Companies under orders given to O.C. Detachments:-
  1 Section 169th Bde M.G. Coy.
  1 " 169th T.M. Batty.
  2 Platoons Cheshire Pioneers
  16 Sappers 2/1st Field Coy R.E.

3rd Coy Victorias in Y 47 L.
" " L.R.B. " Y 48 L.

4th Coys of all three Battalions ("D" Coy of Westminsters) in the R Line.

2nd London Regt in Bde Reserve in HEBUTERNE.

All communication trenches forward of reserve line must be kept absolutely clear.

(Sketch attached) sheet 9.

7. THE OBJECTIVE OF THE BATTALION - To secure ETCH from its junction with FELL and FELLOW to MJ the QUADRILATERAL, occupy the QUADRILATERAL and FILLET as far as 50 yds N. of the junction of INDUS and FILLET - to consolidate the whole as a fire trench facing E. and establish strong points at

  (a) QUADRILATERAL
  (b) Junction of FILLET and INDUS.

is allocated among Companies as follows:-

"A" Coy is responsible for the N.E. Corner of QUADRILATERAL and EXE Trench running into it = 1 Platoon.
(2) S.E. Corner of QUADRILATERAL and EMS Trench running into it = 1 Platoon.
(3) For securing and consolidating ETCH as far as a fire trench facing E = 2 Platoons.

"B" Coy is responsible for (1) the North side of the QUADRILATERAL (exclusive of N.E. corner where EXE runs into it) = 1 Platoon.
(2) The N.W. Corner of QUADRILATERAL and for the EXE Trench running into it from GOMMECOURT = 1 Platoon.
(3) The W. side of the QUADRILATERAL including its junction with EMS at the S.W. Corner of the Quadrilateral = 1 Platoon.

(Leaving 1 Platoon as Company Reserve).
The H.Q. Bombers and "C" Coy will occupy FILLET and establish touch in FILL with the Division attacking on our left and will consolidate FILLET facing E. and establish the strong point at the junction of FILLET and INDUS.

The Section T.M.B. will establish itself in the QUADRILATERAL in positions notified to O.C. Sections.

O.C. "B" Coy will place one of his Lewis Guns at N.E. Corner of the QUADRILATERAL at Junction of EXE to be in support of the "A" Coy Platoon there.

3.

      2 Platoon Cheshire Pioneers will work in the QUADRILATERAL under O.C. "A" Coy in the consolidation of the E Side of this as a strong point.

      1 Platoon Cheshire Pioneers will be under the orders of O.C. "C" Coy in establishing the strong point to be made at the junction of INDUS and FILLET.

      The BATTN PIONEERS will accompany the two Platoons of "A" Coy who are going to establish themselves in and consolidate ETCH.

      O.C. "A" Coy will be prepared to find an escort to the M.G. in junction of Fellow and ETCH.

8.   The Battn will follow the leading two Companies of the QUEEN VICTORIA RIFLES and will advance to the attack crossing FERN, FEED and Fellow on a compass bearing of 37 true and 51 magnetic from top of YANKEE STREET, which bearing crosses the middle of FELLOW and is a direct bearing on to the 2 chalk mounds in the Eastern end of the QUADRILATERAL. "A" and "B" Coys in front in columns of platoons in line abreast at 80 yds distance, the bombers of "A" on the right of their Platoons, the Bombers of "B" on the left of their Platoons.

      All "A" and "B" Coy Scouts and Observation Men will be in their leading Platoons.

      "C" Coy will advance in lines of

          (1) H.Q. Bombers & No 9 Platoon.
          (2) 10, 11 and 12 Platoons.

	"B" Coy		"A" Coy.	
Bomb Sections on L of each Platoon	No 5 Platoon Lewis Gun With Scouts and Observation men in the ranks.		No 1 Platoon	Bomb Sections on R. of each platoon.
80 yds	No 6 Platoon		No 2 Platoon	+ 1 Lewis Gun
80 yds	Lewis Gun		Lewis Gun	
	No 7 Platoon		No 3 Platoon. Batt Pioneers	
80 yds	Lewis Gun		Lewis Gun	
	No 8 Platoon		(No 4 Platoon. Batt Pioneers	1 Lewis Gun
80 yds	1 M.G.		1 M.G.	
	"C" Coy. H.Q. Bombers		No 9 Platoon.	
80 yds				
	(No 10 Platoon	No 11 Platoon.)		
80 yds	(2 M.G.s	1 Section T.M.B.	No 12 Platoon-)	

                    2 Platoons Cheshire Pioneers

One M.G. will accompany the last platoon of "A" Coy.
One M.G.   "   "   "   "   "   "B" Coy.

4.

The remaining two M.G.s will follow "C" Coy and will go to positions notified to O.C. M.G. Section.

The H.Q. Bombers will preceed "C" Coy's advance and in conjunction with the leading Platoon of that Company will bomb up FILLET and secure the junction of INDUS and FILLET. Details will be arranged by the Battn Bomb Officer with O.C. "C" Coy who will give the H.Q. Bombers the support he requires.

"C" Company will proceed up FILLET as soon as it is cleared. The Section of T.M. Battery (and M.G's will follow "C" Coy's last line.

The two platoons of Cheshire Pioneers will follow the T.M. Battery and the two M.G.s.

As it may not be possible to see the advance of the lines in front on account of the smoke, all these advances will be calculated in so many minutes after ZERO TIME and will in no case be delayed beyond the limit of one minute per wave, so that the leading platoon of "A" and "B" will in no case advance later than 4 minutes after ZERO TIME, the 2nd ones not later than 5 minutes after ZERO time and so on, these times being calculated on the time of crossing the front trench of our own system.

During the advance "A" Coy will keep its right on ETCH Trench and "B" and "C" Coys will leave the CEMETERY about 70 yards on their left and will keep on the E. Side of EMDEN communication trench until they pass over FELLOW when they will require to change direction nearly half left in order to get they required direction for their Objective.

All Company Commanders will ensure that all ranks clearly understand the exact limitations of the objectives of the attack and that it is not allowed to proceed beyond them.

Every German Telephone Wire that is seen will be immediately cut and O.C. "C" Coy will cut buried German Telephone Wire running parrallel to the GOMMECOURT - BUCQUOY ROAD about 40 yards to the North of it. Four or five yards at least must be cut out and taken away.

All Platoon Commanders and all Officers will be in the Lines of Platoons. Platoon Sergeants will be behind Platoon Commanders and in rear of Platoons.

<u>WIRE</u>   If front lines are held up by wire all will lie down and wait <u>in reason</u> till a way through is made.

RUNNERS.
-------- 4 Runners per Coy will be at Battn H.Q. and each O.C. Coy will have 4 with him, and will ensure that all these respectively know their way to Battalion H.Q. and to their Coys.

CONSOLIDATION.
-------------- The vital importance of pressing on with the consolidation of the captured trenches and strong points is to be impressed on all ranks. The success of the attack may entirely depend on the energy and absolute determination of all ranks to get this consolidation done promptly and at all costs.

STRAGGLERS. & WOUNDED.
---------------------- The C.O. relies on there being no stragglers from this Regiment, and that all slightly wounded men will remain at duty till night. No unwounded man, except Stretcher Bearers, will accompany wounded (walking cases) to the rear.

5.

COMMUNICATIONS.
--------- Company and Platoon Commanders will establish communication with the Units on their flanks at the earliest possible minute after establishing themselves in their positions.

GRENADES.
-------- The Grenades which will be carried by each man are for a reserve for the bombers and are not except under exceptional circumstances to be used by the man carrying them.

LADDERS.
------ The 5 ladders to be carried by the 2nd Platoons of "A" and "B" Companies for the purpose of getting into the QUADRILATERAL #1 will be taken from our own Assembly Trenches.
    Our own trenches will need bridging as will the first system enemy trenches which the Victorias are undertaking, so that the advance of the rear waves is not delayed.

WIRECUTTERS.
---------- All men carrying wirecutters will wear white tape on each shoulder strap, and if they become casualties the wire cutters will be taken off them. Tape will be drawn from Q.M. Store.

PRISONERS.
--------- Prisoners under an escort of 10 per cent of their numbers will be marched over the open and handed to the Battle Police of the 2nd London in our own Lines.
    If a batch consists of more than 100 it should be put in charge of an Officer when possible.
    Officers should be kept separate from N.C.O.s and men and must not be allowed to speak to them. N.C.Os should also be separated from men if practicable. Prisoners who have been interrogated by the General Staff must be kept separate from the others.
    Escorts and Guards are forbidden to talk to prisoners or to give them tobacco or extra food. Only Staff Officers, A.P.Ms and Intelligence Officers may converse with prisoners.
    Prisoners must be searched for concealed arms and documents as soon as possible after capture, and also at the Collecting Stations, in order to avoid the destruction of orders containing important information. All documents taken from them should be handed over to the General Staff without delay. The search should be carried out in the presence of an Officer when possible.
    Personal effects (except diaries, letters, etc.,) badges etc., will not be collected unless required by the General Staff. Identity discs are not to be taken from them.

    In the event of any of our own Officers, N.C.Os or MEN being unfortunate enough to fall into the enemies hands they are reminded that all the information they can be required to give is their Rank, Name and Regiment. They will under no circumstances give any further information of any kind whatever.

COMMUNICATION TRENCHES.
--------------------- Communication Trenches when made over the NO MANS LAND and in the German lines will all be reserved for up traffic to the front and will not be used for down journeys.
    In our own trench system YANKEE and YIDDISH STREETS are reserved for DOWN traffic and YELLOW and YOUNG STREETS for UP.
    ETCH is reserved for the use of the WESTMINSTERS

STORES.
------- A list of Stores to be carried in the assault by "A" "B" and "C" Coys is attached hereto.

GRENADES.
-------- Bombers will carry 15 Grenades each.

INFORMATION.
------------ The 6th Bn S. Staffordshire Regt will be the BN of the 46th Division on our left. The Rangers on our Right and then the SCOTTISH.

6.

ARTILLERY.
---------- Artillery Lifts for the 2nd Phase will be timed on the assumption that Infantry Will reach EMS (between ETCH and FILLET) 25 minutes after ZERO Time (time of assault), and EXE (between ETCH and FLEET) ** minutes after ZERO TIME.

27

Artillery Lifts for the 3rd Phase will be timed on the assumption that the Infantry reach cross trenches at K.5.a.7.8. by 35 minutes after ZERO Time.

F.O.O.s are being pushed forward to the QUADRILATERAL as soon as it is captured.

CORRESPONDENCE AND MAPS.
------------------- No copies of Maps in which our present trenches are marked and no copies of orders will be take forward by assaulting troops. All private correspondence should be burnt or left behind.

S.A.A., RATIONS" Etc.
------------------- S.A.A. GRENADES, STOKES SHELLS, WATER, RATIONS and VERY PISTOLS and AMMUNITION will be carried up to the captured positions by "D" Coy. Position of Dumps has been notified to O.C. "D" Coy.

WATER.
------- All ranks are warned to be very careful in the use of water as it may not be possible to carry up a fresh supply until nightfall.

LOOTING.
------- All ranks are to be warned that the most *detected* extreme disciplinary action will be taken in the case of any soldier looting, or found in possession of, or to have disposed of, any article from the dead.

HEADQUARTERS.
-------------- Battalion H.Q. will be situated in YANKEE STREET at corner of Orchard.
Brigade H.Q. will be situated in Y Sector Battn H.Q.

FIRING.
------- There should be no firing into GOMMECOURT.

Report centre is in a dug out at the top of YELLOW STREET

Copy no 1. Office copy
2. O.C. A Co
3. " B
4. " C
5. " D
6. " M.G. Section
7. " T.M.B. Section
8. H.Q. 169th I.B.
9. Gap"
10. Major Harding

issued at 1 P.M. 27/6/1916

R Shoolbred
Lieut-Colonel,
Commanding 1/16th London Regiment,
(Queens Westminster Rifles).

STORES TO BE CARRIED IN ASSAULT

"A" to be carried by everyone (Sandbags   3 tucked in belt.
                               (S.A.A.   220 rounds.
                               (Grenades   3
                               (Smoke Helmets 2
                               (Rations   Iron and 1 days
                               (Filled Water Bottle.

"A" Company.

No.1 Platoon.

"A" and
Wirecutters   25
Wirebreakers   1 on every rifle.
Bill hooks   4
Wiring Gloves.   20
Staples.   20

No.2 Platoon.

"A" and
Shovels)   One man in 3 carries a pick and the re-
Picks   )   mainder a shovel. Except Lewis Gunners
                               and Bombers.

Wirebreakers   Balance of issue to Company.
Bill hooks,   4
Bridges   5
Ladders   5
wiring gloves   9

No.3 Platoon.

"A" and
Shovels)   One man in 3 carries a pick and the re-
Picks   )   mainder a shovel. Except Lewis Gunners
                               and Bombers.

French Wire   10 coils (small).
Barbed Wire   5   "
Pickets   22
Staples   20
Bill hooks.   4

No. 4 Platoon,

"A" and
Shovels)   One man in 3 carries a pick and
Picks   )   the remainder a shovel. Except Lewis
and   Gunners and Bombers.
same as
No.3.

5 men to be found to carry Stoke Shells.

"B" Company.

No.5 Platoon.

"A" and
Wirebreakers   1 on every rifle,
Wirecutters.   20
Bill Hooks   4
Wiring gloves   20.

No.6 Platoon,

"A" and
Wirebreakers   Balance of issue to Company.
Shovels)   One man in 3 carries a pick and the re-
Picks   )   mainder a shovel. Except Lewis Gunners a
                               Bombers.

No. 6 Platoon (Contd).

          Bill hooks   4   *wirecutters 5.*
          Bridges   5   *gloves 8.*
          Ladders   5

No. 7 Platoon.

    "A" and
    Shovels) One man in 3 carries a pick and the re-
    Picks   ) mainder a shovel except Lewis Gunners
                   and Bombers.

    French Wire   5 coils (small)
    Barbed Wire   5 coils
    Pickets   22
    Staples   20

No. 8 Platoon.

    "A" and
    Shovels) One man in 3 carries a pick and the re-
    Picks   ) mainder a shovel except Lewis Gunners
                   and Bombers.

    Sandbags   50
    French Wire   4 Coils.
    Barbed Wire   3 "   *10 men carry Stokes SHELLS.*
    Pickets   10
    Staples   10

"C" Company.

No. 9 Platoon
with H.Q. Bombers.

    "A" and Wirecutters ~~15~~ 8
    Shovels   16
    Picks   4
    ~~Wirecutters~~   8
    Bill Hooks   4 *11*
    Wirebreakers   10
    Wiring Gloves   7

No. 10 Platoon.

    "A" and Shovels   16
    Picks   4
    French Wire   10 Coils   *billhooks 3.*
    Staples   20   *wirebreakers 10*
    Pickets   20   *gloves 7.*

No. 11 Platoon.

    "A" and Shovels   16
    Picks   4   *billhooks 3.*
    French Wire   8 Coils   *wirebreakers 10*
    Barbed Wire   4 Coils.   *gloves 7*
    Pickets   18
    Staples   20
    Sandbags   4 men carrying ~~50~~ *40* each.

No. 12 Platoon.

    "A" and 5 Men carrying Stoke Shells.

    Shovels   16
    Picks   4
    Barbed Wire   4 Coils
    French Wire   8 Coils.
    Pickets   10
    billhooks   3
    Gloves   5

ASSEMBLY FORMATION
1/162 METRES

W SECTOR

Y47 O.V.R.

Y47 J B° — "A" ROYALS

Y47 S. — "C" 4 Platoons / H.Q Bombers

10 — 11 — Y47 K — 12 Platoons "C" Coy

Y47 L (Company) O.V.R.

D. Co 1/4 R. Lincs in Reserve
YANKEE ST.

BOYAU

T.M.B Sec ½ Q.W.R.

Y48. — L.R.B.

Y48.S. — Yank St

Y48.S.

Y48 — Third Company

Y48 L. — Third Company

YIDDISH ST

YELLOW ST

R LINE — 4TH COMPANIES

HEDGE

O.V.R. ————
L.R.B. ————
O.W.R. ············

16 Londons

STRONG POINT TO BE CONSOLIDATED HERE.

INDUS — INDUS

FILLET

B Coy. 1 LEWIS GUN.

170x

M.G.

100x

No 6 PLATOON.   No. 5 PLATOON.   No 1. PLATOON

70x

No 7 PLATOON.   No 8 PLATOON IN Coy RESERVE   No. 2. PLATOON.

A. Co. 1 LEWIS GUN.

150x

GERMAN WORK MAY BE M.G. POSITION.

No 3 PLATOON

EMS

(NOTE. Q.V.R. BOMB UP EMS)

H.Q. BOMBERS & "C" COY GOING UP INTO FILLET TO CONSOLIDATE & ESTABLISH STRONG POINT AT JUNCTION OF INDUS & FILLET
H.Q. BOMBERS — No 9 PLATOON
10 PLATOON — 11 PLATOON
2 M.G'S and TM'S — 12 PLATOON
2 PLATOONS CHESHIRE PIONEERS.

No 4 PLATOON
1 LEWIS GUN

ETCH

EMDEN   FELLOW   FELL

I.M.G.

NO SCALE.

169th Brigade.
56th Division.

1/16th BATTALION

THE LONDON REGIMENT

JULY 1916

Report on attack on GOMMECOURT 1st July.
Notes on the attack.

1ST QUEENS WESTMINSTER RIFLES.

(16TH LONDON REGT)

CONFIDENTIAL WAR DIARY.

JULY - 1916.

R Shoolbred Lieut Colonel
Commdg, 1/ Queens' Westminster Rifles

1916

July 1st Attack on GOMMECOURT (detailed report attached)
Survivors of the Battn remained in Road Support
~~Trenches at HEBUTERNE~~ during the night July 1st
to 2nd.
Casualties - Killed Offs 2 O.R. ~~22~~ 16, Wounded Offs
9 O.R. ~~155~~ 124, Missing Offs 9 O.R. ~~318~~ 241, Sick O.R. 1
Other causes 1 Reinforcement 1 O.R.

" ~~2nd~~ Survivors of the Battn numbering 198 marched to
BAYENCOURT and were billetted there for the night

" 3rd Battalion moved to ST AMAND. Casualties Wounded 10 O.R.
Sick 9 O.R.

" 4th At ST AMAND resting. Reinforcement 268 O.R.

" 5th At ST AMAND resting. Casualties Sick 6 O.R.
Other Causes 2 O.R. Reinforcements 8 O.R.

" 6th Battalion moved to FONQUEVILLERS and took over
Trenches from 4th London Regt. Two and a half
Coys in front line. 1 Coy at SNIPER'S SQUARE
Half Coy in cellars at FONQUEVILLERS. Parts of
fire trenches 2'6" deep in water. Communication
Trenches waist deep in parts. Trenches as bad
as any the Battalion has ever taken over. Part
of Trench Z 48 on S. Side of FONQUEVILLERS-LA BRAYELLE
ROAD has been blown in by hostile shelling and in
parts was waist deep in water.

"A" Coy   SNIPERS SQUARE
"B" "   REGENTS ST to ROBERTS AV.
"C" "   2 platoons in Z 47
"D" "   REGENT ST to LE BRAYELLE Road
          2 platoons
          (2 platoons in Village)

Casualties Sick 4 Reinforcement 8 O.R.
Wounded 3.

" 7th Very wet day. Trench Z 48 falling in in places. M.O.
started a drying room in the village enabling the
men to ~~thoroughly~~ change their socks and thoroughly
take care of their feet. There were no cases of
trench feet evacuated to Field Ambulance during
this tour in trenches. The wet in Z 47 and 48 made
it necessary to organise frequent inter Company
reliefs.
Casualties Sick 1 O.R. Reinforcements 6 O.R.

" 8th Very wet day. Started pumping in the trenches.
"A" Coy relieved "B" Coy. "D" Coy moved up one
Platoon from FONQUEVILLERS to hold the BASTION by
night. This platoon moved over to the N. of
LA BRAYELLE Road just before daylight and took over
from the 5th LINCOLNS.
Casualties Wounded 1 O.R. Other causes 1 O.R.
Reinforcements 2 O.R.

" 9th Fine day. Continual pumping day and night.
The remaining 3 platoons of "D" Coy took over
~~from 5th LINCOLNS in Z 49 & 50~~ "C" Coy taking over
from "D"
Casualties Killed 1 O.R. Sick 2 O.R.
Reinforcements 2 O.R.

3

PAGE 2.

1916

July 10th Fine Day. Continual pumping day and night.
           Wiring all along the front and in LA BRAYELLE
           road valley.
           "B" Coy relieved "A" Coy.
           Casualties Wounded 1 O.R. Sick 1 O.R.
           Reinforcements 2 O.R.

"   11th   Fine day. Pumping trenches, baling and
           clearing day and night and wiring.
           L.R.B. relieved "B" Coy who went into cellars in
           FONQUEVILLERS.
           "C" Coy heavily shelled by 5.9"
           Reinforcement 65 O.R.

"   12th   Wet day. Work as yesterday.
                "A" Coy relieved "C" Coy in Z 47 & 48.
           "C" Coy went back to village.
                "B" Coy went to SNIPERS SQUARE.
           Casualties Sick 1 O.R. Reinforcements 2 O.R.

"   13th   A little rain. Work as yesterday. Patrol
           under 2nd Lt DYSON went out at 12-10 a.m. 14th

           Report on Patrol night of 13/14th July.
           ───

           PERSONNEL.
           ─────────
                     1 2nd Lt Dyson.   )
                     2 Sgt Step   ) Patrol leaders
                     3   " Hicks   )
                     4 L/C Jones   )
                    and 20 O.R.s

                Sgt Step states that the above patrol,
           told off in 3 parties, went out together from
           the advanced trench at 12-10 a.m. on 14th
           July as far as the poplar and 80 to 100 yards
           to right of it. The patrol then split up,
           Sgt Hicks taking 6 men to the poplar, Sgt
           Step took 6 men to the corner of Z hedge.
           Lieut Dyson took remainder to the right near
           the "Z"
                SGT STEP. There were three lines of wire,
           not cut. They got through wire on to parapet
           about 30 yards to right of corner. Lieut
           Dyson's patrol closed down to left joining up
           with Sgt Step. Trench appeared quite empty.
           All closed to corner of hedge and found dugout
           under parapet. A German came out of the dugout
           and as soon as he saw the men went back, got a
           rifle and fired at them. Lt Dyson told the
           Germans to come out of the dugout but they did
           not do so. Sgt Step under Lt Dyson's orders
           lay on parapet and threw a bomb into the dugout
           The Bomb exploded and groans were heard. Mr
           Dyson was wounded by a shot fired from behind
           parados, and Germans were seen coming down by
           the hedge and in the open from the rear. The
           Patrol fired on these men and Sgt Step gave
           orders to Retire.

PAGE 3

1916

July 13th (Cont) — Sgt Step and Rfn Lynn helped Mr Dyson over one line of wire and party over the second line, and Sgt Step sent Rfn Lynn on. Sgt Step then called to Mullins to come and help him. Mullins stopped and came back and helped Sgt Step over the second line of German wire. Mr Dyson was by this time quite done and Sgt Step decided to go on and get help and left Mullins with Mr Dyson. Sgt Step reached our own lines and after some delay got help - one S.B. with stretcher and 3 men, and Cpl Smart and himself, but on returning they were unable to find Mr Dyson or Mullins. Sgt Step came back and went out again but was unable to find them and finally returned about 3-30 a.m. L/Cpl JONES states on receiving the order to retire they went half right and so got to the Poplar leaving it on their left hand and saw two Germans at foot of tree. They were taken prisoners - Cpl Jones took one and got him into our own lines at about 1 p.m.
Sgt HICKS' party was on left. Lt Dyson ordered this party to left wheel and circle round Poplar went to catch anyone there. Lieut Dyson, before reaching Poplar went half right and broke connection with Sgt Hicks. He went round the tree and then returned.

Patrol told off in 3 parties left our trench in E.22.d. at 12-10 a.m. Two parties (one under 2nd Lieut Dyson) reached German Line and found it apparently empty. They came to corner of Z where they found a dugout. They called to the occupants to surrender but a shot was the only reply. Sgt Step threw a bomb into the dug out and groans were heard. 2/Lieut Dyson was wounded and Sgt Step ordered the party to return as Germans were seen coming down the hedge.

L/Cpl Jones took his party back via the Poplar, and there saw two Germans, one of whom he took prisoner himself and brought in. The other eventually got away.

Sgt Step left Rfn Mullins with 2nd Lieut Dyson, who was too badly hurt to help himself and went back for help. A party went out with a stretcher but was unable to find either Mr Dyson or Mullins.

Casualties - 2/Lieut Dyson Wounded & Missing
      Mullins Missing.
      Theys) 2/8th Middlesex
      Cotton) Did not return
      Voller) until night of
      Spring) 14/15th July.

L/Cpl Jones knows nothing of these men.
Lynn saw Cotton struggling in German wire, he also saw Voller during the retirement well clear of the German wire and unhurt.

PAGE 4
1916

July 13th (cont) Wounded 1 O.R. ~~Missing~~ other causes 1 Offr O.R.
Sick 3 O.R. Reinforcement 196.

" 14th Last night's patrol casualties definitely ascertained:-
2/Lieut Dyson - Wounded and Missing
Rfn Mullins - Missing
L/C Jones - Wounded

Dispositions - "C" Coy at SNIPER'S SQUARE
"D" " in Z 49 & 50
"B" " " Z 47 & 48
"A" " " FONQUEVILLERS.

Congratulatory message on the achievement of the patrol received from the Corps Commander

"The Corps Commander congratulates the 56th
"Division on the prompt manner in which the
"G.H.Q's request for a prisoner for identity
"purposes was responded to aaa He particularly
"congratulates Colonel Shoolbred and the
"Queens Westminsters for carrying out such a
"successful raid at such short notice."
Casualties 3 wounded Missing 1 Offr 1 O.R.
Sick 9 O.R. Reinforcement 98 O.R.

" 15th CRAWLBOYS LANE and front line trenches now
finally cleared of water and mud. Work
raising floorboards and clearing out foul
bottom of trenches. Revetting in front
Line.
Casualties - Killed 1 O.R. Wounded 5 O.R.
Sick 4 O.R. Other Causes 2 O.R.
Reinforcements 3 Offrs 76 O.R.

" 16th "C" Coy relieved "B" Coy. "B" Coy moved
back to SNIPERS SQUARE. Work as yesterday.
Started digging sump pits in all trenches.
Casualties 4 O.R. Other Causes 1 O.R.

" 17th Started clearing out water and mud from new
trench in front of Z 49 & 50. Other work
as before.
Casualties Killed 2 O.R. Wounded 7 O.R. 1 O.R. sick.
Reinforcement 10 O.R.

" 18th Work as yesterday.
Casualties Sick 4 O.R. Reinforcement 7 Offs
1 O.R.

" 19th "A" Coy took over to the left trenches Z 58
& to 61 from 5th LINCOLNS. Work as yesterday.
Casualties Wounded 1 O.R. Sick 8 O.R.

" 20th "B" Coy relieved "C" Coy. FONQUEVILLERS
shelled during afternoon. "C" Coy went to
SNIPERS SQUARE. Work as yesterday.
Casualties Sick 5 O.R. Reinforcement 12 O.R.

" 21st Work as yesterday.

PAGE 5

1916
July 21st (cont) Casualties Sick 4 O.R. Other causes
        1 O.R. Reinforcements 5 O.R.
                                7

"   22nd Battalion relieved by Queen Victoria Rifles
        during the evening. Battalion moved out to
        ST AMAND.
        Casualties Sick 1 O.R. Reinforcements 2 O.R.

"   23rd At ST AMAND resting.
        Casualties Sick 1 O.R. Other causes 1 O.R.
        Reinforcement 2 O.R.

"   24th At ST AMAND resting. A little Coy Training
        Commenced training fresh LEWIS GUN Teams and
        Bombers. A little range practice.
        (1 Offr + 3 OR) Sick) 4 O.R. other causes 1 O.R.
        Reinforcements 5 O.R.

"   25th At ST AMAND. Training as yesterday.

"   26th At ST AMAND. Training as yesterday.
        Casualties 100 2/8th Middlesex Regt transferred
        to 1/8th Middlesex Regt. Reinforcement 3 O.R.

"   27th At ST AMAND. Training as yesterday.
        Casualties Sick 2 O.R. Reinforcement 4 O.R.

"   28th Inspection of Battalion by Brigadier General
        Commanding 169th Infantry Brigade. Presentation
        of cards from Divisional General to men mentioned
        for gallantry in the attack on GOMMECOURT.
        Casualties Sick 2 O.R.

"   29th At St AMAND Training.
        Casualties Sick 1 Officer 2 O.R. 100 O.R.
        of 23rd and 24th London Regts transferred to
        15th Battn London Regt. Reinforcements 48
        O.R.

"   30th Battalion relieved Queen Victoria Rifles
        in trenches at FONQUEVILLERS.
        Casualties 6 O.R. Sick. Reinforcement 1 O.R.

"   31st Disposition as follows:-

        "A" Coy = SNIPER'S SQUARE,
        "B" Coy = Z 56
        "C" Coy = Z 57 & 58
        "D" Coy = Z 54 & 55.

        Casualties - Sick 1 O.R.

	Offs	O.R.	Total
Strength on June 30th	44	922	966
Reinforcements	10	812	822
	54	1734	1788
Less	23	811	834
Strength on July 31st	31	923	954

Nshooured

Lieut-Colonel,
Commanding 1st Queens Westminster Rifles.
(16th London Regt).

Place	Date	Hour	Summary of Events and Information	Remarks and references to Appendices
HEBUTERNE	1st July	12 noon (Contd)	Our own supply of bombs was exhausted as well as the German ones of which a great number were taken from German Prisoners or found in the trenches in which they were stored in large quantities and at 12.30 p.m. 2nd Lieut J.A.HORNE who had displayed the greatest gallantry during the whole morning, organising and directing men all along YELLOW and shooting with a Lewis Gun when all the team had been knocked out, decided to withdraw to the next line of German Trenches (FERD) and it was in covering this withdrawal that he was hit and believed beyond doubt to have been killed. This left only 2nd Lieut E.H.BOVILL, who had been wounded in the nose very early in the morning, but who carried on most gallantly with his Platoon all day - and 2nd Lieut D.UPTON of all the Officers who went over the top in the morning. This Line of German Trenches becoming also untenable they decided at 1-45 p.m. to withdraw further to the 1st German line, most of them to FERUST where they stayed, still hoping at night to be reinforced and able to hold their own, but at 7 p.m the enemy began to surround them coming in from both flanks and the supply of bombs being entirely used up, as well as all the German ones they could find, they were compelled to retire across the open to our own lines.	
		12.30 p.m.		
		1-45 p.m.		
		7 p.m.		
			2nd Lieut Upton by this time wounded was unable to get away and is missing. He was the Officer who led the bombing party along YELLOW in the morning and he and 2nd Lieut BOVILL had displayed great gallantry all day in re-organising the men and carrying on the attack and defence as long as they had bombs either of our own or enemy ones that could be got, and later when forced to withdraw in carrying out the withdrawal from trench to trench.	
		7.30 p.m.	2nd Lieut BOVILL is reported to have been almost if not quite the last to leave the last enemy trench and it was cruelly hard luck that he should have been killed on the very parapet of our own trench, as he was just stepping into it.	
			MACHINE GUNS. The Vickers Gun which accompanied "A" Coy got as far as the junction of ETCH, FERD, and PRUNY, and was there brought into action by 2nd Lieut ——— (O.W.R. attached 169.Inf.Bde M.G.Coy) who had only one of his team left with him - he fought the gun himself and he was killed at this spot.	

Lieut Colonel
Commdg. 1/Queens Westminster Rifles
J.S. ENGALL

Place	Date	Hour
HEBUTERNE	July 1st	

TRENCH MORTARS. Two of the Trench Mortars were taken up to the enemy front line and probably further - one is thought to have been brought back on the retirement and fired from a shell hole in "No Man's Land" but I have obtained no authentic information on this. The other two, as well as those who were to have gone forward to make the smoke barrage up ETCH and EMS were apparently all knocked out during the bombardment previous to Zero hour.

ACTS OF GALLANTRY etc. Owing to there being no Officer returned from the other side many meritorious acts cannot for the present at any rate be brought to notice, neither those done by men killed and wounded, nor by those who came through it, but I desire to particularly bring to notice the most gallant conduct and bearing of 2nd Lieut J.A.ROWE who by his example and leading inspired and helped all who came within his reach. I have every reason to fully believe that his gallantry and leading merit a recommendation for the Victoria Cross. All who are returned speak in glowing terms of his most gallant conduct. I deeply regret to fear that there is practically no chance of he having survived as he was seen to be wounded very severely.

E.H.BOVILL   I desire also to specially mention 2nd Lieut E.H.BOVILL who though wounded early in the day carried on with his Platoon most gallantly until the final withdrawal during which he was killed.

And 2nd Lieut D.UPTON (2nd London Regiment attached 1st Queens Westminster Rifles) who led the bombing party along FELLOW in the morning and who also did gallant service all day long.

And 2nd Lieut J.S.ENGALL (Q.W.R. attached 169th Inf.Bde M.G.Coy) mentioned above - (Missing and Killed).

Of the N.C.Os and Men - I have the honour to forward the attached reccommendations for immediate reward etc., etc., (See Confidential Papers "Reccommendations for Awards".)

Ashwound Lieut Colonel
Commdg. 1/ Queens' Westminster Rifles

	Place
HEBUTERNE. ATTACK ON GOMIECOURT. ⓑ	
1st July 1916.	Date
	Hour

HEBUTERNE.
July 1st
7.30 a.m.

The Battalion assembled on the night June 30th/July 1st in the assembly trenches in Y.47 area, and at 7.30 a.m. advanced to the attack following the two leading Companies of the Queen Victoria Rifles, - "A" Company on the right - "B" Company on the left - in columns of Platoons in line abreast at 80 yds distance: "C" Company together with the H.Q. Bombers following in similar formation.

"D" Company which had assembled in the old "R" Line and was in support, was moved forward almost immediately by Captain Glasier to the assembly trenches which our front Companies had moved out of - ready to reinforce or take up material for consolidation.

The enemy first and second line trenches were much more strongly held than had been expected and their deep dug-outs seemed practically all to have been undamaged by the artillery bombardment, and both in front of the front line and of the 2nd line enemy trenches a great deal of the wire was not cut at all, so that both the Victorias and ourselves had, in places, to wait and file in close order through the gaps, and many were hit doing this in both these two German Lines. And in both of them a certain number of the enemy who had emerged from their dug-outs or been got out by the Victorias were still engaging their attention. So that, as the advance was being made under heavy Machine Gun Fire from our right from certainly two Machine Guns (one by NAMELESS FARM and one from about 30 yards on the South side of the ETCH communication Trench in the enemy front trench (FEVER) and also under rifle fire from FELLOW itself, the losses were heavy before reaching the bank on the enemy side of the GOMMECOURT - NAMELESS FARM ROAD, which the Victorias were lining. At this point our 3 Companies and two of the Victorias were joined up and intermixed. As no Officer who got as far as this has returned and only one Sergeant, it is extremely difficult to know in detail what happened and still more difficult because signal communication across "No Man's Land" was never able to be established, and as only one messenger from the Companies on the other side of it ever succeeded in getting through, no information except this one message brought by Rifleman Orchard (Signaller) from the GOMMECOURT - NAMELESS FARM ROAD received at 8.30 a.m., was received until the evening,

Ndwrwal
Lieut Colonel
Commdg. 1/ Queens' Westminster Rifles

Place	Date	Hour	Summary of Events and Information	Remarks and references to Appendices
BEAUMONT July 1st (Contd).			what except/was obtained by observation or given by the Royal Flying Corps, and some of what was given by the Royal Flying Corps was, as is not hard to understand, not correct. But clear statements say that Captain G.E.COCKERELL Commanding "B" Coy and Captain H.F.Mott, Commanding "C" Coy were both killed crossing the 1st Line German trench (FERN) and that Captain F.G.SWAINSON Commanding "A" Coy was killed shortly after leaving the 2nd Line German Trench (FEED).	
			It was from this junction of the NAMELESS FARM ROAD with ETCH that 2nd Lieut J.A.HORNE of "B" Company, the senior Officer left, 2nd Lieut A.G.YEATES and 2nd Lieut A.G.NEGUS and 2nd Lieut D.F.UPTON of "C" Coy and 2nd Lieut E.H.BOVILL of "A" Coy, collecting their men together dropped into ETCH Communication trench and bombed up it into and along FELLOW, along which 2nd Lieut UPTON led one bombing party, and thence along FEUD nearly to the Cemetery, where some German bombers held them up for a time. When they had in this way cleared these trenches, they put up one of the Battalion sign boards, on seeing which, the men still lining the NAMELESS FARM ROAD, came over the open and dropped into them.	
			It was by this junction of FELLOW and ETCH that 2nd Lieuts YEATES and NEGUS were killed.	
			2459 Lance Corporal D.Newton, 3513 Rfm A.E.Clark and another bomber tried to bomb up ETCH, but it was too strongly held and they were driven back. They then blocked ETCH and also FELL (the enemy 3rd Line trench to the South of FELLOW) with the assistance of the Platoon of Cheshire Pioneers and of the R.E. Sappers, who are reported to me to have worked most gallantly under the covering fire of a Lewis Gun mounted by 2nd Lieut HORNE and the only gunner left.	
	8.30 a.m.		By this time some more of "B" Coy, among them 3900 Corporal F.E.Hayward, 2nd London Regiment attached Queens Westminster Rifles, some of "C" Coy and some of the H.Q.Bombers worked up by the Cemetery and up EMS and the whole of FELLOW & FEUD were now in our possession.	
			1720 Sergeant W.G.Nicholls who, after Lieut F.Spencer-Smith had been wounded, after crossing the 2nd German Trench (FEUD)had been in command of the H.Q.Bombers Section with some of this Section and I believe led by the	

Place	Date	Hour	Summary of Events and Information	Remarks and references to Appendices
HEBUTERNE	July 1st (Contd)	9.30 a.m.	young Cheshire 2nd Lieut.................. continuing with others, among them, 1687 Corporal R.T.Townsend "C" Company, 2936 Lance Corporal W.C.Ide (2nd London Regiment attached 1st Queens Westminster Rifles) "C" Company, Corporal Hayward "B" Company, 2755 Rfn F.H.Stow "D" Company, up EMS undoubtedly did actually	
		9.0 a.m.	reach the QUADRILATERAL, where a strong enemy bombing party met them and the Cheshire 2nd Lieut ordered our party to retire - apparently trying to cover their retirement himself, as he has not been seen since	
		9.30 a.m.	SUPPORT COMPANY. This Company was ordered at 9.30 a.m. to send a Platoon up with all the bombs they could carry to reinforce the front, thought then to be still held up on the GOMMECOURT - NAMELESS FARM ROAD with written orders to the Senior Officer present to try and bomb up ETCH, EMDEN and EMS. There was by this time only one Officer left with "D" Coy and the Coy Sergt Major had also been killed. 1704 Sergeant H.E.Ironmonger tried to get his Platoon across, but the Machine Gun Fire and Artillery barrage made it impossible and he withdrew the few men who were not hit.	
		11.0 a.m.	At this time another attempt was made to re-inforce the front Companies with the remaining Platoons of "D" Coy and to get bombs up to them, but it was not possible to get through the enemy barrage and Machine Gun Fire. The last remaining Officer of "D" Coy had now been hit.	
		1.0 p.m.	Attempt to reinforce again repeated but it could not be done.	
		1.30 p.m.	It was reported that the front Companies were being driven back from FELLOW. H.Q. Details runners etc turned out to the French trench in front of Cross Street	
		9.0 a.m. to 1.45 p.m.	SITUATION IN ENEMY TRENCHES. These trenches were under heavy Machine Gun fire chiefly from our right. A good many enemy dead were found in these trenches. Many of them, at any rate having been killed during the previous night and this morning's artillery bombardment	
		12 noon	Soon after 12 noon strong bombing counter attacks were made by the enemy both down EMS but principally from the direction of GOMMECOURT and down FIDE.	

SUBJECT:- Attack on GOMMECOURT on 1/7/16.

Headquarters,

169th Infantry Brigade.

Points which occur to me to be worthy of consideration arising out of this day are:-

(1) That nothing like the full value can be got out of Machine Guns if they only have teams of four. The guns so quickly get put out of action through casualties to the personnel. I consider that every Machine Gun should have a team of eight and should go into action with a team of this number.

(2) With reference to Lewis Guns, the drum magazine is so easily damaged, and then, of course, becomes unusable on the gun, and is also bulky and inconvenient to carry. Our Lewis Guns in more than one instance appear on this day to have been unable to be kept in action on account of want of ammunition or of damage to the drums which prevented them from being used, but as none of the Lewis Gun Teams have returned I am unable to give authentic information on the point. Perhaps someone else will be able to say definitely whether there is anything in this or not.

(3) It is again clearly proved that the only way to get up to the number of men who are required for consolidating, and also the stores to do it with, is together with the assaulting troops, otherwise it is impossible to get them up at all. Neither our own Artillery nor the enemy seem able to put in such effective counter battery work as can, on the day of battle, stop the others Artillery barrage.

(4) It is again clearly proved how essential it is for the holding of captured trenches that every man should be a qualified bomber and that a sufficient supply of bombs is taken up with the assaulting troops; it is impossible to get them up afterwards.

(5) COMMUNICATION. To have any chance of standing up to our own front line trenches, all cable must be either armoured or deeply buried; anything else is futile.

(6) R.A.M.C. ARRANGEMENTS. If arrangement had been made to send up 100 <u>fresh</u> bearers with stretchers on the evening of the battle to begin immediately it was dark to look for and collect wounded in "No Man's Land" the whole of the wounded in our Sector could have been collected and evacuated the same night.
The Regimental Stretcher Bearers and Volunteers from the survivors work gallantly and indefatigally as they always do, but there is a limit to what men can do especially after a day of battle and the individual fresh man could have done much more; also there was a considerable shortage of stretchers.

No doubt all these points and others have been already thought out, but I bring them forward just as my own expression of opinion for anything they may be worth.

Nshwollud Lieut-Colonel.
Commanding 1/16th Bn. London Regiment.
(1st Queens Westminster Rifles).

169th Brigade.
56th Division.

1/16th BATTALION

LONDON REGIMENT (Queens Westminster R)

AUGUST 1916

WAR DIARY or INTELLIGENCE SUMMARY

Place	Date	Hour	Summary of Events and Information	Remarks
	August 1st 1916.		Beautiful weather. The three Companies in the front line had large parties out each night putting up barbed wire. In "B" and "C" Companies all other available men were engaged in recovering and improving the new fire trench Z.57 - 61. Enemy shelled LA BRAYELLE ROAD at 9 a.m. with 5.9. No damage. Certain amount of hostile whizz-bangs during the day. Bosch machine guns active during the night and a few light Trench Mortars fell on the advanced trench - not held by us. Enemy seems to be very busy working on his wire and trench. Casualties Sick 4 O.R., Other causes 1 O.R.	
	" 2nd		Work as yesterday. Patrol 1 Sergeant and 6 Men went out to German wire from Z.54 and discovered enemy machine gun but not before the gun had opened on them at a range of about 20 yards. 2 Men wounded but all got safely away. Enemy machine guns active during the night. Our own Machine Guns vigorously replied. Certain amount of whizz-bangs arrived. Casualties - Wounded 2 O.R., Sick 5 O.R. Other causes 1 Officer (2nd Lieut Wagner) posted to R.F.C. with effect from 21/6/16 and 1 O.R., Reinforcement 1 O.R.	
	" 3rd		Work as yesterday. Rather more hostile shelling than usual. Enemy seems to have brought up more anti aircraft guns, but their aeroplanes scarcely ever cross out lines and when they do they do not venture low enough to be able to see anything. Machine Gun duels as usual. Our patrols went out but reported nothing of interest. "A" Company relieved "D" Company in Z.54 & 55. "D" Company moved back to Snipers Square. A good deal of hostile shelling. Casualties Killed 2 O.R., Wounded 1 O.R., Sick 16 O.R., Other causes 2 O.R. Reinforcements 1 Officer (A/Qr.Mr. E.W.N.Jackson gazetted as Hon Lieut & QuarterMaster) and 3 O.R.	
	" 4th		Enemy started an early morning "Hate" on the Division on our left to celebrate the 2nd anniversary of the declaration of the war. A lot of shells and heavy trench mortars were sent over to which our guns made suitable reply. Casualties - Sick 9 B.R.	
	" 5th		Enemy trench mortar paid its unwelcome attentions to Z.54 but did no damage.	

Nihirund Lieut Colonel
Commdg. 1/ Queens' Westminster Rifles

Army Form C. 2118

Place	Date	Hour	Summary of Events and Information	Remarks and references to Appendices

August 5th 1916 (cont)   New R.E. Built firesteps being put in along front line trenches in Z 54 and 55.
         The bursting shells and very lights being sent up can be very plainly seen at night in the direction of the fighting on the N. of the SOMME and make a fascinating picture for those who are not in it.
         Our patrols went out but reported nothing of interest.
         Casualties - Wounded 1 Sick 5, Reinforcement 2 O.R.

" 6th   Enemy shelled FONQUEVILLERS, no damage.
         Casualties - Killed 1 O.R., Wounded 4 O.R., Sick 9 O.R., Reinforcements 3 O.R.

" 7th   Enemy shelled Z 56 & 57 and wounded one men slightly.
         Two enemy staff officers were seen at the top of the Z observing our lines. One was wearing white kid gloves. Our gunners were very slow in getting on to them.
         Battalion was relieved by the Q.V.R. and moved to BIENVILLERS leaving "D" Coy and 30 men of "B" Coy behind in FONQUEVILLERS for R.E. Fatigue.
         Casualties - Wounded 2 O.R. Sick 4 O.R. Other causes 1 O.R. Reinforcement 1 Off 20 O.R.

" 8th   At BIENVILLERS - most of the Battalion engaged on R.E. or carrying fatigue at night.
         Village was shelled for about an hour in the morning - no casualties.
         Casualties - Sick 1 Off., 6 O.R., Other causes 4 O.R., Reinforcements 2 O.R.

" 9th   At BIENVILLERS - fatigues as yesterday.
         Casualties - Missing 2, Sick 8, Other Causes 7 O.R., Reinforcement 2 O.R.

" 10th At BIENVILLERS - Fatigues as yesterday.
         Casualties - Sick 5 O.R., Reinforcements 2 O.R.

" 11th At Bienvillers - Fatigues as yesterday.
         Casualties - Sick 5 O.R. Other causes 1 O.R. Reinforcements 3 O.R.

" 12th At BIENVILLERS - Fatigues as yesterday.
         Casualties - Sick 8 O.R. Reinforcements 2 O.R.

" 13th At Bienvillers - Fatigues as yesterday.
         Casualties - Sick 6 O.R., Other causes 3 O.R., Reinforcements 3 Offs, 3 O.R.

                                   Ashwollid   Lieut Colonel
                                   Commdg. 1/ Queens' Westminster Rifles

Place	Date	Hour	Summary of Events and Information	Remarks and references to Appendices

August 14th 1916.   At Bienvillers - Fatigues as yesterday.
　　　　　　　　Casualties - Sick 8 O.R., Reinforcements
　　　　　　　　　　　1 Off., 2 O.R.

"　　15th　　Battalion relieved Q.V.R.s in trenches Z 54 -
　　　　　Z 61.　Dispositions:-

　　　　　　　　"B" Coy in Z 54 & 55
　　　　　　　　"C" "　" SNIPERS SQUARE.
　　　　　　　　"D" "　" Z 56, 57 & 58.
　　　　　　　　"A" "　" Z 59, 60 & 61.

　　　　　　During the past 8 days out of trenches practically
　　　　　every man has been hard at work on fatigues the whole
　　　　　time, so that it has been impossible to complete the
　　　　　training of Bombers and Lewis Gunners to replace the
　　　　　casualties of the 1st July.
　　　　　　　Casualties - Sick 9 O.R. Other causes 3 O.R.,
　　　　　　　　　　　Reinforcements 1 Offr 42 O.R.

"　　16th　　In trenches.　Carrying on the work of re-
　　　　　claiming the new front line Z 56 - Z 61.
　　　　　　　Casualties - Sick 8 O.R., Reinforcements 8 O.R.

"　　17th　　As yesterday.
　　　　　　　Casualties - Reinforcement 1 Off., 8 O.R."

"　　18th　　As yesterday.
　　　　　　　Casualties - Sick 6 O.R. O. causes 4 O.R.

"　　19th　　Battn relieved by 7th Lincolns (17th Divn)
　　　　　and moved out to ST AMAND.
　　　　　　　Casualties - Reinforcements 6 O.R.

"　　20th　　Battn moved to SUS-ST-LEGER.　Move carried
　　　　　out by Coys at ½ hour intervals.　First Coy
　　　　　started at 7 p.m.
　　　　　　　Casualties - Sick 8 O.R.

"　　21st　　At SUS-ST-LEGER resting.
　　　　　　　Casualties - Sick 5 O.R., Other causes 2 O.R.
　　　　　　　　　　　Reinforcements 2 O.R.

"　　22nd　　169th Inf Bde moved to FROHEN.　Q.W.R. going on
　　　　　to VILLERS L'HOPITAL.　Very trying march - great
　　　　　heat, and many men fell out.　All rejoined in the
　　　　　evening.

"　　23rd　　Brigade moved to ARGENVILLERS, Q.W.R. going to
　　　　　DOMVAST.　Longer march than yesterday but cooler
　　　　　day and fewer men fell out.
　　　　　　　Casualties - Sick 23 O.R.

"　　24th　　At DOMVAST carrying out training.
　　　　　　　Casualties Sick 18 O.R., Other causes 1 O.R.,
　　　　　　　　　　　Reinforcements 8 O.R.

Lieut Colonel
Commdg 1/Queens' Westminster Rifles

Place	Date	Hour	Summary of Events and Information	Remarks and references to Appendices

August 25th 1916.   As yesterday. In the afternoon the Battn marched to the battlefield of CRECY.
              Professor DELBE of CRECY very courteously met the Officers and pointed out various points of interest on the field.
              Missing 1 O.R. Sick 15 O.R. Other Causes 6 O.R. Reinforcements 9 O.R.

"   26th   At DOMVAST training. 217 men of Q.W.R. arrived from 2nd and 6th Entrenching Battalions and 145 men of 8th, 22nd, 23rd and 24th LONDONS were sent down to the base. This exchange almost makes the Battalion one of QUEENS WESTMINSTER RIFLES again.
              The 217 men were delighted to find themselves with their own regiment and the Regiments were are delighted to get them.
              Casualties - Sick 2 O.R. Other causes 1 Off.,
              145 O.R. Reinforcements 1 Off., 206.

"   27th   Battalion attended a Flammenwerfer Demonstration
              Casualties - Sick 2 O.R., Other causes 1 O.R.
              Reinforcement 5 O.R.

"   28th   At DOMVAST training.
              Casualties - Sick 2 O.R. Other causes 1 O.R.
              Reinforcements 3 O.R.

"   29th   As yesterday.
              Casualties Missing 1 O.R. Sick 1 Off.,

"   30th   As yesterday. Heavy rain interfered with training.
              Casualties - Sick 2 O.R.

"   31st   At DOMVAST training.
              Casualties - Sick 1 O.R.

SUMMARY.

	Officers	O. Ranks	Total.
Strength on July 31 -	31	923	954
Add -	10	396	406
	41	1319	1360
Less -	3	407	410
Strength on August 31st	38	912	950

Shepherd Lieut Colonel
Commdg. 1/Queens' Westminster Rifles

169th Brigade.
56th Division.

1/16th BATTALION

LONDON REGIMENT

SEPTEMBER 1916.

WAR DIARY or INTELLIGENCE SUMMARY

(Erase heading not required.)

Place	Date	Hour	Summary of Events and Information	Remarks and references to Appendices

1916

Septr 1st Battn still at DOMVAST training. Casualties 1 Officer sick and 5 O.R. Reinforcements 4 O.R.

2nd Brigade ordered to move to CORBIE. Whole of Brigade Transport left by road for CORBIE. Sick 3 O.R. Reinforcements 1 Officer and 51 O.R.

3rd Battn moved to CORBIE by rail and went into Billets there. Transport arrived at 5 p.m. Casualties NIL.

4th Brigade marched to HAPPY VALLEY - 1½ miles N.W. of BRAY. Battn arrived there after dark and took over 22 tents - about half the Battn bivouaced in the open - night was very wet and cold. Sick 1 O.R.

5th Brigade remained in HAPPY VALLEY. The Battn drew 12 more tents and most of the men managed to get under cover. Casualties O.R. 4 Other causes.

6th Two Battns of the Brigade - the 2nd Londons and L.R.B. moved up in the afternoon. The Q.V.R. and this Battn moved up to trenches just S. of the BRIQUETERIE - about 1 mile N. of MARICOURT - very cold night and nobody got much sleep. The guide could not find the trenches and eventually the Battn did not settle down till about 4 a.m. Casualties NIL.

7th The Battn took over trenches from the L.R.B. about 500 yards N.E. of FAVIERE WOOD. Casualties - 7 O.R. Killed - 1 Officer and 7 O.R. wounded.

8th Battn still in same trenches. Casualties - 3 O.R. Killed 10 O.R. wounded 1 O.R. sick Lieut R.J.H.Bull and servant to Army Signal Service.

9th On the afternoon of 9/9/16 the Brigade attacked N. and E from LEUZE WOOD - Q.V.R. northwards into BOULEAUX WOOD - L.R.B. the sunken road and the trench on the S.E. side of LEUZE WOOD. L.R.B. failed. The Q.V.R. made good part of theirs, but the situation was very obscure and in the evening it was believed that the enemy were in LEUZE WOOD and the Battn was ordered at 7.30 p.m. to move from the MALTZHORN trenches to LEUZE WOOD and drive the enemy out if he had obtained a footing there and to follow him up and capture the trench on the E. side of the Wood which had been the L.R.B's objective in the afternoon.

We had a severe barrage to get through in passing over the FALFREMONT FARM line, but escaped with few losses and got into the wood at just before 11 p.m. and found the Victorias in it but in want of help.

"D" Company was sent to line the Eastern edge of the Wood. "A" Company went to reinforce the Victorias on the North edge of the Wood behind their captured trench. "C" and "B" were got into the Wood and kept in reserve.

Lieut Colonel
Commdg. 1/ Queens' Westminster Rifles

WAR DIARY or INTELLIGENCE SUMMARY

(Erase heading not required.)

Army Form C. 2118.

Place	Date	Hour	Summary of Events and Information	Remarks and references to Appendices
	1916 Septr 10th		At about 1 a.m. on the 10th orders were received from Brigade that the enemy trench on the S.E. side of the Wood must be taken before dawn. The night was very dark and the enemy were pouring heavy shells into the wood without cessation and the position from which to attack this trench as well as the exact bearing of the trench and its distance from the wood were unknown - the maps being known not to be accurate. There was also no communication except by Runner, which took over an hour each way, with Brigade and it was impossible to arrange an earlier hour than 7 a.m. for the attack. "D" Company closed on its left and "C" Company was formed on the right of "D" each attacking in waves of Platoons in line. "D" Company's leading Platoon were ordered to swing to their left to attack the sunken road trench on the N. side of the COMBLES - LEUZE WOOD Road and half the H.Q. Bombers were also given to O.C. "D" Company for the purpose of helping in the attack on this trench. 2nd Lieut Johnston and a patrol from "C" Company reconnoitered the direction of the attack for "C" Company's attack. The casualties during the night were heavy. 2nd Lieuts Apergis and Johnston being killed and some O.R. of "C" and "D" being killed or wounded. I received at 6.55 a.m. a message from Brigade that the artillery barrage had been arranged. A thick mist had come on since 3 a.m. which was still on at 7 a.m., so that you could not see more than 40 to 50 yards, and all promised well, but telephone communication from the Brigade to the Artillery had broken down and the right part of the barrage was never given, in fact there was hardly any at all.	
		7 a.m.	The two Companies went across and got nearly to their objectives when they were held up principally by Rifle & by Machine Gun fire from the trench they were attacking & attacking by Machine Gun fire from the sunken road on the North. The trench was found to be strongly held and Capts Green and Grizelle were obliged to withdraw the remnants of their Companies - some 25 all ranks of each Company - "D" Company pushing a Platoon up to the sap leading from the centre of the wood to the S.E. to guard that flank in case of counter attack.	
		12.30 p.m.	In the middle of the day the Brigadier came up to the wood and ordered a bombing attack up this sap to be made in a last effort to take the enemy's trench. For this purpose "A" Company 2nd Londons, who were also on the East side of the wood, was put under my command, as well as the two Stokes Mortars.	
		3 p.m.	At 3 p.m. the bombing attack started - the 2nd Londons, who were already in our end of this sap being	

RShoolred

Lieut Colonel
Commdg. 1/ Queens' Westminster Rifles

1916
Septr 10th
(Contd).
2.0 p.m.

ordered to clear this sap and its junction with the enemy trench which was the main objective, from which point the Westminsters were to carry on with the capture of the main trench - the attack being made by the remaining men of the H.Q. Bombers supported by "B" and "A" Companies - an artillery barrage working up and along the trench at the rate of 30 yards a minute, was arranged and was given, but it was not successful in keeping the enemy's rifle fire down.

The 2nd Londons pretty well made their objective when Capt Long was killed and the rest came back bringing our men with them and Lieut Webb was unable to stop the retirement. The losses in "B" Company were heavy both during the attack and during the retirement and our casualties during the night of 9th/10th and during this day were

	Killed.	Wounded	Missing.
Officers.	*4	⊗5	-
O.R.	52	166	80

2nd Lieut	*T.S.Apergis.	2nd Lieut	⊗G.W.Cranmore.
"	E.F.Johnston	"	E.GT.Okill.
"	H.Stevenson.	"	H.L.Bell.
"	M.Spencer-Smith	"	C.E.Moy.
		"	W.L.Morgan.

From start to finish we had, as it turned out, no chance. Ordered to attack from a wood we had never been in before on a black dark night and on to a position we were unable to properly locate, and then owing to the breakdown of communication, launched in the morning to the attack without the artillery barrage. And again after some 14 hours exceedingly heavy shelling being sent to it again to bomb up a trench, which as a trench, hardly existed, with hardly any trained bombers to lead the attack, it is no wonder that both the attacks failed, especially as we know, as we learnt later the strength of the sunken road trench from which the enemy were able to bring so heavy a cross Machine Gun fire on both our attacks.

The remains of "B", "C" and "D" were re-organized and lined the Eastern edge of the wood till the evening when the Brigade was relieved by the 5th Division and the Battalion returned to the CITADEL.

Lieut Colonel
Commdg. 1/ Queens' Westminster Rifles

Place	Date	Hour

1916
Septr 10th
(Contd)-
& 11th

I cannot close this account without noting the extreme gallantry and devotion with which Captain A. Ramsbottom (R.A.M.C.) attached, Sergt 964 G.E.Cordery and all the Stretcher Bearers without exception attended to the wounded under such shell fire as we have never experienced before for the whole 20 hours we were in the Wood and practically all the time in the open, as the Dressing Station accomodation was limited to one German dug out in the S.W. corner of the Wood which was the centre of attraction to the enemy gunners the whole time.

Altogether it was a bad day for the Battalion

For Gallant Conduct this day

```
8773  L/C H.R.Wallis    "C" Company
5627  Rfn A.E.Clapham    "    "
4106  "   T.W.Bishop     "    "
```

were awarded the Military Medal.
Casualties 11th Sick 5 O.R.

12th   Battn in huts and tents at the CITADEL.
Casualties 3 O.R. wounded. 1 Officer and 8 O.R. sick.

13th   Battn moved up to trenches at Crucifix HARDECOURT Casualties Sick 4 O.R. Reinforcements 22 O.R.

14th   Battn moved back to trenches in A.5.d.6.1. N.E. of FAVIERE WOOD. Casualties 1 O.R. wounded 7 O.R. Reinforcements.

15th   Attack by Guards and VI Div on our left. Armoured Caterpillar Motor Cars ("Tanks") used in action for the first time. Battn moved up to trenches in ANGLE WOOD VALLEY. Casualties Wounded 3 O.R. Missing 1 O.R. Sick 4 O.R. Reinforcements 122 O.R.

16th   Battn still in NAGLE WOOD VALLEY Casualties Wounded 2 O.R. Reinforcements 2 Officers and 27 O.R.

17th   On the evening of the 17th the Battn was ordered in conjunction with the continued offensive of the 167th Brigade towards BOULEAUX WOOD to attack the German trench along the N. side of the sunken road from BOULEAUX WOOD to COMBLES. The attack to take place at 5.50 a.m. on the 18th. During the evening reconnaissance for this attack 2nd Lieuts Lowndes and Warwick were wounded.

Battn H.Q. moved up to the LONE TREE and the Companies into the assembly trenches dug between LEUZE WOOD and the LOOP TRENCH with the support Company in the N. end of the COMBLES trench.

Lieut Colonel
Commdg. 1/ Queens' Westminster Rifles

Place	Date	Hour

1916

Septr 17th (Contd). The battn was organized now in three Companies and disposed for the attack:-

No. 1 (the remains of A) less 1 Platoon, on the left.

No. 2 (the remains of B and D) less 1 Platoon, under Capt Green on the right both these in the assembly trench, and

No. 3 (the remains of C and the Platoons of Nos. 1 and 2) in support in the W. end of the COMBLES Trench.

Lieut M.M.WEBB was in command of No. 1 Company and 2nd Lieut N.T.Thurston in command of No. 3 Company. 2 Machine Guns were attached to the Battn for consolidating enemy trench when taken.

18th
5.50 a.m. At 5.50 a.m. the two attacking Companies went over the top and both nearly reached the objective when they came under heavy machine gun fire and were unable to get into the enemy trench and the remainder of the two Companies - 3 Officers and 90 O.R. withdrew to the assembly trench - into which 2nd Lieut N.T.Thurston had moved up the supporting Company and in which he had been stopped by Capt Green who saw the uselessness of throwing away more men into the attack.

The L.R.B. attack on the N. end of the LOOP TRENCH had failed to make any progress and the whole thing was hung up.

It was in this attack that Lieut M.M.Webb commanding No. 1 Company was wounded and subsequently killed later in the day in our own trench. 2nd Lieut Eric Jones was killed practically in the German trench - he was probably the only man who reached it and was turning round to encourage his men on when he was killed. 2nd Lieut R. Harrison, the only other "A" Company Officer was killed during the advance and 2nd Lieut Oppitz wounded.

The assembly trench was held all day and in the evening the Battn was withdrawn to ANGLE WOOD VALLEY, the L.R.B. taking over the assembly trench from us.

Casualties 17th 3 Officers wounded 1 O.R. Missing 4 O.R. Sick. Reinforcements 1 Officer and 85 O.R.
Casualties 18th 3 Officers killed and 34 O.R. killed 48 O.R. wounded, 14 O.R. Missing 1 O.R. Sick

19th Battn still in ANGLE WOOD VALLEY.
Casualties 5 O.R. wounded 3 O.R. sick 1 O.R. other causes.

20th Battn relieved L.R.B. in LOOP and COMBLES trenches. Casualties 1 O.R. wounded 5 O.R. Sick Reinforcements 35 O.R.

Lieut Colonel
Commdg. 1/ Queens' Westminster Rifles

Place	Date	Hour	
	1916 Septr 21st		Battn in same position. Casualties 2 O.R. wounded
	22nd		Battn in same position. Casualties 2 O.R. killed 4 O.R. wounded 5 O.R. sick 14 O.R. Reinforcements.
	23rd		Orders received for the Battn to carry out a bombing attack down that part of COMBLES Trench held by the GERMANS. This order was cancelled an hour later and the Battn was relieved by the Q.V.R. who were ordered to carry out the attack. Battn moved back to the FALFEMONT LINE. Casualties 1 O.R. killed 2 O.R. Sick Reinforcements 136 O.R.
	24th		Battn moved back to CASEMENT TRENCH just N. of MARICOURT. Battn in Div Reserve. Casualties 4 O.R. Wounded 3 O.R. Sick.
	25th		Battn still in CASEMENT TRENCH. Casualties 10 O.R. Sick Reinforcements 3 Officers and 51 O.R.
	26th		Battn moved forward to NAGLE WOOD VALLEY. Casualties Sick 2 O.R. Reinforcements 4 O.R.
	27th		Brigade relieved. Battn marched out to Billets in MEAULTE. Casualties Sick 2 O.R. Reinforcements 2 Officers and 3 O.R.
	28th		In billets at Meaulte Casualties Sick 6 O.R. Other causes 5 O.R. Reinforcements 2 Officers and 13 O.R.
	29th		Battn moved up to trenches N. of CARNOY in reserve. Casualties Sick 8 O.R. 2 O.R. Other causes.
	30th		Battn moved to front line trenches E. of MORVAL relieving 9th Suffolks VI DIV - "A" Coy in front line "B" Coy in support "C" and "D" in Battn reserve Reinforcements 2 O.R.

SUMMARY.

	Officers	O.R.	Total.
Strength on July 31st	38	912	950
Add.	13	574	587
	51	1486	1537
Less.	28	543	571
	23	933	956

Lieut Colonel
Commdg. 1/ Queens' Westminster Rifles

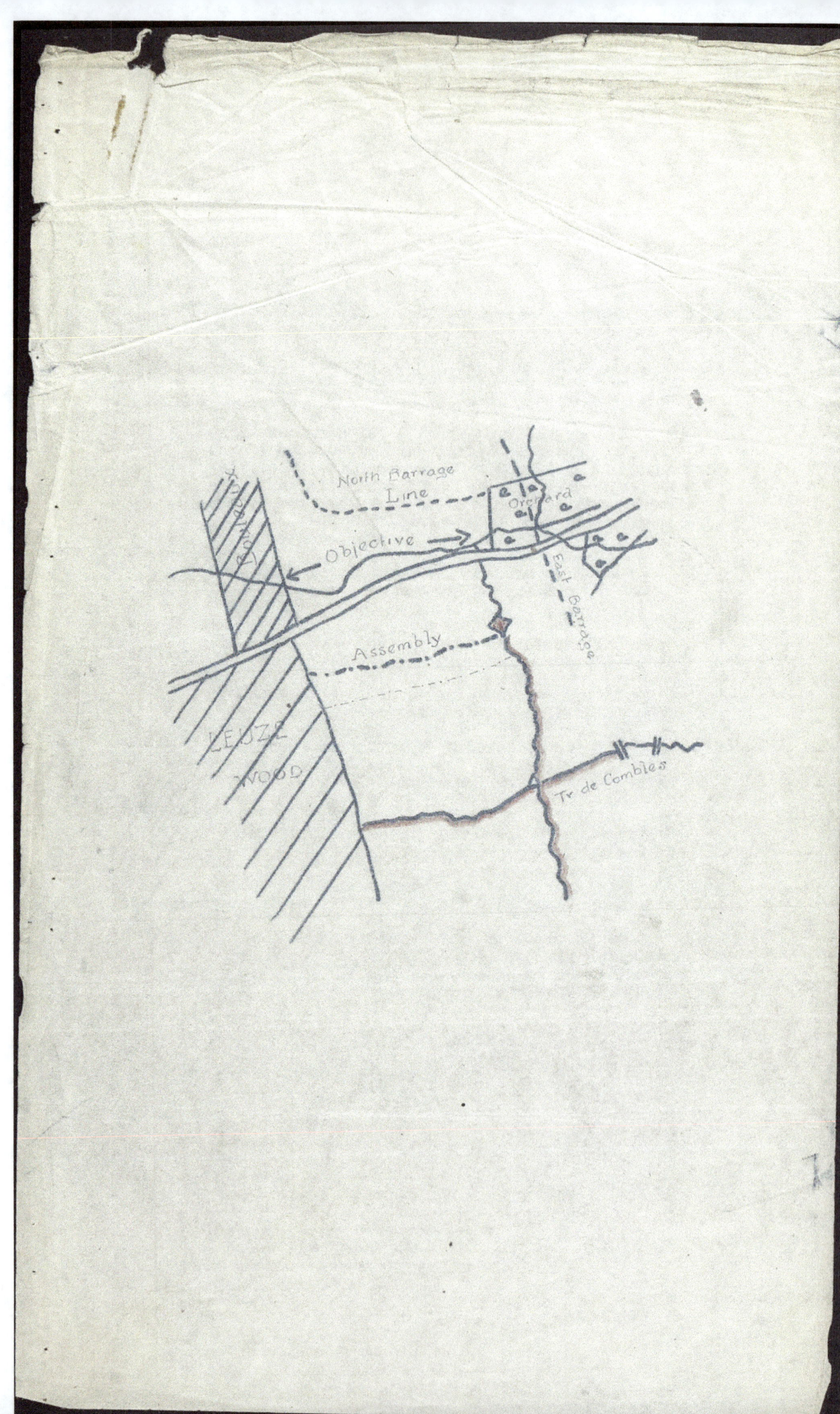

Fourth Army No. G.S.334.

56th Division.

      I desire to place on record my appreciation of the work that was carried out by the 56th Division during the Battle of the Somme. The successful operations in the neighbourhood of BOULEAUX and LEUZE Woods, together with the capture of COMBLES between 9th and 27th September, were feats of arms deserving of the highest praise, and I congratulate the Division on the gallantry, perseverance and endurance displayed by all ranks.

      When after only two days' rest the Division was again called upon to go into the line, they displayed a fine spirit of determination which deserved success.

      The work of the Divisional Artillery in supporting the infantry attacks and in establishing barrages under difficult circumstances was satisfactory and shows that a high standard of efficiency has been reached

      The enterprise and hard work which the Division has shown in sapping forward and constructing trenches under fire has been a noticeable feature in the operations and I specially congratulate the Infantry on the progress they made in this manner at BOULEAUX Wood.

      It is a matter of regret to me that this fine Division has now left the Fourth Army, but I trust that at some future time I may again find them under my command.

                                        Rawlinson

H.Q., Fourth Army,   General,
    27th October, 1916.   Commanding Fourth Army.

WAR DIARY or INTELLIGENCE SUMMARY

1916

Oct. 1st — Battn still in front line E. of MORVAL.
In continuation of the operations of the XIV Corps patrols were ordered to be sent out from all regiments holding the line to endeavour to snatch a little more ground forward. At Zero hour 3.15 p.m. these patrols consisting in each case of One Officer and 20 O.R. were to move forward. The task of our patrol under 2nd Lieut Webster (11th London Regt attached) being to occupy some trenches in T.5.c. central. It was distinctly laid down that this operation was a patrol operation and not an attack. The enemy trench which was our objective was a half dug trench marked on a map but which was not continuous and in point of fact was undistinguishable, at any rate, in places, as a trench and the patrol undoubtedly overshot its mark and fetched up against an occupied enemy trench further away in front of which 2nd Lieut T.W.Webster was killed and the patrol was forced to lie up until dark when another patrol was sent out and brought in the survivors. Had we had any opportunity of reconnoitring our own front or even of studying it ourselves on aeroplane photographs, the sacrifice of a good officer might have been avoided. As with the help of air photographs the L.R.B. succeeded on the night of the 2nd/3rd in locating and occupying the required position which was not held by the enemy. "D" Company moved up to the front line and relieved a company of the French on the right of "A" Company. "A" Company were very heavily shelled all day. Killed 8 O.R. Wounded 23 O.R. Missing 6 O.R. Sick 4 O.R. Reinforcements 65 O.R.

2nd — Battn still in same trenches "A" and "D" Companies heavily shelled all day and it was only the deep narrow trenches which saved them from very heavy casualties.
Two Companies of the L.R.B. relieved "A" and "D" Companies which were moved back to trenches in the FLERS line Killed 3 O.R. Wounded 12 O.R. Missing 2 O.R. Reinforcements 1 Officer 1 O.R.

3rd — Battn still in same trenches relieved at night by the KENSINGTONS. Relief ordered to start at 5 p.m. The first Coy of the Kensingtons arrived at 1 a.m. on the 4th and the relief was not completed until 3 a.m. when the Battn moved back to the CITADEL. Casualties Killed 2 O.R. Wounded 6 O.R. Sick 7 O.R. Reinforcements 1 Officer and 3 O.R.

4th — Battn at the CITADEL Casualties Wounded 1 O.R. Sick 8 O.R.

5th — Battn still at the CITADEL. Casualties Sick 3 O.R. Other causes 7 O.R. Reinforcements 20 O.R.

6th — Battn still at the CITADEL 7 O.R. Sick.

Commdg. 1/ Queens' Westminster Rifles

1916
Octr. 7th — Battn moved at 8 a.m. up to trenches just E. of TRONES WOOD moving on at 7.30 p.m. to trenches just S. of GINCHY and being placed at disposal of 167th I.B. Casualties Sick 3. Reinforcements 4 O.R.

8th — Battn moved up to trenches E. of LES BOEUFS relieving the whole of the 167th I.B. in the front line. "B" and "C" and 1 Platoon of "D" Company in front line — remainder of Battn in support. Casualties 1 O.R. killed 4 O.R. wounded 1 O.R. Reinforcement.

9th — Battn in same position - very heavily shelled all day - intense bombardment of our front line from 6 p.m. to 6.30 p.m. S.O.S. Signal given by the Artillery F.O.O. and our guns put up a heavy barrage.
Battn relieved by three Companies of Lancashire Fusiliers and One Company West Riding (IV Div) Relief not completed until 3 a.m.
Battn moved back and bivouaced W. of TRONES WOOD. Casualties Killed 3 O.R. Wounded 39 O.R. Missing 1 O.R. Reinforcements 46 O.R.
1 Officer (Capt Gazelee) wounded

10th — Battn moved back to CITADEL. Casualties Sick 1 O.R. Reinforcements 2 O.R.

11th — Battn Marched as part of the 169th I.B. to VILLE-SUR-ANCRE, whence it was conveyed in French Motor Buses to LA CHAUSSEE-sur-SOMME. The Transport moved by Road and on its arrival the Transport Officer reported that during the march two of the Lewis Gun hand carts had fortunately completely collapsed and he had abandoned them. These hand carts are worse than useless and simply add to the weight of the Lewis Gun equipment.
The remaining 3 Company Hand Carts which had been with the Battalion for over a year were abandoned for want of transport and also as being of no use in this country. Casualties 1 Officer (2nd Lieut E. Brimelow) from Reserve Battn and 1 O.R. Reinforcement.

12th — Battn resting at LA CHAUSSEE. Casualties NIL.

13th — Battn resting at LA CHAUSSEE. Staff Parade reinstituted for the first time since the Battn left MONCHEAUX. Casualties:- Sick 11 O.R. Other causes 3 O.R. Reinforcements 8 O.R.

14th LA CHAUSSEE. Casualties Sick 18 O.R. Reinforcements 2 O.R.
15th do. " " 5 O.R. " 2 "
16th do. " " 14 O.R. " 4 "
17th do. " " 8 O.R. " 13 "

Commdg. 1/ Queens' Westminster Rifles

Place	Date	Hour

1916

Oct 18th. LA CHAUSSEE.
Lieut-Colonel R. Shoolbred, C.M.G., T.D., D.L., who brought the Battalion to France at the end of October 1914 and has commanded it ever since, went to Hospital today as the first step towards 2 months sick leave in England. Major Harding takes command of the Battalion during Colonel Shoolbred's absence. Casualties. 2 Officers (Lieut-Colonel R. Shoolbred, C.M.G., T.D., D.L., and 2nd Lieut W.J.Ryan, 11th London Regt attached) to Hospital 27 t O.R. Sick.

19th LA CHAUSSEE. Reinforcements 23 O.R.

20th do. Sick 1 O.R.

21st The Battalion marched to HUPPY, about 21 miles. In spite of the lack of recent march training, the Battalion marched very well. Casualties Sick 6 O.R. Reinforcements 8 O.R.

22nd At HUPPY. Warning Order received for move next day to BERGUETTE. Casualties Sick 2 O.R. Reinforcements 8 O.R.

23rd After dinner the Battalion marched 7 miles to PONT REMY to entrain. Entraining complete by 4 p.m. Arrived at BERGUETTE 12 midnight and detrained. A dark and wet night. Casualties NIL.

24th Detraining complete and Battalion ready to move at 2 a.m. Marched to CALONNE-sur-LYS a distance of 9 miles, arriving there at 6.30 a.m. Troops billeted in factories and barns. Casualties 1 Officer (2nd Lieut W. Allan, 10th London Regt) Reinforcement.

25th At CALONNE under orders to be ready to move at One Hours Notice to support either 1st or 4th Corps at GIVENCHY or CUINCHY. Casualties 1 Officer (2nd Lieut F.W.Rouse, 9th Middlesex Regt, attached) and 6 O.R. sick 12 O.R. Reinforcements.

26th Still at CALONNE. Warning order to move to LESTREm the following day. Casualties Sick 12 O.R.

27th March to LESTREM, a distance of about 5 miles Casualties Sick 6 O.R.

28th At LESTREM. Casualties NIL.

29th Battalion marched to BOUT DEVILLE to rest (reserve) billets arriving there by 10 a.m. and relieving the 4th GLOUCESTERS. (61st Division). "A", "C", and "D" Companies billeted in barns in BOUT DEVILLE. "B" Company in huts in LES HUITS MAISONS Casualties 5 O.R. Sick.

P.O. Harding Major.
Commdg. 1/ Queens' Westminster Rifles

Place	Date	Hour	Summary of Events and Information	Remarks and references to Appendices
			1916.
Octr. 30th Companies commence Company Training in the mornings. The C.O. and Adjt. visit the Trenches which the Battalion are to take over.
    Casualties 12 O.R. Sick 1 Officer (2nd Lieut B.C.LEWALL) from Reserve Battn.
31st At BOUT DEVILLE. Company Commanders visit the trenches which their Companies are to occupy. Company Training continued. Casualties Sick 1 O.R.
    Letter received in appreciation of the Divisions splendid work on the SOMME from the Commander of the 4th Army.

    Strength on 30/9/16

	Offrs.	O.R.	Total.
	23	933	956
ADD	5	224	229
	28	1,157	1,185
LESS.	5	294	299
	23	863	886

P.E. Harding Major.
Commdg. 1/ Queens' Westminster Rifles

[Stamp: QUEENS WESTMINSTER RIFLES No. 4/11 Date 4/11/16] | |

WAR DIARY or INTELLIGENCE SUMMARY

Army Form C. 2118.

Place	Date	Hour	Summary of Events and Information	Remarks and references to Appendices
	1916.			
	Nov. 1st.		At BOUT DEVILLE. Casualties: Reinforcements, 8 O.R.	
	Nov. 2nd.		-do- Casualties: Sick, 8 O.R.	
	Nov. 3rd.		Battalion moves up to the trenches in front of NEUVE CHAPELLE taking over from the QUEEN VICTORIA RIFLES. Three Companies in the Front Line & one in Support (A Coy.) The front line Companies from right to left are:- B, C, D. B Company has two platoons in front line, one in defended post behind the line and one in Support. The dispositions of D Coy. are the same as B. C Coy. has three platoons in front line and one in defended post in rear. The whole of A Coy. in Support Line behind the defended posts. The position consists of a trench about two feet deep and the remainder breastwork. The greater part of the front line is badly in need of revetting. There are good communication trenches, some of them slightly waterlogged. All the main C.T's are well boarded and revetted. The line is quiet and with the exception of a certain amount of T.M. activity on the front line. The Sector is fitted with a system of trench railways. Rations are brought up on these as far as the Support Line. Casualties: Sick 2 O.R.	
	Nov. 4th.		Quiet day. The General visited the trenches in the morning and went round three of the Companies with the C.O. Casualties: NIL.	
	Nov. 5th.		Quiet day. Work continued on the front line and C.T's. R.E. working on the parapets of front line, revetting. Our Trench Mortars carry out a bombardment of enemy front line. Enemy retaliate with L.T.M's one landing in front trench of Left Sector and another in NEW CUT ALLEY. No Casualties Casualties: Sick, 1 O.R. " Reinforcements 7 O.R's and 2 Officers (2nd. Lieut. J.H.Falconer, from Highland Cyclist Division Company. and 2nd. Lieut. Musgrove from 5th. Border Regiment.)	
	Nov. 6th.		Quiet day, wet. Casualties: Wounded 1 O.R.	
	Nov. 7th.		Quiet day, but very wet. Trenches falling in badly in many places, part of BALUCHI C.T. & B Line flooded. Work continued all night clearing away the land slides and bailing and pumping the trenches. A wiring party which was sent out at about 6.30 p.m. from D Coy. was attacked, with rifles and	

Commdg. 1/ Queens' Westminster Rifles

1916

Nov. 7th. (contued.) Grenades, by a strong enemy patrol, two Sergeants who were out in front of the wiring, examining the ground, were surprised". One succeeded in getting back to the trench but the other was missing. It is thought that he was wounded and taken prisoner. The wiring party fell back to the trench with two men slightly wounded.
The Middlesex on our flank then opened Lewis Gun fire on the German patrol, who retreated at the double. An Officers patrol was immediately sent out. They searched the ground for an hour and three quarters, but no signs were seen of the enemy or the missing Sergeant.
Casualties: Missing, 1 O.R. (2105 Sgt. Hawkins)
" Sick, 2 O.R.
" Wounded, 2 O.R.
" Reinforcements, 7 Officers. viz:-
2nd. Lieut. H.Pickles   from 4th. Border Rgt.
"   "   A.M.Mackle   "   "   "   "
"   "   C.A.English   "   "   "   "
"   "   J.Betteridge   "   "   "   "
"   "   M.McBean   "   "   "   "
"   "   H.J.Furminger   "   "   "   "
"   "   R.H.Brown   " Highland Division
Casualties: 2 O.R's. To Base Under Age Cyclist Coy.

Nov. 8th. Again wet. Our Stokes Mortars carried out a successful bombardment of the enemy wire and front trench. Many floor-boards etc., were seen flying in the air. There was no enemy retaliation.
Casualties: Sick 5 O.R.   & 2 O.R.
"   Reinforcements, 1 Officer, viz:-
2nd. Lieut. Ryan W.J. from Hospital.

Nov. 9th. Battalion relieved by QUEEN VICTORIA RIFLES. Relief carried out without casualties and complete by 12.30 p.m. The Battalion moved back into Support Billets at CROIX BARBEE. While the Battalion is in CROIX BARBEE large fatigue parties have to be found for work by day and night, on the Front Line and C.T's, under the control of the R.E.

Nov. 9th. Casualties: Sick, 1 Officer - 2nd. Lt. C.S.H.Melhado
                                          to Field Ambulance.
"   Reinforcements, 11 O.R.
"   "   2 Officers viz:-
(2nd. Lieut. Rankin W. and 2nd. Lieut. Waddington J.W. from 4th. Border Regiment.)

Nov. 10th. At CROIX BARBEE. R.E. Fatigue Parties.
Casualties: Sick, 7 O.R.

Nov. 11th. At CROIX BARBEE. Fatigues as usual.
Casualties: NIL.

Nov. 12th. At CROIX BARBEE. Major Harding leaves to attend a Conference of Commanding Officers at 1st. Army Base.

Commdg. 1/ Queens' Westminster Rifles

1916.

Nov. 12th. Casualties: Wounded 1 O.R.
(Continued) " Sick, 1 O.R.
 " " 1 Officer.(2nd. Lt. R.A.Gatfield)
 " Reinforcements, 1 Officer, viz:-
 2nd. Lieut. C.S.H.Melhado from Field Ambulance.

Nov. 13th. Still at CROIX BARBEE. Work as usual.
 Casualties: Wounded, 4 O.R's.
 " Sick, 7 O.R's.
 " Reinforcements, 5 O.R's.
 " " 1 Officer, viz:-
 (2nd. Lieut. W.Hall from 4th. Border Regt.)

Nov. 14th. At CROIX BARBEE.
 Casualties: Wounded 2 O.R's.
 " Sick, 2 O.R's.
 " Reinforcements 8 O.R's.

Nov. 15th. Battalion moves up to the trenches, same Sector as last time, relieving the QUEEN VICTORIA RIFLES. Relief commenced at 12.30 p.m. and complete by 4 p.m. Our Trench Mortars have carried out a straff of the German Front Line during the afternoon. There was no retaliation.
 Casualties: Sick 2 O.R's.

Nov. 16th. In Trenches. Weather fine and cold. Brigadier General on the Corps Staff paid a visit to the trenches in the morning and went up to the front line. Quiet day.
 Casualties: Sick, 5 O.R.

Nov. 17th. In Trenches. Cold and frosty weather.
 Casualties: Reinforcements, 10 O.R's.

Nov. 18th. As yesterday but not so cold. Some rain during the day.
 Casualties: Sick, 1 O.R.
 " Reinforcements, 6 O.R's.
 " " 1 Officer, viz:-
 (2nd. Lieut. R.A.Gatfield from Hospital.)

Nov. 19th. As yesterday. Our T.M's, were active during the afternoon. The Bosch replied on the Left Company with L.T.M's and Shrapnel.
 Casualties: Sick, 1 O.R.
 " " 1 Officer, 2nd. Lt. C.S.H.Melhado to Field Ambulance.
 " Reinforcements, 3 O.R's.

Nov. 20th. Considerably increased enemy artillery activity on front line, chiefly 4.2's. Very little damage was done and there were no Casualties.
 Casualties: 1 O.R. transferred to R.F.C. (Sgt. Yeo)
 " Reinforcements, 11 O.R's.

Commdg. 1/ Queens' Westminster Rifles

1916.

Nov. 21st. Battalion relieved by QUEEN VICTORIA RIFLES and returns to BOUT DEVILLE. Relief complete by 5 p.m.
Casualties: Wounded 1 O.R.
" To Base Under Age 1 O.R.
" Sick 2 O.R's.
" Reinforcements, 1 O.R.

Nov. 22nd. At BOUT DEVILLE.
Casualties: Sick, 2 O.R.
" Reinforcements, 1 O.R.

Nov. 23rd. At BOUT DEVILLE. New small box respirator issued to Battalion.
Casualties: Sick, 4 O.R's.

Nov. 25th. At BOUT DEVILLE. Fatigues as before. Warning Order received, to the effect that owing to changes in the system of holding the Front Line, the Brigade will be relieved on 27th., going back to the LESTREM - LA GORGUE area for 12 days rest and training.
Casualties: Sick, 3 O.R's.
" To No.34 Prisoners of War Company. 1 O.R.
" Reinforcements, 5 O.R's.
" " 1 Officer, viz:-
2nd. Lieut. Bawtree from Reserve Battalion.

Nov. 24th. At BOUT DEVILLE. Two Companies ordered for fatigues. 1 Company for Front Line and 1 Company for work at FOSSE.
Casualties: Sick, 3 O.R's.
" Reinforcements 1 O.R.

Nov. 26th. At BOUT DEVILLE. Church Parade and Communion Service in the morning.
Casualties: Sick, 3 O.R's.
" Reinforcements, 1 O.R.

Nov. 27th. Battalion moves to ROBERMETZ just outside MERVILLE marching there, a distance of about 7 miles. The men are billeted in farm buildings and empty houses. Quite good billets.
Casualties: Sick, 4 O.R's.
" Reinforcements, 5 O.R's.

Nov. 28th. Training commences. 9 - 12 in the morning and 2 - 3.30 in the afternoon.
Casualties: Sick 2 O.R's.
" Reinforcements, 2 O.R's.

Nov. 29th. Training continued. Battalion Route March in the morning.
Casualties: Sick, 2 O.R's.
" Reinforcements, 4 O.R's.

Nov. 30th. Training as above.
Casualties: Sick 4 O.R's.
" Reinforcements, 4 O.R's.

Place	Date	Hour	
	1917. Jany. 27th		In trenches. Bitterly cold. 1 O.R. Sick.
	28th		Orders received at 7 p.m. from Brigade to evacuate the posts and to endeavour to cut all the wire anchors holding back the revetments in the enemy trenches. Both Posts completely evacuated by 9 p.m. and two strong patrols were out all night cutting the wire. All our stores were brought in from the Posts. The two Platoons previously "standing to" all night were sent back to support line, and the Battalion disposed in the same was as before the posts were occupied. Casualties 2 O.R. sick, 3 O.R. to Base for duty with Floating Grain Elevators.
	29th		Enemy shelled the evacuated Posts. Just before dawn 30th "A" Company sent out a small patrol, who lit a small damp fire at BARNET POST, with the object of deceiving the wily HUN into thinking the Post was still held. A strong party was out from "B" Company again cutting wire in BOSCHE Trench. Covering Party of 6 was surprised by the enemy, and retired hurriedly losing One man. 2nd Lieuts Betteridge and Baker took a patrol immediately after the party got in to try to find the missing man, but after thoroughly searching the ground were unsuccessful. One Officer (2nd Lieut E. BAWTREE) and 4 O.R. wounded, 1 Officer (Capt. A.G.BIRD) sick.
	30th		All Companies employed wiring our front line, 40 coils of barbed wire and 32 knife rests being put out. Casualties 2 O.R. Killed 1 O.R. Missing.
	31st		All Companies employed wiring our own front line. For the 1st time this winter, each man brought one blanket to the trenches. Continuous frost since 20th inst. An excellent slide has been made along a flooded ditch near Battn H.Q. Casualties. NIL.

	Offrs.	O.R.	Total.
Strength on 31st Decr. '16.	40	967	1,007
Add.	6	45	51
	46	1,012	1,058
Less.	9	82	91
Strength on 31st Jany '17.	37	930	967

P.B. Harding
Lieut Colonel
Commdg. 1/ Queens' Westminster Rifles

Place	Date	Hour

1916.

Dec 1st — At ROBERMETZ.
Casualties Sick 1 O.R., Missing 2 O.R. (not previously reported).

2nd — At ROBERMETZ.
Casualties Sick 7 O.R., To commission 1 O.R. Reinforcement 1 O.R.

3rd — At ROBERMETZ. Fatigue party of 200 O.R. found for R.E. for work on the Railways.
Casualties 1 O.R. Reinforcement.

4th — At ROBERMETZ.
Casualties:- Sick 4 O.R.

5th — At ROBERMETZ.
Casualties:- Sick 1 O.R., Reinforcements 2 O.R.

6th — At ROBERMETZ.
Casualties:- Sick 3 O.R., Reinforcements 4 O.R.

7th — At ROBERMETZ.
Casualties:- Sick 6 O.R., Reinforcements 4 O.R. and 1 Officer (Capt P.M. GLASIER from Reserve Batn).

8th — At ROBERMETZ.
Casualties Sick 1 O.R., Reinforcements 4 O.R.

9th — The Battalion moved to PONT DU HEM on the LA BASSEE ROAD, and billeted in Reserve Billets. Billets quite good. "D" Company have half the Company as Garrisons of 6 Posts. Battalion supplies R.E. Working Parties every day.
Casualties NIL.

10th — PONT DU HEM. Work as usual.
Casualties 10 O.R. Sick, 3 O.R. Reinforcements.

11th — PONT DU HEM. Work as usual.
Casualties 4 O.R. Sick.

12th — PONT DU HEM. Work as usual.
Casualties 2 O.R. Sick, 4 O.R. Reinforcements.

13th — PONT DU HEM. Work as usual.
Casualties Sick 1 O.R., To commission 7 O.R. Reinforcements 3 O.R.

14th — PONT DU HEM. Work as usual.
Casualties 1 O.R. Wounded, 8 O.R. Sick, 15 O.R. Reinforcements.

P E Harding
Lieut-Colonel.
Commanding 1st Queens Westminster Rifles.

WAR DIARY or INTELLIGENCE SUMMARY

(Erase heading not required.)

Army Form C. 2118.

Place	Date	Hour	Summary of Events and Information	Remarks and references to Appendices

1916.

Decr. 15th — Battalion moves into trenches, relieving Q.V.R. - relief complete at 5.15 p.m. "C" Company in reserve at EBENEZER FARM and "B" LINE. "D" Company on right in S.5.5, S.5.6. "A" " in centre in M.35.1, M.35.2, and M.35.3. "B" " on left in DUCKS BILL CRATER, and M.35.4, to TILLELOY SOUTH. Carried out wiring at night.
    Casualties Sick 1 O.R., Reinforcements 35 O.R.

16th — "A" Company fired rapid at "Stand-to". About 30 "Minnies" over HELL CORNER and NEW CUT ALLEY at 12.30 p.m. Rifle Grenades along our whole line. Wiring at night by all Companies.
    Casualties Killed 1 O.R., Wounded 1 O.R., Sick 2 O.R., 30 O.R. Reinforcements. 1 O.R. Previously reported Missing now reported at Duty.

17th — Very misty early in the morning. Had 2 men sniped. Hostile artillery very active between 10 a.m. and 12 noon and 2 p.m. to 5 p.m. 2 direct hits on NEW CUT ALLEY, also shells of various calibre on HELL CORNER and CHATEAU REDOUBT. Wiring as usual - cleared NEW CUT ALLEY. "B" Company sent out a patrol consisting of 2nd Lieut S.C.YEATES, 1 Sergt and 3 men - were out 3 hours.
    Casualties Killed 2 O.R., Sick 3 O.R. Reinforcement 1 O.R.

18th — "Minnies" and 4.2 on HELL CORNER and NEW CUT ALLEY during afternoon and evening, doing a good deal of damage to the trench. A patrol of 2nd Lieut RANKIN and 2 O.R. went out from S.5.6. - spotted a wiring party and strong covering party and on return we turned Lewis Guns on them. A second patrol 2nd Lieut PICKLES and 6 O.R. went out from M.35.3. to examine enemy wire, but were unable to reach wire owing to the depth of water in road running N.E. from SIGN POST LANE. WORK wiring by all Companies in front line. Work on HUSH HALL and CHATEAU REDOUBT
    Casualties Sick 6 O.R.

19th — Bosche retaliated on head of NEW CUT ALLEY in answer to our Trench Mortar Bombardment. Patrol 2nd Lieut Betteridge and 2 O.R. went out from M.35.b.8.4. to get map reference for certain old Bosche trenches. Work Wiring - trench maintenance - and building Lewis Gun Position in DUCKS BILL.
    Casualties:- 5 O.R. Wounded, 4 O.R. Sick. 3 O.R. Reinforcements.

P.O. Harding
Lieut-Colonel.
Commanding 1st Queens Westminster Rifles

1916.

Decr. 20th. Quiet day. Violent Bombardment of Battn Sector on our right, which put the wind up them to such an extent that there was going to be a gas attack. Patrol under 2nd Lieut W.ALLAN went out from S.S.6., but had nothing to report. Wiring etc. as usual.
Casualties:- Sick 1 O.R.

21st Battalion relieved by Q.V.R and 13th Battn Royal Fusiliers. Royal Fusiliers taking over line to the south of SIGN POST LANE in the morning and we took over temporarily from the 2nd Londons their portion of the line up to the southern end of the CHORD. The Q.V.Rs relieved this portion of the line and the remaining portion of our line from SIGN POST LANE to TILLELOY SOUTH. The relief was complete by 5.25 p.m. The Battalion moved into PONT DU HEM in the same billets as before. Relief was delayed by Heavy Trench Mortars about NEW CUT ALLEY.
Casualties:- Sick 1 O.R.

22nd At PONT DU HEM. Found fatigues about 200 men.
Casualties 1 O.R. to Commission, 2 O.R. Sick, 62 O.R. Reinforcements.

23rd At PONT DU HEM. Fatigues as usual.
Casualties:- 3 O.R. Sick.

24th At PONT DU HEM. Fatigues as usual.
Casualties:- 1 O.R. to Base under age., 1 O.R. Sick.

25th Christmas Day. Rather less fatigues owing to the bombardment by our guns
Casualties:- 1 O.R to commission, 10 O.R Sick.

26th Boxing Day at PONT DU HEM. "Business as usual"
Casualties NIL

27th Relieved Q.V.R. - relief complete by 5 p.m. Line from Southern end of CHORD to SIGN POST LANE. "A" Company on right with 3 Platoons in front line and one in support. "D" Company in centre and "C" Company on left, holding DUCKS BILL, both "C" and "D" with 3 Platoons in front line and 1 in support. "A" and "D" Companies' H.Q. in BRISTOL CASTLE and "C" Company H.Q. in large dug-out in SWITCH. 'B' Company in battalion reserve at Ebenezer Farm
Casualties 2 O.R. Sick, 1 O.R.Reinforcement.

28th All quiet, except for a few "whizz-bangs" round DEAD HORSE COPSE. 2nd Lieut B.C.LEWALL and 7 O.R. went out on patrol from SIGN POST LANE and worked along Bosche wire almost as far as DUCKS BILL

Lieut-Colonel.
Commanding 1st Queens Westminster Rifles.

Place	Date	Hour	
	1916. Decr.28th (Cont'd)		Here they were challenged by a Bosche sentry, who threw a bomb at them. They withdrew without loss. 2nd Lieuts PICKLES and ALLEN also took patrols out. Work Wiring and Maintenance. Casualties:- 1 O.R. to Commission, 3 O.R. Sick, 3 O.R. Reinforcements.
	29th		Quiet all day. Bosche retaliation on TILLELOY SOUTH with 4.2" between 7 and 9 p.m. in answer to our Trench Mortars. Three small patrols went out but did not get far owing to large number of Very Lights sent up by Bosche. Casualties 1 Officer Reinforcement (2nd Lieut V.BELL from 4th Border Regiment).
	30th		All quiet, except for shrapnel about 11.30 a.m. on TILLELOY SOUTH and CARDIFF ROAD. 2nd Lieut-HULL of "A" Company took out a patrol, also Sergt Plumridge of "D" Company - they reported nothing of importance. Work as usual. Casualties:- 1 O.R.Wounded, 2 O.R. Reinforcements.
	31st		Shelling behind our line during the day. Our gunners Strafed the Bosche in the afternoon with short bursts of fire and again at 10.55 p.m., to which he replied energetically with 4.2"s along our support line. Patrols and work as usual. Casualties:- 1 O.R. Wounded, 2 O.R. Reinforcements.

	Officers.	O.R.	Total.
STRENGTH on November 30th	38	875	913
ADD	2	188	190
	40	1,063	1,103
LESS		96	96
Total Strength on Decr 31st	40	967	1,007

P.J. Harding
Lieut-Colonel.
Commanding 1st Queen's Westminster Rifles.

1/1/17.

Place	Date	Hour	

1917.
Jany. 1st.   Hostile artillery very active from 10.30 a.m till 3 p.m. as well as hostile Minnies and rifle grenades. "Moated Grange" Artillery O.P. suffered very badly. Casualties 2 O.R. To commission, Reinforcements 3 O.R.

2nd   Our artillery, T.M.B. and Stokes had an organized "strafe" on enemy front line, support line O.Ps. and H.Q. known to exist, from 12 noon to dusk. There was no retaliation. Casualties 1 O.R. Wounded, 1 O.R. Sick, 1 O.R. Reinforcement.

3rd.   Relieved by KENSINGTONS, relief commenced 4.30 p.m. and was complete by 8.30 p.m. Battalion proceeded to Rest Billets in BOUT DEVILLE Area with Battn H.Q. in RIEZ BAILLEUL Major Glasier left to proceed to a Senior Officers' Course at Aldershot.
     1 Officer (2nd Lieut W.Allan) and 1 O.R. Sick 1 O.R. Reinforcement.

4th   Cleaning up.   Casualties 9 O.R. Reinforcements.

5th   Cleaning up.   Casualties 2 O.R. Sick. 3 O.R. Reinforcements.

6th   Training at BOUT DEVILLE. Casualties 1 O.R. to Commission and 1 O.R. Reinforcements.

7th   At BOUT DEVILLE training. Casualties Sick 1 O.R. 2 O.R. to Base under age.

8th   Working Party of 3 Officers and 200 O.R. on LESTREM - LOCON Road. Casualties Sick 1 O.R. To Commission 2 O.R.

9th   At BOUT DEVILLE training. Casualties NIL.

10th   Inspection by Corps Commander, who expressed the opinion that all ranks looked well set-up, well fed and happy and "so did their Colonel". The Corps Commander thought that about 12 of the mens tunics were too old and on overhearing this the A.A. & Q.M.G. told the A/Adjt that this General is "much too extravagant" and that "you and I have to pay for these things"
     Casualties 1 O.R. Sick, 2 O.R. to Base under age, 4 O.R. Reinforcements.

11th   Battalion Boxing Tournament was held - Six weights A ring was borrowed from the R.E. and for a first attempt the afternoon was a great success.
     Casualties Sick 4 O.R. Reinforcements 2 Officers (Lieut W.G.Orr and 2/Lieut P. Palmer from 19th and 18th Bns London Regt respectively)

12th   Working Party of 15 at LESTREM. Billet occupied by No. 5 Platoon "B" Company completely destroyed by fire. Fire broke out about 6 p.m. and died down at about 11 p.m. Lewis Guns were saved but the majority of

P B Harding
Lieut Colonel
Commdg. 1/ Queens Westminster Rifles

WAR DIARY or INTELLIGENCE SUMMARY

Place	Date	Hour	Summary of Events and Information	Remarks and references to Appendices

1917.
Jan. 12th mens kits etc were lost, the owners being at the
(Contd). "BOW BELLS" at the time. 2nd Lieut A.M.MACKIE
(Border Regt) attached 1st Q.W.R., Sergt Ing and
Rfn Buckley acted very promptly and efficiently.
Casualties 3 O.R. Sick, Reinforcements 2 O.R.

13th   One Officer with a party of 23 O.R. including
a Lewis Gun Team from each of "B" "C" and "D" Companies
went to trenches to take over three posts held by us in
German abandoned front line, FAUQUISSART SECTION. The
Post to be taken over by "B" Company was rushed by the
Bosche just before the relief took place and was left
in the Bosche's possession. Casualties 4 O.R. sick,
1 O.R. to Commission, 3 O.R. Reinforcements.

14th   Battalion relieved 7th Middlesex. Snow on
the ground and freezing on and off.
"B", "C", and "D" Companies in front line
and support. "A" Company in Battalion reserve. One
Platoon of "B" Company moved up at night to front line
to stand by in support of posts held by "C" and "D"
Companies.
Casualties 4 O.R. Sick 1 Officer (Lieut W.T.
W.BIRTS and 1 O.R. Reinforcement.

15th   Still very cold. Our patrols very active
and established the fact that the old German front line
opposite our centre and left Companies was completely
abandoned by the enemy and that he had two posts,
including the post captured on the 13th inst, and a
detached sentry group from one post opposite our
right Company. 2nd Lieut .AM.MACKIE (4th Border Regt),
Lieut W.G.ORR (19th London Regt) and 2nd Lieut B.C.
Lewall did excellent work with their patrols.
Casualties 1 O.R. Reinforcement.

The whole of "A" Company were employed
through the night wiring the posts in the old
German front line. Mud knee deep. The country
immediately behind the old German front line completely
flooded and the trenches blown or fallen in.

16th   The whole of "A" Company again employed
wiring.
    Wiring Party 28 O.R.
    Covering   " 28 "
    Carrying   " 24 "
    Casualties 1 O.R. Sick, 4 Officers (Lieut
R.A. Gatfield 2nd Lieuts Waddington J.W., Rankin F.A.
and McBean H.) transferred to Machine Gun Corps
(Heavy Branch). 2 O.R. to commission. 2 O.R. Reinforcements.

17th   As for 16th. Heavy fall of snow. ENFIELD POST
temporarily evacuated for about ½ hour owing to hostile T.M.
1 Officer (Lieut C.W.RENTON, 20th London Regt) and 1 O.R.
Reinforcements.

Lieut Colonel
Commdg. 1/ Queens' Westminster Rifles

Place	Date	Hour

1917.
Jany 18th   "A" Company wiring as yesterday. Quiet day.
     Casualties - 1 Officer (2nd Lieut A.G.BEVILLE)
Reinforcement, 1 O.R. Sick.

19th   "A" Company wiring as yesterday. Quiet day.
During this six days spell in trenches "A" Company
put out 272 coils of barbed wire and 370 pickets and a
knife rests.
     Casualties 1 O.R. Killed and 1 O.R. TO Commission.

20th   Battalion relieved by the L.R.B. "A" and "B"
Companies remained in defended posts on RUE BACQUEROT.
"C" and "D" Companies moved back to LAVENTIE to billets.
Freezing.
     1 O.R. wounded, 1 O.R. Sick. 3 O.R. reinforcements.

21st.   Bitterly cold. At 7 p.m. very heavy hostile
shelling was heard on the Brigade front. The Battalion
was ordered to "stand to". The enemy, we afterwards
heard, had bombarded and raided the posts held by the
left Battalion. The posts we re-occupied by the left
Battalion before dawn. "Stand to" dismissed at 8 p.m.
     Casualties 2 O.R. Sick, 1 O.R. Wounded, 1 O.R.
to commission, 1 Officer (2nd Lieut C.K.GRAY from
18th Battn London Regt) and 2 O.R. Reinforcements.

22nd   Battalion in Billets in LAVENTIE and defended
posts. Large working parties found for trenches. Severe
frost.
     Casualties 5 O.R. Reinforcements.

23rd   Ditto.
     Casualties 1 O.R. Wounded, 1 Officer (2nd
Lieut G.J.FARMER) transferred to R.F.C. 1 O.R. to
commission.

24th   Ditto.
     Casualties 3 O.R. Wounded, 6 O.R. Sick. 1 O.R.
Reinforcements.

25th   Ditto.
     4 O.R. Wounded, 1 O.R. Sick, 2 O.R. to
commission, 2 O.R. Reinforcements.

26th   Battalion relieved L.R.B. in same sector.
Ground too hard to put in wiring pickets. Very little
wiring done in consequence.
     "A", "B", and "C" Companies in front line
"D" in support.
     "A" and "B" Companies holding BARNET and
ENFIELD Posts respectively.
     Most of the wire on the right of ENFIELD had been
blown away by the enemy, the previous evening, when
they made an unsuccessful raid on the L.R.B. "A" and
"B" Companies each had one Platoon "standing to" all
night in our front line ready to reinforce the posts at a
moments notice
     Casualties 1 O.R. Sick.

Lieut Colonel
Commdg. 1/ Queens' Westminster Rifles

Place	Date	Hour	Summary of Events and Information	Remarks and references to Appendices
	1917 Feby 1st		Battalion relieved by L.R.B. and moved to billets at LAVENTIE in Brigade Reserve. At 3 a.m. the Hun heavily strafed our front line - Companies in front stood-to. Casualties 1 O.R. Killed, 2 O.R. Wounded 6 O.R. Sick.	
	2nd		In Billets at LAVENTIE - Training and Working Parties. Casualties 6 O.R. Sick, 1 O.R. Reinforcements.	
	3rd		Ditto. Casualties 2 O.R. Sick, 1 O.R. Other Causes, 4 O.R. Reinforcements.	
	4th		Ditto. Casualties 5 O.R. Sick, 1 Officer (2nd Lieut W.J.Ryan, 11th Ldn Regt) transferred to R.F.C., 1 O.R. to Commission., 2 O.R. Reinforcements.	
	5th		Ditto. Casualties 2 O.R. Sick.	
	6th		Ditto. Casualties 2 O.R. Sick.	
	7th		Battalion relieved L.R.B. in trenches. Casualties 1 O.R. Sick, 2 O.R. Reinforcements.	
	8th		In trenches. Every available man employed wiring. Casualties 2 O.R. Sick.	
	9th		Ditto. Casualties 1 O.R. Other Causes.	
	10th		Ditto. Lieut-Colonel R. Shoolbred, C.M.G., T.D., D.L., rejoined and reassumed command of the Battalion, 1 O.R. Sick, 1 O.R. To commission. 1 O.R. Reinforcement.	
	11th		Ditto. Casualties 2 O.R. Sick.	
	12th		Ditto. The frost at last shewing signs of breaking. Casualties 2 O.R. Sick.	
	13th		In trenches. Every available man employed wiring. Casualties 1 O.R. Killed 4 O.R. Sick.	
	14th		Battalion relieved by L.R.B. and moved back to Billets at LAVENTIE in Brigade Reserve. Casualties 3 O.R. Sick, 2 O.R. To commission, 2 O.R. Reinforcements.	

RShoolbred Lieut Colonel
Commdg. 1/ Queens' Westminster Rifles

Place	Date	Hour	Summary of Events and Information	Remarks and references to Appendices
	1917 Feby 15th		In Billets at LAVENTIE - Training and working parties. Casualties 3 O.R. Sick, 3 O.R. Reinforcements.	
	16th		Ditto. Casualties 4 O.R. Sick, 2 O.R. To commission 1 O.R. Reinforcement. 1 Officer (Capt A.G.BIRD) invalided.	
	17th		Ditto. Casualties 3 O.R. Sick, 31 O.R. Reinforcements.	
	18th		Ditto. Wet season commences. Casualties 4 O.R. Sick.	
	19th		Ditto. Casualties 2 O.R. Sick. 1 Officer (2nd Lieut R.I.Richens, 18th London Regt) and 51 O.R. Draft.	
	20th		Battalion relieved L.R.B. in trenches, which are beginning to shew signs of wholesale collapse as a result of the thaw and rain. Casualties 1 O.R. Sick, 20 O.R. Reinforcements.	
	21st		In trenches - very quiet. Casualties 5 O.R. Sick, 2 O.R. Reinforcements.	
	22nd		Ditto. Casualties 2 O.R. Sick.	
	23rd		Ditto. Casualties 1 O.R. Sick.	
	24th		Ditto. Casualties 1 O.R. Sick, 1 O.R. Reinforcements.	
	25th		Battalion relieved by L.R.B. and moved into Brigade Support. Casualties 1 O.R. Sick, 1 O.R. To commission 2 O.R. Reinforcements.	
	26th		Battalion in Brigade Support. Casualties 1 O.R. Reinforcements.	
	27th		Ditto. Casualties 13 O.R. Sick, 3 O.R. Reinforcements.	

NShoolbred Lieut Colonel
Commdg. 1/ Queens' Westminster Rifles

1917.
Feby 28th   Battalion in Brigade Support.   C.O. of
            relieving Unit of the 49th Division arrived to
            look round preparatory to taking over tomorrow.
                   Casualties 1 O.R. Died, 3 O.R. Sick, 5 O.R.
            Reinforcements.

	Officers	O.R.
Strength on 31.1.17....	38	938.
Add.	2	132.
	40	1,070.
Less.	2	96.
Strength on 28.2.17....	38	974.

            N Shoolbred   Lieut-Colonel.
         Commanding 1st Queens Westminster Rifles.

Place	Date	Hour	Summary of Events and Information
	1917. Mar. 1st		Relieved from RED HOUSE - POSTS - & LAVENTIE, by 1/5th West Yorkshire Regt - 49th Division. Battalion "treked" to BOUT DEVILLE. We are now going out for six weeks training to the WILLEMAN Area. Casualties 1 Officer (2nd Lieut J. BETTERIDGE) and 4 O.R. Sick.
	2nd		Brigade moved independantly to the ST. FLORIS Area - Battalion to CORNET MALO about a 9 mile march. Battalion marched very well. Casualties 3 O.R. Sick. Rev. T. Tiplady, C.F. brought on Officers establishment vide A.R.O.
	3rd		Brigade moved to PERNES Area via LILLERS. Battalion had a midday halt for dinners in the grounds of a CHATEAU which we afterwards discovered to be the H.Q. of the G.O.C. 1st Army. A Major General came to speak to the Colonel and said "THE" General had no objection to our being there. Afterwards it transpired that he did object to the Transport, which was drawn up in the drive. The Battalion was billetted in FLORINGHEM. Distance of this day's "trek" 14½ miles. A few men fell out on the march. Casualties 2 O.R. Sick, 7 O.R. Reinforcements.
	4th		Brigade moved on to the WILLEMAN (No. 1 Area). The march was made very uncomfortable for us by the fact that we were preceded by the "odds and sods" of the Brigade and were continually being held up by the 2/3rd Field Ambulance. Marched via ST POL, where we were badly hung up by level crossings. A long "trek" of 16¼ miles. Battalion billetted in OEUF. Casualties 1 O.R. Sick, 2 O.R. Other Causes.
	5th		Brigade reached final destination - WILLEMAN (No. 3) Area. A heavy snowstorm on the night of the 4/5th made going very heavy - fortunately the "trek" was a short one - about 9 miles. Battalion billetted in LE QUESNOY with Brigade H.Q. Accomodation very limited. When the Battalion had eventually shaken in a warning order was received from Brigade that the march would be resumed on the morrow. Orders for the move arrived at midnight. Length of march this day about 9 miles Casualties 3 O.R. Sick, 3 O.R. Other Causes.
	6th		Brigade Moved to FROHEN Area. Battalion billetted in BONNIERES - Another long "trek" of about 14½ miles. Operation orders received from Brigade at midnight. Casualties 1 O.R. Sick 2 O.R. Other Causes.
	7th		Battalion moved to Area IVERGNY - SUS ST LEGER.

Shoobrid Lieut Colonel
Commdg. 1/ Queens' Westminster Rifles

Place	Date	Hour	

1917.
Mar. 7th (Contd).   Owing to bad condition of the roads Brigade "treked" a very round-about way. A bitterly cold day. Battalion billetted in SUS ST. LEGER where we had been billetted for two nights in August 1916. Rumours that we are going into trenches near ARRAS. Distance of "trek" about 13 miles.
    Casualties 3 O.R. Sick 1 O.R. Other Causes.

8th   Brigade moved on. Column commanded by Lieut-Colonel R. SHOOLBRED, C.M.G., T.D. D.L. - about 9 miles trek. Billetted in Area - GOUY EN ARTOIS - WANQUETIN - FOSSEUX - SIMENCOURT etc. 2nd Londons and ourselves placed at disposal of 175th Brigade.
    Brigade in Corps Reserve prepared to move up into Corps line in case of a German attack on a line BELLACOURT - WAILLY.
    We are now again in the VIIth Corps - the Corps which attacked at GOMMECOURT in July 1916.
    Battalion billetted in SIMENCOURT - uncomfortable billets - part of the Battalion in huts - damn cold.
    From the 1st to 8th of March inclusive the Brigade treked about 98 miles. A very big strain on men who had been in trenches continously since the 29th of November and who had had no marching at all since that date.
    About 40 men fell out on the march. March discipline was good and the whole trek a creditable performance.
    In our present position we are now 21 miles south of our starting point LAVENTIE.
    Casualties 1 O.R. Other Causes.

9th   The Commanding Officer reconnoitred CORPS line. O.C. Companies reconnoitred approaches from SIMENCOURT to Corps Line and assembly trenches.
    Day spent in general cleaning up.
    A full issue of fresh meat was issued this day and a very limited supply of charcoal.
    Rations throughout have been unsatisfactory and on one occasion we received about 300 rations of rice and flour in lieu of bread or biscuit - a useful commodity while on trek.
    Casualties 1 O.R. Sick. 1 O.R. Other Causes.

10th   Remained in SIMENCOURT. Inspection of Gas Helmets. Cut down number of employed men in accordance with G.H.Q. Letter. Companies practised Platoon formations for the attack. Casualties 2 O.R. Sick. 1 Officer (2nd Lieut W. ALLAN) transferred to R.F.C. 1 Officer (2nd Lieut J. BETTERIDGE) returned from Hospital, 2 O.R. Reinforcements.

RShoolbred Lieut Colonel
Commdg. 1/ Queens' Westminster Rifles

Place	Date	Hour	
	1917. Mar. 11th		The Sabbath Day. Voluntary Services. Continued practice in Platoon formations. Great aerial activity the whole day. Weather warmer. Roads awful. Conference at Brigade H.Q. The Divisional General commented on the excellent "chits" received by Division from the 1st Army and XIth Corps. Casualties 1 O.R. Sick, 1 O.R. Other Causes. 18 O.R. Reinforcements.
	12th		In SIMENCOURT. Companies trained for 4 hours in morning. Bayonet fighting - rapid loading - dummy bomb throwing etc. Casualties 2 O.R. Sick, 2 Officers (2nd Lieuts S.E.TROTTER & J.H.M.HOOPER from Reserve Battn) and 41 O.R. Reinforcements.
	13th		Same as for the 12th. Much noise of artillery fire. Casualties 2 O.R. Sick.
	14th		Battalion moved from SIMENCOURT to ACHICOURT starting at 5.30 p.m. We are told that town is frequently treated to Gas Shells. Casualties 3 O.R. Sick, 1 O.R. Other Causes.

	15th		"D" Company garrison for the ACHICOURT defences. The other 3 Companies were at work at night clearing HOPE STREET of mud - duration of work about 4½ hours.
			    "Good" document received on economy in FAT. Almost as amusing as the "Pork and Bean Ration" pamphlet. The following is an extract from the former document. "Water in which greasy plates, dishes etc are washed, should be allowed to cool and the grease collected from the surface"
			    Casualties 1 O.R. Other Causes. 1 Officer (2nd Lieut W.E.CRAWFORD from 18th Res.-Bn. London Regt) and 2 O.R. Reinforcements.

	16th		Battalion at work again at night. About 450 O.R. on GREEN STREET C.T. About 40 men continued work of previous night on HOPE STREET. 50 men of "D" Company on R.E. and ammunition fatigues. 3 Companies worked on GREEN STREET C.T. clearing mud. Germans very active in the air - much artillery activity. Casualties 3 O.R. Sick.
	17th		Same working parties as for previous day. Many German aeroplanes over our lines during the day. Our artillery very active. Casualties 1 O.R. Sick.

Ashworth Lieut Colonel
Commdg. 1/ Queens' Westminster Rifles

1917.
Mar. 18th   45 men of "B" Company sent up to do daylight
work on GREEN STREET. At 9.30 a.m. a wire received
from Brigade to cancel all working parties, the
Battalion prepared to move up to take over from 2nd
Londons or to take over the German front line. A
later message received states that the Germans are supposed
to be retiring in front of the Brigade on our right.
2nd Londons ordered to keep in touch with Battn on
their right and to send out patrols to discover if
the Germans have gone in front of us.
  Battn moved by Companies to 2nd London front.
  Brigade orders received stated that the
advance of the 169th Infantry Brigade would be made
on a two Battalion front and readjustments would be
made accordingly.
  "A" and "B" Companies were sent over to join up
on the left with the 2nd Londons (who were by this
time through BEAURAINS) and to obtain touch with
the Div. on our right, -the XIVth Divn.
  "C" Company moved up to old British front line.
"D" Company was in support about M.4.c. Battalion
near MAISON BRULEE in M.4.c.
  Communication with front as usual very bad
runners experienced great difficulty in finding
the Companies owing to the extreme darkness.
The Germans had filled the village of BEAURAINS
with wire - spikes for horses etc. At about
midnight a report came in from "A" and "B"
Companies to say they were in position in MELTON
Trench in M.11.c.1½.½ to M.11.a.9.2.
  Casualties 4 O.R. Sick, -4 O.R. Reinforcements.

19th   In the early morning orders were received to
move two Companies into the PREUSSEN WEG. "A"
Company then took up position on the right &
"B" on the left. "A" Company to where PREUSSEN
WEG joins NEUFCHATEL LANE there to get touch with
2nd Londons.
  "C" Company were ordered up to MELTON TRENCH in
support.
  Approximate position of our front line.
PREUSSEN WEG M.11.b.8.2. to M.18.central.
The C.O. then decided to move Battalion H.Q.
into BEAURAINS. 2nd Lieut HARROW was ordered
forwarded to reconnoitre position for Battn H.Q.
He found an excellent German dug out marked on the map as
Company H.Q. at M.10.d.9½.8. Battn H.Q. moved forward
to this dug-out - there was the Officers mess room about
15 feet down - below this about another 15 feet down
were the sleeping quarters, which consisted of four
more rooms in each of which was a stove - during an
investigation of telephone wires etc, some fuze was
found at the main entrance to the dug-out. This lead
to a mine let into the wall. A further examination
resulted in the finding of similar mines at the other
two entrances to the dug-outs.

                            Lieut Colonel
                    Commdg 1/ Queens' Westminster Rifles

1917.
Mar. 19th (Contd).

There was a German Officer captured in BEAURAINS along with two O.R. on the 18th. We suppose that he had used this dug-out-up to the last minute, as bread, butter, salt and pepper were on the table. Owing to the promptness of the 2nd Londons in entering BEAURAINS he had not been able to fire the fuze. All other dug-outs in the village seem to be very thoroughly blown up. Nothing was left by the Germans in the village except a few hundred bombs, Very Light ammunition etc. The materials that we did find were of the most excellent quality and all their signal wire was of copper.

Companies worked on converting German trenches, digging fire steps etc.

"C" Company took up a position from a point in MELTON T. about M.11.c.8.8. to N. end of CIRCULAR WORK M. 11.d.0.2. thence round W. side of WORK to M.17.b.2.6. thence to GRUNDHERR LANE about M.17.b.0.4.

Patrols were sent out up PREUSSEN REDOUBT and up NEUFCHATEL LANE towards NEUVILLE VITASSE, the former saw no enemy. The latter heard and saw enemy in NEUFCHATEL LANE.

Casualties 3 O.R. Wounded, 2 O.R. Sick. 27 O.R. Transferred to "TANKS".

20th

Work on consolidation continued. "A" Coy took up position along SWITCH Trench to M.18.c.7.4.

At night "A" Company were ordered to establish 2 Lewis Gun Posts - one at M.18.b.4.5. in the PREUSSEN REDOUBT - the other at M.18.d.7.8. NEUFCHATEL LANE. On going out to establish the latter post the party saw a working party of the Germans about 50 strong filling in trenches at spot where post was to be established. A fighting patrol was sent out by O.C. "A" Company, but when they reached the spot the Germans had gone. Both Posts were established.

Q.V.R. established a Lewis Gun Post in VITASSE LANE.

Casualties 2 O.R. Wounded, 6 O.R. Sick, 12 O.R. posted T.M.B., 9 O.R. Reinforcements.

21st

Work continued.

At night "A" Company were ordered to construct Lewis Gun Posts at M.18.b.2.9. and M.18.b.4.9. The first Post was established as ordered. The second position was considered to be an unsuitable one by O.C. "A" Company owing to a "bluff" which would mask the fire of this Post about 100 yards in front He, therefore, constructed a Post at M.18.b.2.6. - both these Posts were occupied on the night 21/22nd The three Posts in M.18.b. were joined up by using old German trenches. Two Companies of the L.R.B. were placed at the disposal of O.C. Q.W.R. for work on reclaiming DEODAR LANE between M.18.d.6.3. and

Place	Date	Hour	

1917.
Mar. 21st (Contd)   M.18.b. 75.20. and connected thence with PREUSSEN REDOUBT at M.18.b.4.5. by a well traversed trench.
    Q.V.R. established Posts in NEUVILLE LANE at M.24.b.b.3. and in VITASSE LANE about M.24.b.5.7.
    "B" Company sent a patrol to PINE TRENCH and brought back no satisfactory information.
    Casualties 5 O.R. Sick.

22nd   Work continued.
    At night "B" Company put out a line of wire covering their frontage from approximately M.11.b.72.20 to M.18.b.0.5. Other work on fire steps and Company H.Q. Hostile artillery active during the day.
    Casualties 3 O.R. Killed, 2 O.R. Wounded, 1 Officer (2nd Lieut R.H.BROWN) and 6 O.R. Sick.

23rd   Capt J.A.GREEN 1st Queens Westminster Rifles, who was attached to 169th Inf. Bde as learner, was killed by a shell while superintending salvage work - his death was instantaneous. Buried the same night in new cemetery near Cross Roads in M.4.c.
    "A" Company put out two more Lewis Gun Posts - one at M.18.b.75.15, the other at M.18.d.6.3½. Patrol from "B" Company visited PINE TRENCH again and reported that it was occupied by the enemy.
    Casualties 3 O.R. Wounded, 3 O.R. Reinforcements.
    Capt J.A.GREEN Killed in action.

24th   Work as usual.
    Patrol of "B" Company, under orders of O.C. "A" Company sent to investigate TELEGRAPH REDOUBT and to bring back definite information. This patrol started about 6 p.m. Patrol returned at 8.45 p.m. but it was 3.30 a.m. (new time) before any information reached Battn H.Q. - TELEGRAPH REDOUBT was reported to be in occupation of the enemy.
    Relief by L.R.B. Began at 6 p.m. Heavy "strafe" by the enemy artillery about 7 p.m. One shell landed in a Post occupied by "A" Company and wounded 4 men. L.R.B. also had 2 Killed and 5 Wounded. Three Companies were relieved by 9.30 p.m. "A" Company reported complete at 10.50 p.m. At 11 p.m. all watches were put forward 1 hour - (Summer Time) Battalion in billets at ACHICOURT.
    Casualties 4 O.R. Wounded, 1 O.R. Sick, 3 O.R. Reinforcements.

25th   Day of rest and bathing. Orders received to relieve 2nd Londons in support on the following day.
    Casualties 4 O.R. Wounded, 5 O.R. Sick, 5 O.R. Reinforcements.

26th   Relieved 2nd Londons in support, starting from ACHICOURT at 6.30 p.m. New dispositions 2 Companies in old German front line - 2 Companies in old British front line at M.4.c.
    After relief Companies went straight on to dig new C.Ts

Lieut Colonel
Commdg 1/Queens' Westminster Rifles

1917.
Mar. 26th (Contd).
– a zig zag trench from M.17.b.6.8. to M.18.a.5.8. – another from M.12.c.80.05. to WILLY TR. at M.18.b.2.6.
O.C. "D" Company had charge of the digging of the former trench and for the work the whole of "C" Coy and half of "A" Company were attached to him. O.C. "B" Company was in charge of the latter one. Half of "A" Company were attached to him.
Casualties:- 8 O.R. Sick, 8 O.R. Reinforcements.

27th
Work on new C.T.s continued.
Trench from M.17.b.6.8. – M.18.a.5.8. reported to be 6 feet deep except where the ground was chalky where it was only 4 feet – trench was 5 feet wide at the top. Trench from M.12.c.80.05 to M.18.b.2.6. was completed as ordered, except that it was not made 5 feet wide at top – but averaged 4 feet wide throughout. This trench was only ordered to be dug 3 feet deep. Casualties 1 Officer (2nd Lieut E.A. HUDSON) and 2 O.R. Wounded, 3 O.R. Sick, 2 O.R. Reinforcements.

28th
Work on new C.Ts completed. From N.E. Corner of CIRCULAR WORK in M.17.b. to junction of BATTERY TRENCH in M.18.a. completed to 6 feet deep everywhere. About 50 yards of N. face of CIRCULAR WORK cleared and deepened to 6 feet. Salvage work carried on by a Platoon each of "A" and "B" Companies during the day on old front line. Intermittent shelling of BEAURAINS and back areas. Our artillery active.
Casualties 2 O.R. Wounded, 2 O.R. Sick, 1 O.R. Other Causes, 1 O.R. Reinforcements.

29th
Work as usual.
"A" Company carried up wire and pickets to new trench on bank in M.24.c. which was being dug by Q.V.R. Later 50 men of this Company put up wire in front of new trench. "B" Company during the day salvaged wire and pickets. At night 50 men carried up wire etc to the strong point in M.24.c.35.30 from R.E. Dump in BEAURAINS, for work under KINGSAP.
"C" Company also collected wire etc from R.E. Dump and carried it up to the Company H.Q. in M.18.b.1.2. for work under KINGSAP. Two Platoons of this Company worked at night on the MANOIR TRENCH under the L.R.B. Hostile artillery less active during the day and the night quiet.
Casualties 6 O.R. Sick, 2 O.R. Reinforcements.

30th
The Battalion relieved the L.R.B. in the evening New dispositions as follows:- "D" Company on the right from M.18.c.89.63. to M.18.b.10.20. "C" Company in the centre from M.18.b.10.20. to BATTERY TRENCH exclusive. "B" Company on left from BATTERY TRENCH to M.11.b.72.20. Each Company held the line with three Platoons in front line with One Platoon in support immediately in rear.

Ashworth Lieut Colonel
Commdg 1/ Queens' Westminster Rifles

Date	
1917. Mar. 30th (Contd).	The six posts in front were divided between the Right and Centre Companies, "D" Company holding Posts 1, 2 and 3 and "C" Company holding Posts 4, 5 and 6. The relief started at dusk and was completed by 10.55 p.m. (Summer time). Hostile Artillery fairly quiet during the day. Casualties 5 O.R. Sick.
31st.	Most of the work in the left sector having been taken over by 168th Infantry Brigade, the Battalion was ordered to work on the trenches which it occupied prior to handing over. That part of the PREUSSEN WEG held by the Centre Company required deepening owing to it being in full view of NEUVILLE VITASSE. This work was carried out by "C" Company. On the rest of our front work was done on new fire steps and Company Headquarters. Casualties 3 O.R. Wounded, 1 O.R. Reinforcement, 2 O.R. Sick.

	Offrs.	O.R.
Strength on 28.2.17.	38	974.
Add.	6	168.
	32	806.
Less.	5	108.
Strength on 31.3.17.	37	914.

Ashwoourd Lieut-Colonel.
Commanding 1/16th London Regiment.
(1st Queens Westminster Rifles).

Place	Date	Hour	
	1917. April 1st.		During the day work was continued on the trenches held by us. In the evening the Battalion was relieved by the RANGERS of the 168th Infantry Brigade. Relief started at about 8 p.m. and was completed at 1 a.m. During the day hostile artillery was fairly quiet but during the night our front and support lines were shelled. Our relief was completed without any casualties, the RANGERS, however, being less fortunate. Companies proceeded by march route to MONCHIET, a distance of about 10 miles. Casualties 6 O.R. Sick, 2 O.R. Reinforcements.
	2nd		Battalion "all in" by 5.30 a.m. Day of rest and cleaning up. Casualties 1 O.R. Sick.
	3rd		Another day of rest and cleaning. During the afternoon the Divisional Band played in the village and the Battalion was also allotted 400 seats at the "BOW BELLS" Casualties 2 O.R. Reinforcements.
	4th		Training was carried out during the day. The new Platoon formation, bayonet fighting and rapid loading was especially practised. Casualties 1 O.R. Sick, 1 O.R. Other Causes, 1 O.R. Reinforcement.
	5th		Training still carried on in Battalion area, the new formations etc still being practised. O.O. No. 85 issued at 5 p.m. (Copy attached). Casualties 12 O.R. Sick, 1 Officer (Major P.M. Glasier) and 1 O.R. Reinforcement.
	6th		Training still carried on. In the afternoon special attention was given to Artillery Formation. Orders for the move to ACHICOURT postponed 1 day. Administrative Orders in conjunction with O.O. No.85 for Z Day were issued. (Copy attached). Casualties 3 O.R. Wounded (Ammunition Loading Party) 14 O.R. Sick.
	7th		In the evening the Battalion marched to Billets in ACHICOURT. The same areas were occupied as on March 25th. Casualties 13 O.R. Sick, 1 O.R. Other Causes, 21 O.R. Reinforcements (serving with T.M.B.)
	8th		At about 1 a.m. a few shells were fired into ACHICOURT with the result that a barn adjoining one of the "A" Company billets caught fire. "A" Company turned out immediately and their efforts prevented the fire from spreading. At about noon the town was again shelled. "B" Company H.Q. received a direct hit, causing part of the building to collapse, thereby inflicting many casualties on a Platoon of men of this Company who were taking shelter in the building. The shelling ceased at about 1 p.m., but started again at 2 p.m. This time a lorry loaded with 9.2" ammunition was hit and immediately burst into flames. The fire spread to adjacent lorries, until in all there were twenty burning. After a time the ammunition began to explode and some of the houses in the Square began to blaze. A great deal of damage was caused by this fire, many billets being

1917.
April 8th (Contd). burned and a large quantity of stores and equipment buried beneath the ruins. At 8.15 p.m. the Battalion moved up from ACHICOURT to the RESERVE AREA, West of BEAURAINS. Battalion "all in" by midnight.
     Casualties 1 Officer (2nd Lieut A.G.BEVILLE) and 16 O.R. Killed, 31 O.R. Wounded.

9th Zero Day. Orders to be prepared to move forward from Zero plus 2 hours. No orders for move received.
     Casualties NIL.

10th Battalion still in RESERVE AREA. In the evening a wire was received stating that the Division had gained its objective. All Units to reform. But this information as to the objective having been gained turned out not to be true.
     Casualties 1 O.R. Other Causes, 2 O.R. Reinforcements.

11th Orders to move were received by 'phone at 2.30 p.m. The Battalion moved up to the Area in N.14.c. - E.N.E. of NEUVILLE VITASSE, in trenches which were supposed to be the HINDENBURG LINE. Battalion H.Q. in German dug-out in TELEGRAPH LANE.
     Casualties 1 O.R. Sick, 1 O.R. Reinforcement.

12th In the afternoon orders were received to move South the Area occupied by the 2nd Londons. While this move was in progress, cancelling orders were received and later, the Regiment was ordered to send three Companies up to the NEPAL TRENCH in N.21.d. with One Company in support in N.20. "A", "B", and "D" Companies moved forward, while "C" Company who were shifting a dump remained in support. This move was not completed until the early hours of the 13th April.
     Casualties 4 O.R. Sick, 1 Officer (2nd Lieut H.J. FURMINGER) Transferred to "TANKS"

13th Our attack on the SENSEE RIVER Line was intended this day in conjunction with the Corps on our left and right the objectives of the 56th Division being the village of CHERISY from its North end inclusive to the Wood in U.2.a. (Map 51.b.S.W. just North of the village of FONTAINE LEZ CROISILLES exclusive.

     The 169th Infantry Brigade was to do the attack with the 2nd Londons on the right and the L.R.B. on the left, supported respectively by the Victorias and the WESTMINSTERS and all four Battalions were moved in the early morning to the Assembly Area due South of WANCOURT under the ridge of which the WANCOURT TOWER was on the N.E. Spur. The Battalion reached its assembly area at 9 a.m. The attack of the Brigade was to be dependant on the Divisions on our Left and Right getting into the alignment we occupied (at present our position was a considerable salient - the enemy still holding GUEMAPPE and the high ground North of CROISILLES.).

                                    Lieut Colonel
                        Commdg. 1/ Queens' Westminster Rifles

Place	Date	Hour
	1917. April 13th (Contd).	

Neither the Division on our left or on our Right did get on this day and the attack was not delivered and at night we relieved the L.R.B. on the Left of the WANCOURT TOWER RIDGE and the Victorias relieved the 2nd Londons on the Right. This afternoon the Division on our left attacked GUEMAPPE which was heavily shelled by both the enemy and ourselves and the position in it was very obscure.

At 10 p.m. a Warning Order came in that the attack as detailed at the beginning of the day - April 13th - was to be carried out on the following morning and at 11.45 p.m. the final orders were received ordering the attack at 5.30 a.m. the following morning - the Victorias attacking on the Right and the WESTMINSTERS on the Left, and no longer making our attack dependent on what happened on our left or right, but making it an independent and apparently isolated attack.

The men were also entirely whacked and there was no time or possibility of any proper explanation to them of their objectives - or of more than the mere organization of the advance to the attack objective, which no one had ever seen.

These objectives were firstly the establishing of a position along the ridge some 500 yards West of CHERISY - a ridge running N.E. & S.W. and parallel to and 1,000 yards from the Tower Ridge on which we were established. And, secondly, the capture and consolidation of the village of CHERISY itself and the establishment of strong points on the northern flank of our attack and of outposts along the line of the SENSEE RIVER to the East of the village.

The first objective was the task of "A" and "B" Companies - "A" on the right and "B" on the Left.
The second objective was the task of "C" and "D" Companies - "C" on the right and "D" on the Left.
After about 1 hours sleep in the 24 for the last three days the Battalion proceeded to its task.
The enemy was known to be digging in on the ridge West of CHERISY some 1,000 yards in front of the WANCOURT TOWER RIDGE and parallel to it, but the strength of his artillery or of his dispositions for defence were entirely unknown, though during the last few days he had been shewing a much stronger resistance than at any period since the beginning of his withdrawal from the Corps front.

14th   At Zero Hour - 5.30 a.m. - the Battalion advanced to the attack.

"A" and "B" Companies forming the first wave - "A" on the Right and "B" on the Left.

"C" and "D" Companies forming the second wave - "C" on the Right and "D" on the Left.

NShoolbred   Lieut Colonel
Commdg. 1/ Queens' Westminster Rifles

1917.
April 14th.
(Contd).

each wave advancing in two lines of men extended at 6 paces interval and at 200 yards distance. The distance between the first wave last line and the first line of the 2nd wave was 300 yards in order to conform to the advance of the Victorias on our Right. It was a beautiful morning and quite light with the remains of the moon to help the dawning day. It appears that the enemy were launching an attack against the WANCOURT TOWER, which was our left flank, at the same time as our attack was taking place, as the enemy barrage started a few minutes before ZERO HOUR and before our own barrage commenced. Our own barrage is described by our attacking waves as seeming to be negligible as compared with the enemy. It certainly did not keep the Machine Gunners heads down or stop their fire.

The Battalion went into action 497 all ranks.

"A" Company with Capt. H. AGATE in command.
  2nd Lieuts W. HULL, H. PICKLES, and R.I.RICHENS.
"B" Company with Lieut S.C.YEATES in command.
  2nd Lieuts J. BETTERIDGE and T.S.BAKER.
"C" Company with Lieut W.G.ORR in command.
  2nd Lieuts B.C.LEWALL, W.M.MUSGROVE and C.A.ENGLISH.
"D" Company with 2nd Lieut P. PALMER in command.
  2nd Lieuts S.E.TROTTER, V. BELL and C.K.GRAY.

Headquarters followed the last line of "C" and "D" Companies and established itself just under the crest of the hill at about 6 a.m.

Information was at this time brought back by Sergt HAWKINS of "C" Company that some enemy were quite close and it appears that as soon as the front waves had gone over the ridge and were descending into the valley between us and the ridge, which formed the first objective, a number of the enemy appeared in their left rear.

Heavy Machine Gun fire was also opened from front and from both flanks and the advance was held up - the casualties from Machine Gun fire being severe. It was this Machine Gun Fire and not the enemy barrage which caused nearly all our casualties.

At shortly before 8.30 a.m. two Companies of the L.R.B. were sent up, one to line the trench out of which our first wave had gone and the other to form a defensive flank by the river. At about 9 a.m. a formed body of the enemy were seen some 200 yards on their side of the TOWER RIDGE moving to the S.W. to a position about half way between the TOWER and the junction of the tracks in 29.d.8.9. They were about 50 strong and looked remarkably like the front wave of a counter attack, but they contented themselves with some sniping which the L.R.B. replied to and I did not turn the artillery on to them because of the numbers of our wounded, who I feared were in their neighbourhood, neither in view of the obscurity of the position in our front did I attack them with the bayonet.

Ashmound   Lieut Colonel
Commdg. 1/ Queens' Westminster Rifles

1917.
April 14th
(Contd).

It appears that our lines advanced keeping touch with the VICTORIAS on our Right across the enemy practice trenches on our side of the valley over which the attack was advancing and that the few remaining Officers and Men of the two front Companies established themselves the furthest of these trenches, the two rear Companies in one of the nearer of them.

They were no longer in sufficient strength to press the attack any further and were under heavy Machine Gun fire as well as enemy shell fire, but it was the Machine Gun fire which caused nearly all the casualties.

Quite early in the morning Capt H. AGATE was wounded and Lieut S.C.YEATES and 2nd Lieut T.S.BAKER were killed, 2nd Lieut R.I.RICHENS mortally wounded and at different times 2nd Lieuts BETTERIDGE and PICKLES were wounded leaving in these two Companies - "A" and "B" - only 2nd Lieut W. HULL.

Lieut W.G.ORR established himself with some 20 O.R. of his Company in a spit locked trench forming one of the rear ones of this German practice system and collected into it some 20 other men of our Regiment and also some DURHAMS and some VICTORIAS and proceeded to dig in.

The messenger whom he sent back to report his position never reached Battalion Headquarters and was presumably killed.

Lieut ORR was attacked at about 11 a.m. from his left front but with the help of his Lewis Guns and by rifle fire he drove off the attack.

His losses were heavy during the day and at dusk, including 3 Officers of the DURHAMS and a few VICTORIA men, he had only 27 all told.

2nd Lieut B.C.LEWALL of "C" Company was wounded early in the day, and in going to help, although already wounded himself, a wounded rifleman, he was again wounded. 2nd Lieut W.M.MUSGROVE was also wounded.

Of "D" Company 2nd Lieuts P.PALMER, V.BELL and S.E. TROTTER were all wounded and 2nd Lieut C.K.GRAY and his whole Platoon, with the exception of two or three men who got detached, is missing. They were the left Platoon of the last wave and it is feared that the survivors of it have been captured.

There is no doubt that under the immense difficulties of the hurried issue of orders and of the absolute impossibility of any sort of previous reconnaissance of the ground that the Battalion attack swung too much to its Right, drawing indeed into the Victoria area. In some cases also, the sunken road leading to FONTAINE LEZ CROISILLES seems to have been mistaken for the correct one, viz, the one leading to CHERISY, which was the inter - battalion division between the VICTORIAS and ourselves.

This rendered our left all the more vulnerable to the enemy formed for their attack on the WANCOURT TOWER position.

Ashwood   Lieut Colonel
Commdg, 1/ Queens' Westminster Rifles

1917.
April 14th
(Contd).

Furthermore, our left was, from the initial plan of the attack, entirely in the air, there being no attack made between GUEMAPPE and the left of our Brigade objectives, this ground being the reverse slope of a hill ending at the East end of the WANCOURT TOWER SPUR. At the last Minute and while on the trek to some other destination the -------- Brigade were diverted and ordered to fill in this gap and establish a defensive flank from CHERISY to GUEMAPPE, but coming up in the dark and with no previous reconnaissance at all they got too much to the Right - deployed for their advance in the middle of our assembly area and eventually crossing the line of our advance by a further diagonal half right advance came into support of the Victorias on our right instead of being on our left, and being held up on the TOWER RIDGE, established themselves there where they remained all day.

There was no communication from the front, and knowing how close a formed body of the enemy were to the TOWER RIDGE, I had no hope of establishing any from the rear, except that 2nd Lieut A.M.MACKLE went out in the early afternoon to collect all the men he could find in our near front so that the remains of the Battalion could be reassembled as order by Brigade in our morning assembly area. In this way some 65 O.R. were collected. At this time we had no knowledge of the men of "C" Company and oddments who were maintaining themselves in the German practice trench (alluded to above).

At 5 p.m. an order was received from Brigade that Battn H.Q. was to move to and re-establish itself in the H.Q. in WANCOURT which we had occupied the previous night and 2nd Lieut A.M.MACKLE was left on the ridge to collect stragglers and wounded from the field at dusk, and misinterpreting his orders, as he failed to distinguish between stragglers and a formed body, however, small, holding a position won in battle. 2nd Lieut A.M.MACKLE instructed LIEUT W.G.ORR when he got into touch with him after dark to withdraw to the assembly area. Owing to the unfortunate withdrawal of Battn H.Q. it was 9 o'clock at night before I heard of Lieut ORR's position and of his having withdrawn from it. After consultation with Brigade Lieut ORR was ordered to re-establish himself in the post he had occupied and informed that he would be relieved by the 4th Londons of the 168th Brigade who were taking over the line and for whom he was instructed to leave guides. He left 2nd Lieut C.A.ENGLISH and three other guides who knew perfectly well what they had to do and where they had to go, but who, on account of the darkness of the night, failed when guiding the platoon to find the position. Lieut ORR having only 15 men with him - his original 27 less oddments of other Regiments and less the guides for the relieving platoon of the 4th London Regiment, and having had no orders to hold the position at all costs, and estimating his force as insufficient to be able to hold

Lieut Colonel
Commdg. 1/ Queens' Westminster Rifles

1917.
April 14th
(Contd)

the position in the face of any attack during the day, withdrew his men at dawn, judging himself just before dawn to be practically surrounded by the enemy, whose Very Lights were crossing over his trench from both front and back. A withdrawal for which, wrong or right, I accept full responsibility.

Lieut ORR had behaved with the greatest gallantry and resource all day and owing to the failure of communication was placed in a position of extreme difficulty in making his final decision. As a matter of fact the enemy never did occupy the trench he withdrew from and the following night the LONDON SCOTTISH re-established themselves in it without any fighting or casualties.

But this whole incident is another instance shewing the importance of Battalion Headquarters not being moved from its Battle position until for good or for ill the position in front is definitely and fully cleared up.

The Battalion came out of action that night to the NEUVILLE VITASSE Area.

	Officers.	O.R.
"A" Company.	1	23.
"B" "	-	40.
"C" "	2	42.
"D" "	-	50.
	3	165.
Headquarter "Details"	4	53.
	7	218.

Casualties - 13th - 2 O.R. Killed 11 O.R. Wounded.

Casualties - 14th - 2 Officers Killed (Lieut S.C.YEATES and 2nd Lieut T.S.BAKER) and 11 O.R. Killed. 5 Officers (2nd Lieuts S.E.TROTTER, B.C.LEWALL, J. BETTERIDGE, P. PALMER and V. BELL) and 143 O.R. Wounded. 3 Officers (Capt H. AGATE, 2nd Lieuts C.K.GRAY and H. PICKLES) and 96 O.R. Missing. 1 O.R. Reinforcement.

15th

At noon the Battalion paraded for "Roll Call" after which the Companies were amalgamated, "A" and "B" Companies forming No. I Company and "C" and "D" Companies No. 2. At 3.30 p.m. the Battalion again paraded and marched back to trenches in the old German front line 500 yards South of BEAURAINS. The Battalion now being so small in numbers all the men were able to find accomodation in cleared German Dug-outs and shelters erected

N Shoolbred   Lieut Colonel
Commdg. 1/ Queens' Westminster Rifles

Place	Date	Hour	
			1917.
		April 15th (Contd).	by the 167th Infantry Brigade. Casualties 2 Officers Died of Wounds (2nd Lieut R.I.RICHENS and 2nd Lieut W.M. MUSGROVE) and 1 O.R. Died of Wounds. 2 O.R. Other Causes.
		16th	The whole day was given up to temporary reorganization and rest. Casualties NIL.
		17th	The day was again devoted to rest and cleaning up. The weather was bad and did not in any way add to the comfort of the men. The Battn was allotted baths at AGNY, but no clean change of underclothing was available for the men. Casualties 1 O.R. Died of Wounds, 5 O.R. Sick.
		18th	Baths were again allotted to the Battalion at AGNY. Reorganization and refitting during the day. Casualties 2 O.R. Sick, 1 O.R. Reinforcement.
		19th	Reorganization, refitting and deficiencies were attended to during the morning. Also a conference of the N.C.Os of the Battalion to endeavour to account for some of the Missing men. Casualties 2 O.R. Sick, 1 O.R. Reinforcement.
		20th	The Battalion paraded at 9.30 a.m. and proceeded by march route to the embussing point 500 yards N.E. of the junction of the ACHICOURT - DAINVILLE and ARRAS - DOULLENS Roads. Dinners were served at noon and at 5.30 p.m. the Battalion was taken by buses and lorries to ST AMAND, a distance of about 15 miles, arriving at 7.30 p.m. Casualties 1 O.R. Sick, 3 O.R. Reinforcement. 1 Officer returned from Hospital (2nd Lt R.H.BROWN).
		21st	Orders from Division stated that the first two days were to be entirely devoted to rest. Beyond reorganization no work was done. Casualties 2 O.R. Sick. 1 O.R. Other Causes. 1 O.R. Reinforcements.
		22nd	Day of Rest. At 10.30 a.m. there was a Parade Service for members of the Church of England and throughout the day services were held locally of all other denominations. On this day the Officers and Men of the "SURPLUS PERSONNEL" rejoined the Battalion from BOUQUEMAISON. Casualties 1 Officer (2nd Lieut H.J.HOLLAND) and 87 O.R. Reinforcements.
		23rd	Training was carried on during the morning

RShoolbred Lieut Colonel
Commdg. 1/ Queens' Westminster Rifles

Place	Date	Hour	

1917.
April 23rd (Contd). Reorganization, refitting and foot inspection were the special points attended to.
   Casualties 2 O.R. Killed, 1 O.R. Other Causes. 6 O.R. Reinforcements.

24th Training was carried on during the morning, physical training, bayonet fighting and platoon organization being specially attended to. At noon a warning order was received stating that the Brigade was to be ready to move forward at 2 p.m. Later orders received detailed the Battn to proceed by march route via POMMIER - BERLES - BEAUMETZ to WANQUETIN. The Battn moved off from ST AMAND at 2.10 p.m. and arrived at WANQUETIN at 6.45 p.m., the distance covered being 12 miles.
   Casualties 4 O.R. Sick, 1 Officer (Lieut C.W. RENTON) exchanged for 2nd Lieut F.W. RUSSELL of this Regiment who was serving with the 2nd Londons.

25th Reorganization and refitting was carried on throughout the day.
   Casualties 1 O.R. Died of Wds, 7 O.R. Sick 1 Officer (2nd Lieut E.W. SMITH) and 30 O.R. Reinforcements.

26th Orders from Brigade warned us of a further move of the Brigade Group. At 12 noon the Battalion paraded and proceeded by march route to BERNEVILLE via WARLUS. Dinners were served on the roadside between WARLUS and BERNEVILLE and the Battalion entered its billeting area at 3 p.m.
   Casualties 1 O.R. Sick, 2nd Lieuts W.E. CRAWFORD and C.A. ENGLISH were sent to 4th London Regiment and 2nd Lieut S. MINEAR of this Regiment joined us from that Battalion, 1 O.R. Other Causes.

27th Reorganization and training throughout the day At 9.30 p.m. warning orders for further move of the Brigade Group were received.
   Casualties 7 O.R. Sick, 26 O.R. Other Causes, 2 Officers (2nd Lieut E.C. HAYES from L.R.B. and 2nd Lieut A.B. RUSSEL from 2nd Londons) and 26 O.R. Reinforcements.

28th At 12.35 p.m. the Battalion paraded and proceeded by march route to the old German trench system known as the HARP, 600 yards South of TILLOY. The route ordered was via BAC DU NORD - ARRAS - NEUVILLE VITASSE ROAD. The Battalion arrived at its new area at 3.45 p.m., but did not take up its position in trenches until 9 p.m., the 7th Middlesex not having evacuated.
   Casualties 1 O.R. Sick.

29th Training was carried on during the morning, especially of Lewis Gunners. At 3.10 p.m. warning orders were received detailing DICK and SHOU to proceed to the line.

Ashworth
Lieut Colonel
Commdg. 1/ Queens' Westminster Rifles

1917.
April 29th (Contd). Detailed orders arrived at 4.40 p.m. by the Brigade Major. For tactical purposes the Companies were again combined, "A" and "B" forming No. I Company and "C" and "D" forming No. 2 Company. At 7 p.m. the Battalion proceeded via TILLOY-WANCOURT ROAD to Brigade Headquarters in the NIGER TRENCH 600 yards N. of the TILLOY-WANCOURT ROAD (N.16.B.1.8.) Here guides from the 1st and 3rd Londons met the Companies and took them to their respective positions. Battn H.Q. was established N.E. of WANCOURT in N.17.D.1.1. No. 2 Company positions as follows:- 3 platoons behind the bank in N.18.c. from Road Junction South to the Marsh 1 Platoon in semi-circular trench E. of the Sunken Road in N.18.A.& C. Up to midnight No. 1 Company had not reported
Casualties 1 O.R. Wounded. 4. O.R. Sick. 93. O.R. Reinforcement.

30th At 1.10 a.m. No. 1 Company reported complete and relief was accordingly wired to Brigade. At night all Companies worked on assembly trenches in the Battn area. Intermittent shelling throughout the day which increased in violence in the evening.
Casualties 1 O.R. Sick.

	Officers	O.R.
Strength on 31.3.17	37	914.
ADD.	9	278.
	46	1,192.
LESS.	18	441.
Strength on 30.4.17	28	751.

Ashwood
Lieut-Colonel.
Commanding 1st Queens Westminster Rifles.

SECRET.

1st Battn Queens Westminster Rifles.

OPERATION ORDERS

No. 85.

Lieut-Colonel R. Shoolbred, C.M.G., T.D., D.L., Commanding.

Ref. Map. Sheet 51.B.S.W.

1. ENEMY's DEFENSIVE LINE.
The enemy's main defensive line now runs in the Corps front from TILLOY - southwards along top of TELEGRAPH HILL - on the West Side of the Eastern part of NEUVILLE VITASSE and thence south eastwards along the COJEUL SWITCH - through M.1.a. and c., N.7.a and c., N.13.a and c., N.19.a and eastwards along top of N.19.d. and thence through N.20.c., N.26.b., N.27. a., b.and d.

2. ATTACKING FORCES.
In conjunction with an attack by the 1st Army on VIMY and the 6th Corps on our immediate left, the VIIth Corps will shortly resume the offensive. The 56th Divisional task will be the capture of NEUVILLE VITASSE as its first objective and the establishment of a line just W. of WANCOURT from N.16.d.2.2. to N.22.b.2.3. as its second objective.
The 30th Division attacks on the Right of the 56th Division, and the 14th Division attacks on the Left of the 56th Division.

3. 56th Divisional ATTACK.
The attack of the 56th Division will be carried out by the 167th Brigade on the Right and the 168th Brigade on the left. The 169th Brigade is in Divisional Reserve.

4. PROGRAMME OF ATTACK.
The probable programme of attack is as follows:-
At Zero VIth Corps will assault so as to bring it level with the left of the VIIth Corps.
At Zero + 2 hours 14th and 56th Division to assault and capture the BLUE Line.
At Zero + 6 hours and 40 minutes - 30th - 56th and 14th Divisions to assault and advance to the BROWN Line.

5. DAY OF ATTACK.
The attack will take place on Z Day.

6. PRELIMINARY ASSEMBLY AREA.
On Z - 2 day the Brigade moves to its preliminary assembly area.

7. TOOLS.
On Z - 1 day, packs will be stacked, and tools, bombs and ground flares will be drawn under orders issued later.

8. BATTLE ASSEMBLY AREA.
On night of Z - 1/Z day the Brigade moves to the Battle Assembly Area.

9. LEWIS GUNS.
All Lewis Gun Magazines and all spare parts for Lewis Guns, except the spare barrels and the tin magazine boxes will be taken in with the Companies.
O.C. Companies are responsible that everything is taken with the exception of anything which is deficient which they will notify the Adjutant of by 10 a.m. on the 8th inst.

10. WARNING ORDER "Z" DAY.
The Battalion will be ready to move from 2 hours after Zero on Z Day.

11. CARE OF TOOLS.
All tools taken in will be required (subject only to Battle Casualties) to be returned when the Battalion is withdrawn.

12. ARMS - PLATOON COMMANDERS.
Platoon Commanders (Officers) will carry a rifle and sword.

13. WATERBOTTLES.
On no account are men's waterbottles to be touched to drink from on Z - 1 Day, or during Z Day without permission from O.C. Company.

14. DISTRIBUTION - BATTLE AREA. Battn H.Q. will be in a dug-out in M.4.c.25.55 on the S side of ACHICOURT - BEAURAINS Rd. due S. of MAISON BRULEE. Company distribution in Battle Area will be in depth and in following location:-

"A" Company In Reserve Line in M.4.c.

"B"   "   In Reserve Line in M.4.a. and c.

"C"   "   In HAIG ST. & trenches leading out of it in M.3.d.

"D"   "   In HARDY ST. in M.3.d.

If the Battalion is called upon, the Companies will move in the following order, "A", "B", "C" and "D".

15. COMPANY H.Q.
Company Headquarters must be in close proximity to, if not absolutely in their Company areas.

16. RUNNERS.
From Zero 2 hours on Z Day, one runner per Company and 2 for Headquarters will be at Brigade Headquarters - G.33.d.4.0.

17. ARTILLERY FLAGS.
Artillery Flags will be drawn and carried 4 per Company. It must be distinctly understood by all ranks that if these are stuck in the ground they will be disregarded by the artillery, who will only keep their fire in advance of them

- 3 -

so long as they are being waved by hand in the air. They will be in charge and kept close to hand by the Platoon Commander.

The Division on our right will be using RED and YELLOW (diagonal) flags for the same purpose.

18. GROUNDFLARES.
Orders as to times and conditions of use of the groundflares will be issued later.

19. LEATHER JERKINS.
Leather Jerkins will be worn under the tunic and ground sheets will be carried rolled on the belt by each man.

20. MAPS.
Maps to be carried.

    Sheet 51.B. S.W. 1/20,000
    "   51.B.   1/40,000

NEUVILLE VITASSE.

21. OBSERVERS' TELESCOPES, & TELESCOPIC RIFLES.
These will not be taken into action, but will be carefully stored in their cases at Quartermaster's Stores.
Telescopic Rifles will be sent to Q.M.Stores by hand and not carried on wagons.

22. LOOTING.
All ranks are warned that the most extreme disciplinary action will be taken in the case of any soldier detected looting or found in possession of, or to have disposed of, any article from the dead.

23. ARTILLERY.
If a re-bombardment of any portion of an objective becomes necessary, it will normally, unless special orders to the contrary are issued, last for 30 minutes, and the barrage will then lift and move forward to admit of the attack of the objective.

24. TANKS.
Four "TANKS" are being allotted to the Division for the attack on NEUVILLE VITASSE. Special attention will be paid to any signal from "TANKS".

25. MEDICAL ARRANGEMENTS.
The position of the Regimental Aid Post will be notified later. Advanced Bearer Posts will be established at:-
(1) M.4.c.15.70. near the X Roads (MAISON BRULEE)
(2) In cellars at BEAURAINS at M.4.d.65.00.
The Divisional Advanced Dressing Station at ACHICOURT at M.3.b.40.95.
Walking Cases will proceed to Corps wounded walking Collecting Post - AGNY.

26. PRISONERS.

Prisoners will be sent to Collecting Post at M.4.d.1.1.

J.S. Price Capt & Adjt.
1st Queens Westminster Rifles.

Copies to:-

(1) O.C. "A" Company.
(2) "   "B"   "
(3) "   "C"   "
(4) "   "D"   "
(5) Major Harding, M.C.
(6) Adjutant.
(7) 169th I.B.
(8) War Diary.
(9) QuarterMaster.
(10) Office.
(11) Signal Officer.
(12) Spare.

Issued at S.H.Q. 8.4.17.

1st Battalion Rhodesian Rifles.

ADMINISTRATIVE INSTRUCTIONS

with reference to Operation Order No. 60

dated 5/4/17.

6th April 1917.

1. BOMBS:-
    The following Bombs will be carried into action:-

    Mills No. 5. - 12 bombs per man of a bombing squad.
    Mills No. 23. - 6 bombs per man of a rifle bombing squad.

    These will be drawn from the Divisional Dump at N.2.c.7.9.
    In drawing these the following procedure will be adopted:-

    Half of the Bombers and half of the Rifle Grenadiers of each Company will report to the Battalion Bombing Officer - 2nd Lieut. .... - at Battalion Headquarters in ACHICOURT at 9 a.m. on "Y" Day. The Battalion Bombing Officer will supervise the drawing of bombs and rifle grenades and will ensure that sufficient bomb buckets or belt bags are taken up to the dump. Bombers and Rifle Grenadiers will be marched to the dump in separate parties. Each bomber will thus draw 24 Mills No. 5 and each rifle grenadier 12 Mills No. 23, 6 in each bucket. The 12 cartridges for these will be issued as a separate packet.

2. WATER: (a)
    10 Petrol Cans full of water will be drawn by each Company.

    (b) Ground Flares on the scale of one per man per Company will be drawn by each Company.
    The water tins and the ground flares will be drawn on "Y" Day from the Dump mentioned in para (1) above, as follows:-

    "A" Company will be at dump at 9.30 a.m.
    "B"   "   "   " "   " 10.0 a.m.
    "C"   "   "   " "   " 10.30 a.m.
    "D"   "   "   " "   " 11.0 a.m.

3. TOOLS and SANDBAGS.
    20 Shovels and 10 Picks per Company and 2 Sandbags per man will be drawn on "Y" Day from the 512th Field Company R.E. Dump in the School, ACHICOURT, as follows:-

    "A" Company will be at Dump at 11.0 a.m.
    "B"   "   "   " "   " 11.30 a.m.
    "C"   "   "   " "   " 12.0 a.m.
    "D"   "   "   " "   " 12.30 p.m.

    N.B. All parties drawing stores and materials as laid down in paras (2) and (3) will be as small as possible.

4. PACKS.
    Packs will be stacked by Companies in the R.E. Stores ACHICOURT at 2 p.m. at the following times on "Y" Day.

    "A" Company at 2.0 p.m.
    "B"   "   " 2.30 p.m.
    "C"   "   " 3.0 p.m.
    "D"   "   " 3.30 p.m.

RATIONS.

The three days Iron Rations for consumption on [illegible] [illegible] days are dumped in house at [illegible]. They will be issued daily by Supply Officer to Quartermaster of Bn. and will be carried to Q.M.Stores under Line Transport. No Train Supply Wagons will be in use for conveying rations on these days. The three days Iron Rations for Transport Personnel are dumped at the Transport Lines and will be issued daily by [illegible]. The three days oat rations are dumped at the Transport Lines and will be issued daily by the Brigade Transport Officer.

6. SHELTERS.

The Brigade Transport Officer will draw from [illegible] ACHICOURT on [illegible] 100 bivouac shelters and will distribute on scale of 25 per Battalion. These are for use of fighting troops in assembly areas and are not intended for Transport personnel. Capt [illegible] will arrange to get these shelters up to the Battalion on night of Y/Z. Further orders will be issued to him later. When Companies vacate assembly areas sufficient men will be left behind to guard petrol tins and bivouac shelters until there is an opportunity to move them to the new position.

7. SANITATION.

One latrine per Company must be provided in assembly areas - all to be dug at least three feet deep. Excreta must not be allowed within 2 feet of the ground level. Latrines must then be filled in and fresh ones dug if necessary. Latrines must not be dug near fire trenches or dug outs. Areas of ground fouled must be as small as possible and FOUL GROUND should be marked with lumps of chalk.

8. VERY PISTOLS.

All Very Pistols will be handed in to Q.M. Stores ACHICOURT on afternoon of "Y" Day. The Company Q.M.Sgts are responsible for the safe custody of these. In the event of a Company needing the Pistols, O.C. Company will make his own arrangements for getting them up.

(Sd) H.S.PRICE.

Capt & Adjt.
1st Queens Westminster Rifles.

Copies to:-

(1)	C.O.	(7)	O.C. "A" Company.
(2)	Adjutant.	(8)	O.C. "B" "
(3)	2nd in Command.	(9)	O.C. "C" "
(4)	Transport Officer.	(10)	O.C. "D" "
(5)	Quartermaster.	(11)	War Diary (2).
(6)	Bombing Officer.	(12)	Signal Officer.

(13), (14) and (15) Spare.

Place	Date	Hour	

1917.

May 1st. No work was done during the day, except the collecting of dead. In the evening the Battalion was relieved by the L.R.B. The Companies continued work on the assembly trenches up to the time of relief, which started at 8.30 p.m. but was not completed up to midnight. During the day the shelling of our trenches was severe.
Casualties. 3 O.R. Killed. 5 O.R. Wounded. 1 Officer 2nd.Lieut W.Hull and 4 O.R. Sick.

2nd. At 1.30 a.m. H.Q. moved back to new quarters in the WANCOURT LINE although relief was not at the time reported. Relief was reported complete to Bde.at 4.30 a.m. Severe hostile shelling made the relief very difficult and caused many casualties to both ouselves and the L.R.B. During the day the Companies were resting and at night provided working and carrying parties for the BDE.
Casualties. 2 O.R. Killed 5 O.R. Wounded 5 O.R. Sick 1 O.R. Other Causes. 1 O.R. Missing.

3rd. Zero day. The Battalion was in Brigade Reserve and was not called on during the day except for small carrying parties. At 8 p.m. orders were received to move up and occupy the line as held on the 1st.inst. The Battn was now in support. The front line as then held was CAVALRY FARM TRENCH and LANYARD TRENCH. At 7.35 p.m. a very heavy barrage was put down by both sides apparently along the whole of the CORPS front, and it was assumed that a counter attack was imminent against CAVALRY FARM and LANYARD TRENCH. On the arrival of Battn. H.Q. in TANK TRENCH news was received that the garrisons of the front line had withdrawn and Major Burnell of the L.R.B. immediately went forward to order a re-occupation of the front line, but found that the garrison had not withdrawn. In the meantime a wire from BDE. had ordered a withdrawl which was not at the time complied with as it was believed that the real situation was not known at BDE.H.Q. Eventually the BDE. Intelligence Officer with verbal but definite orders for the L.R.B. and 2nd.Londons to withdraw to the W. of the WANCOURT LINE and the original front line of May 1st. to be occupied by the Q.V.R. on the left and ourselves on the right, with the exception that instead of being in Support, the Battn. was now holding the front line and GORDON SUPPORT with one double Company, and one in TANK TRENCH. It became apparent afterwards that the BOSCH did not counter attack but as far as can be gathered the whole strafe started owing to the S.O.S. Signal of both sides being the same and the mistake was mutual. Relief was complete by 3.30 a.m.
Casualties. 1 O.R. Killed. 16 O.R. Wounded. 1 O.R. Sick. 1 O.R. Other Causes. 1 O.R. Reinforcement.

4th. No work was done during the day. At night the Battn was relieved by the 4th.LONDONS. The day was fairly quiet and casualties very light. Relief was reported complete by 2.30 a.m. and the BTN. proceeded to trenches in WANCOURT LINE as on the 2nd.inst.

N Shoolbred
Lieut Colonel
Commdg 1/Queens' Westminster Rifles

WAR DIARY or INTELLIGENCE SUMMARY

(Erase heading not required.)

1917.

Date		
May 4th. contd.	For tactical purposes the Batn. was attached to the 168th.I.B. Casualties. 1 O.R. Killed. 2 Officers, 2nd.Lieut. H.J.Martin 10th.Lon.Att. & 2nd Lieut. F.W.Russell and 4 O.R.Wounded 5 O.R.Sick	
5th.	No work during the day. At night working parties were sent up for digging etc. under the R.E. Casualties. 2 O.R.Killed. 6 O.R. Sick.	
6th.	During the day the Coys. collected old shell cases, and at night worked on wiring on the WANCOURT LINE in front of the Battn. area. Casualties 2 O.R.Sick.	
7th.	Some shell cases were collected during the day and parties were detailed from each Coy. for the burying of horses. At night, parties were sent up collecting dead in the LONDON SCOTTISH area and wiring was also continued on the WANCOURT LINE. Casualties. 1 O.R.Wounded. 1 O.R.Sick. 1 O.R.Other causes. 1 O.R.Reinforcements.	
8th.	During the day only local work was done. At night the Battn. moved forward into "Left Support" and relieved the 3rd.LONDONS. Relief was reported complete to BDE. at 11.55 p.m. Severe hostile shelling during the night. Casualties. 1 O.R.Wounded. 5 O.R.Sick. 1 O.R. Reinforcement.	
9th.	Severe shelling throughout the morning on all the support trenches. Orders received to move forward and relieve the "KENSINGTONS" in "LEFT SECTOR" front line. All arrangements were accordingly made and 169th.I.B. was informed of coming relief. At 7 p.m. orders were received cancelling the relief and a further operation order directed that the LONDON SCOTTISH would relieve us on the night of 10/11th, this Btn. to move back to WANCOURT LINE. Usual work on deepening trenches and collecting dead. Casualties. 2 O.R.Killed. 6 O.R.Wounded. 2 O.R.Sick 1 O.R.Reinforcement.	
10th.	Shelling during the day was intermittent on the Btn. area. At dusk the Companies moved from their trenches and were employed on shifting dumps forward. On completion, the companies proceeded to trenches S.E.of TILLOY and not the WANCOURT LINE as at first ordered the Q.V.R. having moved forward to relieve us. Casualties. 4 O.R.Wounded. 1 Officer 2nd.Lieut S.Minear Other Causes. 1 Officer 2nd.Lieut.E.Caudwell and 1 O.R.Reinforcements.	
11th.	The Btn. arrived in its new area at 5 a.m. Relief was accordingly wired to BDE. No work was undertaken during the day. Casualties. 5 O.R.Killed 4 O.R.Wounded 2 O.R.Sick. 1 O.R.Reinforcement.	
12th.	The day was given to rest and cleaning up. No work was done during the day. Casualties. 5 O.R.Sick. 1 O.R.Other causes.	

N.S.Woollard
Lieut Colonel
Commdg. 1/ Queens' Westminster Rifles

	Place	Date	Hour	Summary of Events and Information	Remarks and references to Appendices

1917.

May 13th. The Coys. did three hours work during the morning. Special attention being paid to Physical Training and Bayonet Fighting.
Casualties. 3 O.R. Sick. 2 O.R. Reinforcements.

14th. Training during the morning. Specialists carried on throughout the whole day. No other work.
Casualties. 1 O.R. Sick. 1 O.R. Reinforcement.

15th. Training as usual. Small fatigue parties during the afternoon collecting old shell cases. No other work.
Casualties. 2 O.R. Sick. 1 O.R. Other Causes. 7 O.R. Reinforcements.

16th. Training and fatigue parties as usual. No other work.
Casualties. 1 O.R. Other Causes. 3 O.R. Reinforcements.

17th. Heavy rain during the night made any sort of work on the ground difficult. Morning was devoted to lectures and smoke helmet drill. No other work.
Casualties. 2 O.R. Sick. 1 O.R. Other Causes. 1 O.R. Reinforcement.

18th. Work as usual during the morning. Fatigue parties during the afternoon collecting old shell cases.
Each day while the Btn. was in the area, fifty seats were allotted for the "Bow Bells".
Casualties. 1 O.R. Sick.

19th. The Battn. was relieved by the East Lancs. Regt. 8th. Bn. Orders had been issued for the Btn. to be clear of the trench area by 11.30. At 11.30 a.m. the Battn. which was marching as three Coys. moved off. Dinners were served on the Transport Lines, half a mile S.W. of TILLOY and the march resumed at 1.30 p.m. via cross country tracks to ARRAS thence by infantry track to DUISANS, the destination. The Btn. arrived in at 4.15 p.m. and was billeted in huts on the AGNEZ-DUISANS Road.
Casualties. 1 O.R. Other Causes.

20th. Day of Rest. Services were held throughout the day by all denominations. Parade Service at 11 o'clock for members of the Church of England. Beyond rifle inspection, no work or training was done.
Casualties. 2 O.R. Sick. 9 Officers Lieut. E. Ridehalgh. 22nd. Lon Regt. 2nd Lieut. S. North 19th. Lon Regt. E.M. Payne, 23rd. Lon. Regt. A.C. Cooper 19th. Lon. Regt. R.L. Whittle, 19th. Lon. Regt. F.E. Whitby, 19th. Lon. Regt. R. Herring, 20th Lon. Regt. W.F.D. Young, Q.W.R. E. Brimelow. Q.W.R. and 164 O.R. Reinforcements.

21st. Three hours training was done during the morning by all Coys. No work during the afternoon.
Casualties. 3 O.R. Sick. 1 Officer, 2nd Lieut. H.K. Moulton & 17 O.R. Reinforcements.

22nd. Heavy rain during the night and morning made night work in the open difficult. The Coys. carried on for three hours in the huts during the morning. No work during the afternoon.
Casualties. Nil.

23rd. Five hours training was done on this day. Coys. paraded at 9 a.m. and worked till 12 noon. Coys again paraded at 2 p.m. and worked till 4 p.m.

N.Shoolbred Lieut Colonel
Commdg. 1/ Queens' Westminster Rifles

Place	Date	Hour

```
1917.
May 23rd.    Specialists under specialist Officers also trained
contd.       during the above hours.
                 Casualties. 1 O.R.Sick. 1 Officer Other Causes.
                     2nd.Lieut.E.M.Payne, 23rd.Lon.Regt.
    24th.    The Btn.Paraded at 9.45 a.m. on the parade ground
             W. of DUISANS", and proceeded at 9.55 a.m. by march
             route to the new billetting area in AGNEZ LES DUISANS.
             No other work was done on this day beyond preparation
             for the coming G.O.C's inspection.
                 Casualties. 2 O.R.Reinforcements.
    25th.    The day was given to final cleaning of equipment
             etc. for the inspection. At intervals throughout the
             day Coys. were inspected by the Commanders. No other
             work was done.
                 Casualties. 5 O.R.Sick. 1 Officer Other Causes
                     Major.P.E.Harding, M.C., 2 O.R.Other
                         Causes. 1 O.R.Reinforcements.
    26th.    Divisional Commander's Inspection. The Btn.
             marched on to the Parade Ground at 10.45 a.m. and was
             inspected by the Divisional Commander at 11.30 a.m.
             During the afternoon no work was done.
                 Casualties. 7 O.R.Sick 1 O.R.Other Causes.
                     1 Officer 2nd.Lieut.S.I.Wilson &
                     21 O.R.Reinforcements.
    27th.    Sunday. Day of Rest. A Parade Service was held at
             11.30 a.m. for members of the C.ofE. on the Parade Ground.
             Services of the other denominations were held through-
             out the day.
                 Casualties. 3 O.R.Sick.
    28th.    Four hours work was done during the morning.
             C Coy. were allotted the Rifle Range. Bayonet fighting
             Physical Drill and Bombing was carried out by the
             other Coys. In the afternoon, short tactical schemes
             were carried on by the N.C.O's.
                 Casualties 5 O.R.Sick. 12 O.R.Reinforcements.
    29th.    Work as usual during the morning and afternoon.
             Coys. had the use of the Bayonet Assault Course in
             turn during the day.
                 Casualties. 3 Officers.Capt.N.T.Thurston,Lieut.
                     C.E.Moy,and 2nd.Lieut.O.A.M.Heaton,
                     and 11 Other Ranks Reinforcements.
    30th.    Work as usual during the day. D Coy. had the use of
             the Rifle Range. In the evening a Football Match V
             the Q.V.R.was played. The Q.V.R. won 2 nil.
                 Casualties. Nil.
    31st.    Training as usual during the day. Bombing,bayonet
             fighting,physical training etc.
                 Casualties. 1 O.R.Sick.
```

	Officers	O.Rks.
Strength on 30.4.17	28	751
Add.	13	248
	41	999
Less.	6	156
Strength on 31.5.17	35	843

Lieut Colonel
Commdg. 1/ Queens' Westminster Rifles

Place	Date	Hour	
	1917.		
	June 1st.		Work as usual during the day. A Coy had the use of the Rifle Range throughout the whole of the day. Casualties 10 O.R. Sick. 7 O.R. Other Causes 10 O.R. Reinforcements.
	2nd.		Training as usual during the morning. In the afternoon Gas Helmets were examined by the Divisional Gas N.C.O. Casualties 2 O.R.Sick. 8 O.R.Reinforcements.
	3rd.		Day of Rest. Parade Service for members of the Church of England in the morning and Services of the other Denominations throughtout the day. Casualties. 1 O.R.Sick. 1 Officer 2nd.Lieut. S.I.Wilson 23rd.Lon.Regt. to L.R.B. and 4 O.R.Other Causes
	4th.		Training as usual during the day. B Coy had the use of the Range throughout the day. Casualties. Nil.
	5th.		Work and training as usual throughout the day. Casualties. 2 O.R.Sick. 1 Officer, 2nd.Lieut.J.P.D Kennedy 19th.Lon.Regt.Reinforcement.
	6th.		Training as usual through the day. C.Company had the use of the range. Casualties. 1 Officer Capt.A.J.Beadel,R.A.M.C. Sick. 1 Officer Capt.D.Rees,R.A.M.C. & 1 O.R.Reinforcement
	7th.		Work and training during the morning. Orders for the move received. The afternoon was spent in packing up etc., During the period spent in AGNEZ, the men were bathed once. All respirators were thoroughly examined and all men due for inoculation were treated at the Aid Post. Casualties 2 O.R.Sick. 7 O.R.Reinforcements.
	8th.		At 5.30 a.m. the Battn.paraded and proceeded by march route via DAINVILLE-ACHICOURT-BEAURAINS to TELEGRAPH HILL arriving at 9.30 a.m. The day was spent in the German trench system known as the HARP about 1000 yds. South of TILLOY. Casualties. 8 O.R.Sick.
	9th.		At 8.10 p.m.the Battn proceeded by platoons at 200 yds. interval, to front trenches to relieve the 6th.S.L.I. of the 14th.Div. The front line as held then was from about O.20.A.Central S.to the railway (O.20.D.05.50) thence S.W. to O.26.A.3.2. D Coy held the trench N.of the railway and C Coy south of the railway. The support coy (B) held BOOR & BISON trench O.20.A.3.4. to O.20.C.2.9. thence S to the trench junction in O.20C.55.25. The Reserve Coy (A) held BUCK & LION trench which ran N from the railway O.19.B.8.4. to O.19.D.55.70. and O.19.B.3.4. to O.19.C.95.85. (Map Sheet 51B.S.W.Edition 4a.) Relief complete by 1.5. a.m. Casualties. 6.O.R.Sick.
	10th.		At night all coys. worked on their own trenches. C Coy worked on deepening the front line and making fire steps. D Coy.on improving fire positions. LION SWITCH was deepened also LION TRENCH by A Coy B.Coy. on work in BOOR & BISON TRENCH. Day was quiet. Casualties. 1 O.R.Wounded. 3 Officers 2nd.Lieuts. K.Palmer, 22nd.Lon.Regt.W.B.Marsh, 19th.Lon.Regt. & J.C.Goadby 13th.Lon.Regt. & 1 O.R.Reinforcements.

Ashwound Lieut Colonel
Commdg. 1/ Queens' Westminster Rifles

Place	Date	Hour

WAR DIARY or INTELLIGENCE SUMMARY
(Erase heading not required.)

Army Form C. 2118

1917
June 11th. Work as usual during the night. Wire was thickened in front of the two right platoons of C Coy. The remainder of C Coy plus one platoon of B worked on deepening the front line from the left of C Coy to SPOOK LANE. D Coy also worked on the continuation from SPOOK LANE. Trench was deepened to 2ft.6in. Wire was also put out in front of D Coy where JUNGLE ALLEY joins the front line. A Coy provided carrying parties for front line. B Coy worked on BOOR & BISON. Day was quiet.
Casualties. 1 O.R. Wounded. 4 O.R. Sick.

12th. Work as usual during the night. About 90 yds of Apron wire was put out in front of C Coy. Deepening of front line from C Coy flank N for about 125 yds. D Coy also deepened a further 80 yds. of the front line helped by one platoon of A Coy. 70 yds wire was put out in front of APE. B Coy supplied men to help both C & D. Spare men of B Coy were employed in improving parts of BOAR. A Coy on rations.
Casualties. 1 Officer. Lieut W.T.W.Birts & 7 O.R. Sick. 10.R. Other-Causes. 4 O.R. Reinforcements.

13th. At night C Coy on widening and deepening front line from KESTREL to MANSE LANE. 150 yds of single apron wire put out. D Coy on widening and deepening APE & SPOOK Lane. B Coy supplied Post & Rations etc. A Coy on rations and local work. Day fairly quiet.
Casualties. 2 O.R. Wounded.

14th. Work as usual during the night. C Coy continued work on JACKDAW TRENCH. 30 yds of wire put out and Patrols and covering parties were also supplied by this Coy. D Coy on deepening and improving APE. B Coy on salvage work in the Battn area. A Coy. 1 Platoon on carrying wire and pickets. Three platoons on Battn. rations less B Coy. In the early morning the Division on our left made an attack against a work known as the MOUND in O.2.D.(Map 51B. S.W.). This attack was apparently successful. Later in the afternoon, our left Coy.Commander observed Bosch massing for an attack or counter attack round the S.W. corner of the Bois du Vert. This was immediately reported to BDE. and the information was sent to the Division concerned by 5.20 p.m. At 5.30 p.m. the Bosch put down a heavy barrage on all trenches North of the COJEL River, but thanks to the Quickness of Capt. Relton the Artillery etc. had all been warned in time. Captain Relton, by his excellent observation on the German trenches and communications, materially assisted in smashing what looked like a very heavy counter attack. Later in the evening a wire was received, expressing appreciation of the excellent work done by this Officer
"Copy of wire received from Division on our left"

SHOU.
BMR. 38.   15/6   aaa
Following message received from MOSES. aaa
Very many thanks for your co-operation in yesterdays operations aaa. Your assistance materially contributed to our success aaa. ends.aaa
                              KEB. 3.40. p.m.
Casualties. 2 O.R. Sick. 1 O.R. Other Causes.

AShvollnid
Lieut Colonel
Commdg. 1/ Queens' Westminster Rifles

Place	Date	Hour	Summary of Events and Information	Remarks and references to Appendices

1917.
June 15th.   The day was quiet. At night the Battn. was relieved
             by the Q.V.R. Relief commenced at 10 p.m. and was
             completed by 1 A.M. After coys. continued working for
             the Q.V.R. till dawn.
                Casualties. 1 O.R.Killed 4 O.R.Wounded. 4 O.R.Sick.
     16th.   On completion of work Coys moved back to the support
             trenches. D Coy in EGRET TRENCH in immediate support
             to the front line. C Coy in CURLEW TRENCH. B Coy half
             in DUCK TRENCH and half in BUZZARD TRENCH. A Coy in
             continuation of BUZZARD N of the RAILWAY. At night
             all Coys less D worked for the Q.V.R.
                Casualties. 1 O.R.Wounded 5 O.R.Sick.
     17th.   Local work on trenches during the day. At night
             A.B & C Coys working for the Q.V.R. The day was quiet.
                Casualties. 3 O.R.Sick.
     18th.   Work as usual on local trenches during the day.
             At night the usual companies worked on posts, wiring
             etc. for the Q.V.R.
                Casualties. 1 O.R.Wounded. 1 Officer, 2nd.Lieut.
             E.W.Smith, Other Causes. Reinforcements 4 O.R.
     19th.   Quiet during the day. Local work improving trenches
             fire bays & fire steps, salvage etc. At night
             A.B & C Coys on work for the Q.V.R.
                Casualties. 5 O.R.Wounded 6 O.R.Sick. 4 O.R.Reinforcements.
     20th.   In the evening the Battn. was relieved by the LONDON
             SCOTTISH. Relief started at 11 p.m. and was completed
             by 2.10 a.m.
                Casualties Nil.
     21st.   On relief the Companies proceeded by march route
             over cross country tracks to ACHICOURT and was billeted
             in houses and barns in the village. The Battn was reported
             "all in" to Brigade at 8 a.m. No work was done during the
             day, the time being given to rest and cleaning up.
                Casualties. 3 O.R.Sick.
     22nd.   No work during the day beyond cleaning up and re
             fitting and baths.
                Casualties. 1 Officer 2ndLieut R.H.Brown, Higl.Cyc.
             & 1 O.R.Sick. 3 Officers,2nd.Lieuts.T.J.Hudson 9th Lon
             T.J.M.Van der Linde & W.J.Smith 21st.Lon.Regt.Reinforcements
     23rd.   Continued re fitting and remainder of Battn Bathed.
                Casualties. 4 O.R.Sick 7 O.R.Other Causes. 179
             O.R.Reinforcements.
     24th.   Church Parade at 10 a.m. Battn free for remainder of
             the day.
                Casualties 1 O.R.Sick.
     25th.   Commenced training. Lewis Gunners and one Company
             on ground behind Range. remainder of Coys on ground
             N.W. of Railway. 40 men worked on removing wire from
             neighbourhood of range.
                Casualties 1 O.R.Other Causes.
     26th.   Continued training. A & B Coys fired on the Range
             (13 targets) in morning. Afternoon, removal of wire
             continued.
                Casualties. 2 O.R.Sick. 12 O.R.Reinforcements.
     27th.   Continued training. All coys had the use of the
             Bayonet Gallows. Removal of wire continued.
                Casualties. 1 Officer Lieut E Ridehalgh & 2 O.R.Sick

                                    Ashwolind
                                    Lieut Colonel
                            Commdg. 1/ Queens' Westminster Rifles

Place	Date	Hour	

1917.
June 28th.   Continued training. Battn had the use of the "THRESH"
Disinfector. during a portion of the morning and afternoon.
In the afternoon, heats for the Battn Swimming Races
at the Baths in the CITADEL. ARRAS. Heavy rain in the
evening. Continued removing wire.
   Casualties. 2 O.R.Sick. 1 O.R.Reinforcement.
29th.   Training continued. Rained all the afternoon. Removal
of wire continued S of SHORT STREET & range.
   Casualties 2 O.R.Sick.
30th.   Training continued. B Coy fired on range from 9 a.m.
to 11.30 a.m. when it came on to rain & continued till
the evening. when the Lewis Gunners fired. Removal of
wire continued.
   Casualties 4 O.R.Sick.

```
                                        Offrs.   O.RKS.
        Strength on May 31st.1917.       35       843
                Add                      10       227
                                        ─────   ──────
                                         45      1070
                Less                      7       120
        Strength on June 30th.1917.      38       950.
                                        ═════   ══════
```

[signature] Lieut Colonel
Commdg. 1/ Queens' Westminster Rifles

WAR DIARY or INTELLIGENCE SUMMARY
Army Form C. 2118

1917.

July 1st. Church Parade service for members of the C. of E. was held on the Rifle Range. Services of the other denominations were also held throughout the day. No other work. Battn Swimming Sports were held during the afternoon at THE CITADEL, ARRAS. The Divisional Band played during the afternoon.
Casualties 6 O.R. Sick, 13 O.R. Transferred 169th Trench Mortar Battery, 1 Officer (2nd Lieut E.E.ELLIS 9th London Regt) and 29 O.R. Reinforcements.

2nd In the afternoon the Battn paraded and proceeded by march route via WAILLY - BEAUMETZ - MONCHIET - to GOUY EN ARTOIS. Owing to the heat etc, the march was very trying for the men, several of whom fell out en route.
Casualties 3 O.R. Sick, 1 Officer (2nd Lieut W.T.W. BIRTS) Reinforcement.

3rd In the afternoon the Battn paraded and proceeded by march route via BARLY - SOMBRIN - to SUS ST LEGER, the destination. On this march many men fell out and did not arrive until very late.
Casualties 7 O.R. Sick, 1 O.R. Reinforcement.

4th. No work was done during the day: all the time was devoted to rest and cleaning up.
Casualties 1 Officer (2nd Lieut G.L.LLOYD, 21st London Regiment) and 36 O.R. Reinforcements.

5th. Training was again started. Bombing, Bayonet fighting, physical training etc. Baths with a clean change of clothing were allotted to the Battalion.
Casualties 1 O.R. Other Causes, 4 O.R. Reinforcements.

6th. A rehearsal was held during the morning of the Brigade Church Parade. All units of the Brigade attended. The Battn proceeded at 9.30 a.m. to the Chateau at GRAND RULLECOURT, where the practice was held.
Casualties 1 O.R. Killed, 2 O.R. Reinforcements, 1 O.R. Other Causes.

7th. Training as usual was carried out during the day. Special attention was paid to Bombing and Bayonet Fighting.
Casualties 1 Officer, 2nd Lieut A.C.COOPER, 19th London Regiment, Transferred to R.F.C.

8th. Day of Rest. The Brigade Church Parade at which His Majesty the King was to have been present, was cancelled. Owing to the bad weather conditions, Services of the other denominations were held throughout the day. No other work.
Casualties 1 O.R. Sick.

NShoolbred Lieut Colonel
Commdg. 1/ Queens' Westminster Rifles

WAR DIARY or INTELLIGENCE SUMMARY

	Place	Date	Hour	Summary of Events and Information	Remarks and references to Appendices

1917.

July 9th. Work as usual during the day. "A" and "B" Companies had the use of the Range. Other training as usual. Bayonet work etc.
Casualties 5 O.R. Sick, 3 O.R. Reinforcements.

10th. Training as usual during the day. "A" and "B" Companies had the use of the Bombing Trenches and Bayonet Assault Course.
Casualties 1 O.R. Sick, 22 O.R. Reinforcements.

11th. At 8.5 a.m. the Battalion paraded and proceeded to join the 169th Inf. Bde in a Brigade Route March. On completion two more hours training was done.
Casualties 4 O.R. Sick.

12th. Training as usual during the day. "A" and "B" Companies had the use of the Live Throwing Pits - "C" and "D" Companies using the Bayonet Assault Course.
Casualties 2 O.R. Sick, 17 O.R. Reinforcements.

13th. Training as usual during the day. "A" and "B" Companies had the use of the range during the day the Lewis Gunners firing on completion of "A" and "B" Companies.
Casualties 4 O.R. Sick, 1 O.R. Reinforcements.

14th. At 8 a.m. the Battn paraded and proceeded by march via IVERGNY - LE SOUICH - BREVILLERS - LUCHEUX WOOD - SUS ST LEGER. In the afternoon the Battn held a Sports Meeting. Though the weather the early part of the day was bad, by noon the ground was in good condition.
Casualties 1 O.R. Sick, 5 O.R. Other Causes, 5 O.R. Reinforcements.

15th. Day of Rest. Parade Service was held in the morning for members of C. of E. Services were also held for the other denominations throughout the day.
Casualties 1 O.R. Sick, 4 O.R. Reinforcements.

16th. Training as usual during the morning. "A" and "B" Companies route marched during the morning, while "C" and "D" Companies had the use of the Baths. In the afternoon the 169th I.B. held their HORSE SHOW and also ran off heats for the Brigade Sports Meeting.
Casualties 1 Officer (2nd Lieut H.J.HOLLAND) and 1 O.R. Sick.

17th Training as usual during the morning. "A" and "B" Companies on the Range. "C" and "D" Companies using the Bomb Pits. In the afternoon the 169th I.B. held their Sports Meeting in the Grounds of the CHATEAU at GRAND RULLECOURT. The weather remained fine and the Battn for the second successive time won the Brigade Championship. Prizes were afterwards presented by the Comtesse KERGOLAY.
Casualties 1 Officer (Lieut E. RIDEHALGH, 22nd London Regiment) and 3 O.R. Reinforcements.

N.Shoolbred Lieut Colonel
Commdg. 1/ Queens' Westminster Rifles

Place	Date	Hour	Summary of Events and Information	Remarks and references to Appendices

1917.
July 18th.   Weather interfered with the work of the Battn during the day. The time was mostly therefore given to lectures.
            Casualties 3 O.R. Sick, 2 O.R. Other Causes.

19th.   At 9.5 a.m. the Battn paraded for a Brigade Route March. Route via HUMBERCOURT - COULLEMONT - SOMBRIN to SUS ST LEGER. Usual work was carried out in the afternoon.
            Casualties 4 O.R. Sick, 3 O.R. Reinforcements.

20th.   Work as usual throughout the day.
            Casualties 3 O.R. Sick, 8 O.R. Reinforcements.

21st.   Training as usual during the morning. The programme of training was not followed. O.C. Companies reporting to the Orderly Room the nature of their training for the day. Operation Orders for the Move to the Vth Army Area were issued this day.
            Casualties 6 O.R. Sick.

22nd.   Day of Rest. Services of all denominations were held throughout the day. Parade service for members of the C. of E. was held at 10 a.m.
            Casualties 5 O.R. Sick, 2 O.R. Other Causes, 2 Officers (2nd Lieut G.A.N.LOWNDES and 2nd Lieut A.G.BROOKE) Reinforcements.

23rd.   Only two hours training was done during the morning. The rest of the day was given to cleaning up billets etc prior to the Divisional Move.
            Casualties 9 O.R. Sick, 1 Officer (2nd Lieut R.S. HERRING 20th London Regiment) Transferred to R.F.

24th.   At 2.30 a.m. the Battalion paraded for the move. Tea was issued from the Q.V.R. Cookers and at 3 a.m. the Battalion proceeded by march route to BOUQUEMAISON Station. Rations for the day were issued on arrival at the Station and entrainment then started. The train left at 6.50 a.m. and arrived at WIZERNES, three miles S.W. of ST OMER at noon. Detrainment started immediately and dinners were served in a field adjoining the station. At 3.15 p.m. the Battalion again paraded and proceeded by march route to LA COMMUNE, 10 miles N.W. of ST OMER. Teas were served on the road and the Battn arrived all in at the destination at 10 p.m.
            Casualties:- 1 Officer (Major J.B.WHITMORE) and 2 O.R. Reinforcements.

25th.   No work was done during the day. The Battn was resting after the previous days march, a total distance of 18 miles having been covered.
            Casualties 2 O.R. Sick.

26th.   Training again commenced. The area allotted for this purpose being three miles away. The Companies worked from 9 a.m. till 4 p.m., dinners being served on the training ground
            Casualties 5 O.R. Reinforcements.

                    Lieut Colonel
            Commdg. 1/ Queens' Westminster Rifles

Place	Date	Hour	Summary of Events and Information	Remarks and references to Appendices

1917.
July 27th.   Training was again carried out on the allotted ground.
              Casualties 1 Officer (2nd Lieut A.C.BROOKE) and
              3 O.R. Sick.

     28th.   The Battalion paraded and route marched via LA COMMUNE
              LE COMMUNAL - LA PANNE - RECQUES and NORDAUSQUES. During
              this march "D" Company acted as advance Guard. On
              arrival at the QUARRIES in NORDAUSQUES, Artillery formation
              was practised as a Battn. Parade was at 8.15 a.m., the
              Battn arriving back at 1.30 p.m.
              Casualties 1 O.R. Reinforcement.

     29th.   Day of Rest. Parade service for members of the C. of E.
              was arranged at which the Assistant Chaplain General was
              to have been present. A severe thunderstorm in the morning
              caused the service to be cancelled, but later in the day
              services were held of other denominations.
              Casualties 1 O.R. Sick, 2 O.R. Other Causes.

     30th.   Training as usual on the parade ground. Special
              attention being given to Outposts.
              Casualties 6 O.R. Sick.

     31st.   Usual training throughout the day, Musketry, Live
              Bombing throwing etc., Lewis Gunners under L.G.O.
              Snipers under Scout Officer.
              Casualties 1 O.R. Sick.

                                              Offrs.   O.R.
                                              ------   ----
              Strength on June 30th 1917   38.   950.

                           ADD.   7   146.
                                              ------   ------
                                               45.   1,096.

                           LESS.   4   106.
                                              ------   ------
                                               41.   990.
                                              ======   ======

                    NShoothed   Lieut-Colonel.
              Commanding 1/16th Battn London Regiment.
                (1st Battn Queens Westminster Rifles).

1.8.17.

Confidential

War Diary

of

1/16th Battn The London Regt.
(Queens Westminster Rifles)

from 1st August 1917 to 31st August 1917.

Vol. 33

WAR DIARY or INTELLIGENCE SUMMARY

Army Form C. 2118

Place	Date	Hour	Summary of Events and Information	Remarks and references to Appendices

1917

August 1st. Training as usual throughout the day. The lecture on the new gas arranged for the evening was cancelled owing to bad weather.
Casualties:- Capt T.L.RELTON to Chinese Labour Depot 1 Officer (2nd Lieut A.C.BROOKE) from Hosp.

2nd Training as usual during the morning. A lecture on the new gas was given in the afternoon by the Divisional Gas Officer.
Casualties 3 O.R. Sick.

3rd. The Battalion paraded at 9 a.m. for Route March. "C" Company marched as an Advanced Guard to the Battn. On conclusion of the march the Battalion was addressed by Lieut-Colonel R. SHOOLBRED, C.M.G., T.D., D.L.
Casualties 2 O.R. Sick.

4th. Training as usual throughout the day. On this day Lieut-Colonel R. SHOOLBRED handed over the command the Battalion to MAJOR P.M. GLASIER.
Casualties 1 O.R. Sick. 1 Officer (Lieut-Colonel R. SHOOLBRED) to England, 4 O.R. Reinforcements.

5th. Day of Rest. Services as usual throughout the day. The Transport moved at 2.30 a.m. and proceeded by road to the ABEELE Area, taking two days.
Casualties 2 O.R. Sick, 3 O.R. Reinforcements.

6th. Battalion paraded and proceeded by march route to WATTEN STATION, entraining at 5 p.m. Arrived ABEELE STATION at 8 p.m. and marched to the Camp in the WIPPENHOEK Area N. of the CASSELL - ABEELE ROAD.
Casualties 2 O.R. Sick, 1 O.R. Other Causes 6 O.R. Reinforcements.

7th No training was done on this day.
Casualties NIL.

8th The Commanding Officer inspected the Battalion during the morning. No training during the afternoon.
Casualties 3 O.R. Sick.

9th Training as usual throughout the morning.
Casualties 4 O.R. Sick, 7 O.R. Reinforcements.

10th Four hours training was done during the morning, including 2 hours route marching.
Casualties 4 O.R. Sick, 2 O.R. Reinforcements.

11th A warning order was received in the early hours of the morning and at 12.20 p.m. the Battn paraded and proceeded by march route to ABEELE STATION. Here the Battn entrained and proceeded to OUDERDOM. From there the Battn marched to the camp at CHATEAU SEGARD and encamped there for the night. The Transport proceeded by road to DICKEBUSH.
Casualties 1 Officer (2nd Lieut K. PALMER 22nd Ldn Regt) and 7 O.R. Sick 1 O.R. Reinforcements.

Major.
Commanding 1st Queens Westminster Rifles

1917.
August 12th. Orders to move were received at 2.30 p.m. and the Battalion paraded and moved via cross country tracks to YEOMANRY POST, 1,000 yds N.E. of ZILLEBEKE LAKE, arriving at 5 p.m. At 8 p.m. guides led the Companies forward to take over front line trenches W. of GLENCORSE WOOD, from J.8.c.2.2. to J.14.a.8.6. "A" Company on the Right, two Platoons in front line, two in support, "B" Company on the left, two Platoons in front line, two in Support. "C" Company in trenches N. of MENIN ROAD, at J.13.b.0.3. "D" company in trench N. of YEOMANRY POST I.17.d.7.0. Relief was reported complete to Brigade at 1.10 a.m.
 Casualties 1 Officer (2nd Lieut W.F.D.YOUNG) and 4 O.R. Wounded.

13th. In trenches. Heavy intermittent shelling throughout the day. At night the Battalion was ordered to establish posts in GLENCORSE WOOD, 100 yds forward from our front line. Operations were ordered to start at 9 p.m. At that time our heavy guns were shelling close to our front line trenches on the right. This delayed the start of "A" Company but on the left "B" Company got their posts out. At 9.7 p.m. the enemy put down a heavy barrage on our front line, but this did not interfere with the left Company posts. The right Company, however, could not move owing to our own heavies and protective barrage was later called for by lamp signal which was immediately put down.
 Casualties 7 O.R. Killed, 2 O.R. Wounded.

14th. Heavy shelling again throughout the whole 24 hours. In the evening the Battn was relieved by the 2nd Londons, proceeding to trenches at HALFWAY HOUSE. Relief was not complete till 5 a.m. on the 15th.
 Casualties 24 O.R. Killed, 51 O.R. Wounded. 6 O.R. Sick.

15th. In the evening the Battalion again went into the line in Brigade Reserve in trenches round Battn H.Q. at J.13.d.0.3. Shelling still heavy and continuous. "D" Company commanded by Capt E. BRIMELOW. took up a position behind the JARGON SWITCH and were ordered to follow the fourth wave of the attack as "Moppers-up" to both attacking Battalions.
 Casualties 3 O.R. Killed, 12 O.R. Wounded. 10 O.R. Sick.

16th. Zero Day. The Battalion was not called on during the day for any active part in the operations, except small carrying parties. At night the Battalion again moved into the line to relieve the L.R.B. With the exception of two Platoons of "A" Company, the whole Battalion was in the front line. "C" Company holding the forward posts. "B" Company during the operations had very little
 D

 Major.
 Commanding 1st Queens Westminster Rifles

WAR DIARY

INTELLIGENCE SUMMARY

1917.

August 16th. mopping up to do and eventually became involved with fourth wave of the attack and fell back later to the front line.
    Casualties 2 Officers (2nd Lieut S. NORTH 19th London Regiment) and 16 O.R. Killed, 1 Officer (2nd Lieut A.M. MACKLE 5th Border Regt) Died of Wounds, 4 Officers (2nd Lieut W.D. SMITH 21st London Regt, Lieut E. RIDEHALGH, 22nd London Regiment, 2nd Lieut E.E. ELLIS, 9th London Regt and Capt E. BRIMELOW) and 109 O.R. Wounded, 29 O.R. Missing, 3 O.R. Sick.

17th. After the previous days heavy shelling, the enemy's artillery was much quieter during the day on front areas. At night, however, he again put down his usual barrage. Relieved by the Ox and Bucks of the 14th Division - started at 9 p.m. and was complete by 2 a.m. The Battalion proceeded to CHATEAU SEGARD.
    Casualties 2 O.R. Killed, 1 O.R. Wounded. 11 O.R. Sick.

18th. The Battalion arrived at CHATEAU SEGARD at about 7 a.m. and at 12 noon embussed and proceeded to WUPPENHOEK Area as before, arriving at about 4 p.m.
    Casualties 1 O.R. Wounded, 2 O.R. Sick. 5 O.R. Reinforcements.

19th. Day of Rest. A Thanksgiving and Memorial Service was held at 6 p.m. in the camp.
    Casualties:- 1 O.R. Killed. (Died of Wounds)
    2 O.R. Reinforcements.

20th. Reorganization of Companies throughout the day.
    Casualties 3 O.R. Sick, 6 O.R. Reinforcements.

21st Reorganization and training throughout the morning.
    Casualties:- 26 O.R. Reinforcements.

22nd. Three hours training was done during the morning. Lectures for Officers during the afternoon.
    Casualties:- 5 O.R. Sick, 5 O.R. Reinforcements.

23rd. Training as usual during the morning. In the afternoon, the Transport moved to the new area at MOULLE.
    Casualties 6 O.R. Sick.

24th. No work during the morning. At 2 p.m. the Battalion paraded and proceeded by march route to ABEELE STATION. Entrainment was due to commence at 3.15 p.m., but owing to the late arrival of the train was not commenced until 5.30 p.m. The distance to be covered by rail was approximately 30 miles, the time taken being over 6 hours. On arrival at WATTEN STATION, the Battn

Major.
Commanding 1st Queens Westminster Rifles

WAR DIARY or INTELLIGENCE SUMMARY

(Erase heading not required.)

Place	Date	Hour	Summary of Events and Information	Remarks and references to Appendices

1917.

August 24th. detrained and proceeded by march route to MOULLE on the ST OMER - CALAIS ROAD, arriving all in at 3 a.m.
  Casualties 1 O.R. Sick, 4 O.R. Reinforcements.

25th No training was done on this day. Battn Area very scattered - H.Q. and "A" Company being at MOULLE - "B" "C" and "D" Companies, Transport and Q.M.Stores at ZUDROVE 1½ miles E. of MOULLE.
  Casualties 1 Officer (Capt P.C.COOTE) rejoined from 169th T.M.B. and 4 O.R. Reinforcements.

26th Divine Services as usual for all denominations throughout the day.
  Casualties 2 O.R. Reinforcements.

27th. Training as usual throughout the morning. Special training for N.C.Os and lectures for Officers during the afternoon.
  Casualties 3 O.R. Sick, 9 O.R. Reinforcements.

28th. Training as usual, Lectures for Officers and N.C.Os and riding lessons for Junior Officers in the afternoon.
  Casualties 2 O.R. Reinforcements.

29th. Training as usual throughout the day.
  Casualties 1 O.R. Sick, 9 O.R. Reinforcements.

30th Training during the morning and cleaning up of billets prior to move to 3rd Army Area.
  Casualties 5 O.R. Sick, 1 O.R. Reinforcements.

31st. The Battalion paraded at 7.45 a.m. and proceeded by march route to WIZERNES where entrainment commenced at 10.15 a.m. The move by train to 3rd Army Area was accomplished in about 10 hours. At 11 p.m. the Battalion proceeded by march route via ACHIET - le PETIT, ACHIET - le - GRAND, BIEFVILLERS to a camp One mile E. of BAPAUME, arriving in at 3 a.m.
  Casualties 2 O.R. Sick.

	Offrs.	O.R.
Strength on July 31st.	41	990.
ADD.	2	98.
	43	1,088
LESS	9	357
	34	731.

Major.
Commanding 1/16th Battn LONDON REGIMENT.
(1st Queens Westminster Rifles).

Confidential

Vol 34

169/56

War Diary

of

1/16th Bn The London Regt.

from 1st September 1917   to 30th September 1917

WAR DIARY or INTELLIGENCE SUMMARY

Army Form C. 2118.

Place	Date	Hour	Summary of Events and Information	Remarks and references to Appendices

1917.
Septr 1st.   Battn in Camp: no training during the day. Casualties :- 1 Officer (2nd Lieut W.T.W.BIRTS) to Medical Board in Eng. and 7 O.R. Sick 2 O.R. Reinforcements.

2nd   Day of rest. The usual Church Services were held throughout the day.
Casualties:- 2 O.R. Sick, 1 O.R. Reinforcement.

3rd.   Four and Half hours training throughout the day. Night operations were cancelled.
Casualties 1 Officer (2nd Lieut R.L.WHITTLE) and 4 O.R. Sick and 80 O.R. Reinforcements.

4th.   Two hours training during the morning. At 7 p.m. the Battalion paraded and proceeded by march route FREMICOURT to LEBUCQUIERE. H.Q. and "A" Company billetted in the village and the reaminder of the Battn in a camp between LEBUCQUIERE and VELU. Relief complete by 10 p.m.
Casualties 3 O.R. Sick 1 O.R. Reinforcements

5th.   In the evening the Battn moved forward into front line trenches, relieving the 2nd Battn ROYAL SCOTS of the 3rd Division. The trenches taken over were astride the BAPAUME CAMBRAIN Road. "B" Company taking the Right Company Sector, "C" Company on the left, with "D" Company in support. For this purpose, 1 Platoon of "A" Company was attached to "B" Company and the remaining Platoons of "A" were attached to "C" Company. Relief was completed by 11.30 p.m.
Casualties 1 O.R. Wounded, 1 O.R. Sick, 1 O.R. Other causes, 1 O.R. Reinforcement.

6th   In trenches. Work continued throughout the day on improvement to communication trenches, drainage etc. At night, patrols from both front Companies were out but no BOSCH were encountered.
Casualties 2 O.R. Sick, 9 O.R. Reinforcements

7th.   Work as usual throughout the 24 hours. Patrols at night as usual from both Companies.
Casualties:- 1 O.R. Wounded, 4 O.R. Sick, 1 O.R. Reinforcement.

8th   Work as usual on wiring and communication trenches. To help with the large amount of work to be done in the Sector, One Company of the Q.V.R. were attached. Patrols as usual. Whole Sector very Quiet.
Casualties:- 4 O.R. Sick, 1 Officer (2nd Lieut C.E.MOY) seconded for duty with 169th T.M.B., 3 O.R. Reinforcements.

WAR DIARY or INTELLIGENCE SUMMARY

(Erase heading not required.)

Army Form C. 2118.

Place	Date	Hour		Remarks and references to Appendices

1917.

Septr 9th. Work as usual on trenches. C.Ts. were started by the Q.V.R. to join up the Posts not connected. All the work done was with the idea of making a continuous front line trench. At present many posts are isolated.
Casualties 3 O.R. Sick.

10th. Work as usual throughout the day. The usual patrols at night.
Casualties 3 O.R. Sick, 2 O.R. Reinforcements.

11th. Usual work on posts, communication trenches and wire. Patrols by both Companies at night. Hostile artillery and snipers showed a tendency to be more active.
Casualties 4 O.R. Sick, 5 Officers (2nd Lieut W.H. GATFIELD H.A.KILBURN, 13th London,-W.J. THOMAS 13th London, W.H.ORMISTON, 13th LONDON, R.S.JACKSON, 13th London) Reinforcements.

12th Work as usual during the day. Hostile activity was maintained. Patrols as usual.
Casualties 1 O.R. Wounded, 4 O.R. Sick, 1 O.R. Reinforcement.

13th Work as usual during the day. At night the Battn was relieved by the Q.V.R., two Companies "B" and proceeding to billets in LEBUCQUIERE. "A" Company took over trenches in LOUVERVAL WOOD and were attached the 2nd Londons for work. "D" Company proceeded to the Sunken Road running S.W. from DOIGNIES in J.16.c for work under the Q.V.R. Owing to relieving Lewis Guns not arriving, relief was not completed until 2.15 a.m.
Casualties 3 O.R. Sick, 1 O.R. Other Causes

14th In Billets: H.Q. and "B" Company in huts at LEBUCQUIERE. "C" Company in tents ½ mile S.W. of the village. No work or training during the day.
Casualties 1 O.R. Reinforcement.

15th. Three hours training was carried out during the morning near Battn billets. No other work.
Casualties 4 O.R. Sick, 11 O.R. Reinforcements.

16th. Day of Rest. Services of the various denominations were held throughout the day.
Casualties:- 4 O.R. Sick, 1 O.R. Other Causes, 1 Officer (Major J.Q.HENRIQUES) rejoined from England, 2 O.R. Reinforcement

17th. Training as usual throughout the morning. At night "B" and "C" Companies moved up to relieve the two forward Companies. "B" Company to the Sunken Road S.W. of DOIGNIES to relieve "D" Company:- "C" Company to LOUVERVAL WOOD to relieve "A" Company. Relief was complete by 11 p.m.
Casualties 2 O.R. Sick, 1 O.R. Reinforcements.

WAR DIARY or INTELLIGENCE SUMMARY

Place	Date	Hour	Summary of Events and Information	Remarks
	1917. Septr 18th.		Some work and training during the day. Cleaning up, refitting etc, by the two Companies in camp. In the afternoon a rehearsal took place for the Corps Commanders Inspection. Casualties 1 O.R. Sick, 4 O.R. Reinforcements.	
	19th		No work or training during the day. At 11 a.m. the Battn (less "B" and "C" Companies) was inspected by the Corps Commander (4th Corps). Casualties 2 O.R. Sick, 4 O.R. Reinforcements.	
	20th		No work or training during the day. Casualties 6 O.R. Sick, 3 O.R. Reinforcements. 2 Offrs (2nd Lieuts R.L.WHITTLE & K.PALMER).	
	21st		Training during the morning. In the evening the Battn moved up to relieve the 4.V.R. in the Right Sub-Sector. H.Q. and the two Companies in camp entrained at LEBUCQUIERE for LOUVERVAL, the two forward Companies marching direct. Trenches were taken over with "A" Company on the left, "B" Company in the centre and "D" Company on the right, with "C" Company in support at the QUARRIES. Relief was complete by 12.15 a.m. Casualties 1 Officer (2nd Lieut T.J.HUDSON) and 15 O.R. Sick.	
	22nd		Work was carried on throughout the day on new posts, communication trenches etc. Patrols at night by the Companies in the line. Casualties 4 O.R. Sick, 8 O.R. Reinforcements.	
	23rd		Work as usual throughout the day. Patrols at night by the front Companies. Casualties 4 O.R. Sick, 1 O.R. Reinforcements.	
	24th		Work was continued on all trenches - widening and deepening. Patrols as usual. Casualties 2 O.R. Sick, 21 O.R. Reinforcements.	
	25th		Work on new Posts, C.Ts, etc was continued. Patrols at night from the front Companies. Casualties 6 O.R. Sick, 1 O.R. Other Causes 4 Officers (Capt A.J.M.GORDON, 2nd Lieut F.W.RUSSELL, 2nd Lieut W.E.GRUSELLE, 13th London, and 2nd Lieut J.L.HEWITT, 13th London) and 3 O.R. Reinforcements.	
	26th		Work was continued throughout the day. The usual patrols at night went forward to suspected occupied posts etc in NO MANS LAND. Casualties 4 O.R. Sick.	
	27th		Work as usual throughout the day. Patrols at night. Hostile artillery continued active. Casualties 2 O.R. Wounded, 5 O.R. Sick, 1 O.R. Other Causes.	

Place	Date	Hour	Summary of Events and Information	Remarks and references to Appendices
	1917. Septr 28th.		Work as usual throughout the day. Patrols at night. "C" Company sent out a patrol under 2nd Lieut W.H. ORMISTON and 30 O.R. This party came into contact with a German patrol of 15 and in the encounter which took place, 11 of the enemy were killed and two taken prisoners (one wounded), the remaining two of the German patrol getting away. Our own casualties amounted to 6 O.R. Wounded. Casualties 4 O.R. Sick, 5 O.R. Reinforcement.	
	29th.		Relief by the Q.V.R. On completion the Battn proceeded to the camp at LEBUCQUIERE in Divisional Reserve. Relief was complete by 11 p.m. and Battn all in at 1 a.m. Casualties 6 O.R. Wounded, 1 O.R. Sick, 5 O.R. Reinforcements.	
	30th.		Day of Rest. Services as usual throughout the day. Casualties 2 O.R. Sick, 1 O.R. Reinforcement.	

	Officers	O.R.
Strength on August 31st	33	731
ADD	12	167
	45	898
LESS	4	128
Strength on 30th Septr	41	720

Signature

Lieut-Colonel.
Commanding 1st Queens Westminster Rifles.

<u>Confidential</u>

War Diary

of

1/16th Bn The London Regt.

from 1st October 1917 to 31st October 1917

Place	Date	Hour	
	1917. Octr. 1st.		Training during the morning as usual. Casualties 1 O.R. Sick, 4 Officers off strength (Capt S.R.SAVILL M.C. to Senior Officers' Course, 2nd Lieut J.L.HEWITT (13th Ldn Regt), 2nd Lieut W.J.THOMAS (13th Ldn Regt) and 2nd Lieut W.E.G GRUZELLE (13th Ldn Regt) all posted to 2nd London Regiment,- 1 O.R. Other Causes, 3 Officers - 2nd Lieuts R.A.BASSHAM, H.T.HARPER and I.d'A.S.STITT - and 17 O.R. Reinforcements.
	2nd.		Training as usual, including musketry, rapid wiring etc. Lewis Gunners on the Range. Bombers on the Live Throwing Pit. Casualties 3 O.R. Sick.
	3rd.		Training as usual throughout the day. Casualties 2 O.R. Sick, 2 O.R. Reinforcements.
	4th.		Training during the day consisting of :- Company attack by flag control, Live Bomb throwing, Rifle Grenade etc. Casualties 5 O.R. Reinforcements.
	5th.		Usual training throughout the day. Casualties, 1 Officer (2nd Lieut J.C.GOADBY, 13th London Regt - and 1 O.R. Sick.
	6th.		Rapid Wiring, Platoon Drill, Flag control attacks and G.O's inspection of Companies throughout the day. Casualties 1 Officer (2nd Lieut W.H.GATFIELD) and 1 O.R. Sick.
	7th.		In the evening the Battalion moved up to relieve the Q.V.R. Company dispositions - "D" on the Right, "C" centre, "A" on the left with "B" in support at the QUARRY. Relief was reported complete to Brigade by 11.30 p.m. Casualties 4 O.R. Sick, 1 O.R. Reinforcement.
	8th.		Work on trenches and Posts throughout the day. Patrols at night from "B" and "D" Companies went out to the enemy wire and suspected Posts. Casualties 2 O.R. Sick, 1 O.R. Reinforcements.
	9th.		Usual work throughout the day. Patrols at night as usual from "B" and "D" Companies. The patrol under 2nd Lieut H.T.HARPER came into contact with a Bosch patrol in NO MANS LAND. Lewis Gun fire was opened, scattering the German patrol and leaving one wounded prisoner in our hands. Congratulations were again received from the B.G.C. and G.O.C. Casualties 1 O.R. Sick, 1 Officer (Capt & Adjt H.S.PRICE) to England, 1 Officer (2nd Lieut T.J. HUDSON) and 3 O.R. Reinforcements.

Lieut Colonel
Commdg. 1/ Queens' Westminster Rifles

Place	Date	Hour	

1917.
Octr 10th.   Work as usual throughout the day. Patrols at night to the usual German Posts.
            Casualties 1 O.R. Sick, 5 O.R. Reinforcements.

11th.   Work as usual during the day. The Q.V.R. having asked for information regarding the objective of their proposed raid, 2nd Lieut T. CAUDWELL with 10 O.R. went out to reconnoitre the approaches and wire in front of the craters K.8.b.3.1. The place was found to be unoccupied and was thoroughly inspected by 2nd Lieut T. CAUDWELL, whose report furnished all the information required. Special congratulations were sent to this Officer by the B.G.C.
            Casualties 3 O.R. Sick and 3 O.R. Reinforcements.

12th.   Usual work on wire, posts and C.Ts throughout the day. Patrols at night from both "B" and "D" Companies went forward to the usual points in enemy wire etc.
            Casualties 4 O.R. Sick.

13th.   Work as usual throughout the day. Patrols at night. On this day one Company of the 4th Battn NORTH STAFFORDSHIRE REGIMENT were attached to the Battalion for instruction.
            Casualties 3 O.R. Sick, 1 Officer (2nd Lieut W.F.HALL - 10th Ldn Regt) Posted to 169th Trench Mortar Battery, and 1 O.R. Reinforcement.

14th.   Work continued on C.Ts, posts and wire. Usual patrols at night.
            Casualties 4 O.R. Sick 4 O.R. Reinforcements.

15th.   The Battalion was relieved at night by the Q.V.R. and 2 Companies ("A" & "D") proceeded on relief by march route to the Brigade Reserve Camp in LEBUCQUIERE. Relief was reported complete to Brigade by 10.15 p.m. The attached Company of the NORTH STAFFS remained in the trenches and were taken over by the Q.V.R. "B" Company proceeded to the SUNKEN ROAD S of DOIGNIES. "C" Company to SOLE TRENCH. Both these Companies remained for work in the RIGHT and LEFT Sub-Sectors.
            Casualties 2 O.R. Reinforcements.

16th.   In billets. No training during the day. Large fatigue parties daily made it impossible to parade more than one Company for training.
            Casualties 1 O.R. Reinforcements

17th   No training during the morning as all available men were sent to the Baths.
            Casualties 2 O.R. Sick, 1 O.R. Other Causes. 39 O.R. Reinforcements.

Lieut Colonel
Commdg. 1/ Queens' Westminster Rifles

Place	Date	Hour	Summary
	1917. Oct. 18th.		"D" Company trained for three hours during the morning. "A" Company provided all fatigue parties. Casualties 2 O.R. Sick. 1 Officer (2nd Lieut F.H.FAVELL - R.F.C.) - joined Battn for 1 months' attachment.
	19th.		"A" Company carried out training for three hours during the morning. "D" Company provided all fatigue parties. Casualties 6 O.R. Sick, 1 O.R. Reinforcement.
	20th.		Inter-Company relief. "A" Company relieved "C" in SOLE TRENCH. "D" Company relieved "B" Company in the SUNKEN ROAD S. of DOIGNIES. Relief was reported complete by 10.30 p.m. Casualties 5 O.R. Sick, 1 O.R. Other Causes 1 Officer (2nd Lieut W.H.GATFIELD) from Hospital and 8 O.R. Reinforcements.
	21st.		Day of Rest. The usual services were held for all denominations. Casualties 1 O.R. Sick, 3 O.R. Reinforcements.
	22nd.		"B" Company carried out training during the morning. "C" Company providing all fatigue parties. Casualties 4 O.R. Sick, 7 O.R. Reinforcements.
	23rd.		In the evening the Battalion moved up into the line to relieve the Q.V.R. Relief was reported complete to Brigade at 10.15 p.m. No patrols were send out. Company dispositions as follows. "D" on the Right, "C" in Centre, "B" on the Left with "A" in Support. Casualties 4 O.R. Sick, 1 O.R. Reinforcements.
	24th.		Work during the day on C.Ts, posts and wiring. Patrols at night by "A" & "C" Companies to suspected occupied posts in the German advance line. The patrol of "A" Company came into contact with BOSCH near the Cross Roads in K.8.a.9.4. Fire was opened by both sides and it is believed that many casualties were inflicted on the enemy. Our own casualties were 2 men killed. 2nd Lieut H.A. KILBURN was in command of the patrol. Congratulations won again received from the divisional commander. Casualties 2 O.R. Killed, 2 O.R. Sick, 10 O.R. Reinforcements.
	25th.		Work during the day on C.Ts, Posts and wiring. Patrol from "A" Company to ruined house on DEMICOURT - MOEUVRE ROAD. No enemy were seen. Usual wire patrols. The Company of NORTH STAFFS took over a complete Company frontage in the centre of the Battalion sub-sector. Casualties 3 O.R. Sick, 1 O.R. Other Causes.

Lieut Colonel
Commdg. 1/ Queens' Westminster Rifles

Place	Date	Hour	Summary of Events and Information	Remarks and references to Appendices

1917.
Octr. 26th.   Work during the day on C.Ts, posts and wiring. Patrol from "A" Company to ruined house to cover search party. from "A" Company ordered to bring in bodies of two Germans reported to have been seen in front of the house.
           The bodies of two men of the 120th R.I.R. were found and brought in. These men had evidently been killed in the encounter on the night 24/25th October. Enemy movement was heard but no enemy were seen during this operation. Amongst the papers on one of the bodies there was a post card containing a rough sketch of the area to be patrolled and lines indicating apparently the route of the patrol.
           Casualties 3 O.R. Sick, 2 O.R. Other Causes, 1 O.R. Reinforcement.
           A Patrol from "D" Company - strength 2 Officers and 10 O.R. under 2nd Lieut MOULTON down DEMICOURT - GRAINCOURT ROAD to enemy's outpost wire on left. No signs of enemy met with.

27th.   Usual work on trenches, posts and wire.
           Patrol from "B" Company - strength 1 Officer and 10 O.R. to ruined house on MOEUVRES ROAD. No signs of enemy seen or heard.
           Patrol from "D" Company - strength 2 Officers and 10 O.R. under 2nd Lieut R.K. MOULTON to shell hole in K.8.a.3.8. About 50 of the enemy were seen. They opened fire with four machine guns. We replied with Lewis Gun, which jammed after half a drum had been fired. Casualties are believed to have been inflicted on enemy. We suffered no casualty.
           (A dead German of the 414th Infantry Regiment, who had apparently been dead 2 days, was found in K.8.a. by a patrol from the 109th Infantry Brigade on the 29th October. This man had probably been killed in this
(patrol encounter)   Casualties 2 O.R. Sick.

28th.   Usual work on posts, trenches and wire.
           Patrol from "A" Company under 2nd Lieut E.C.HAYES strength 1 Officer, 29 O.R. and 2 Lewis Guns along DEMICOURT - MOEUVRES ROAD. No enemy seen or heard. The Company of 4th Battn NORTH STAFFS left the line and were relieved by Companies in the line who were redistributed. Relief complete by 7.30 p.m.
           Company dispositions as follows:- "B" on Left, "C" in centre, "D" on right, "A" in support.
           Casualties 1 Officer (2nd Lieut W.B.MARSH - 19th LONDON REGIMENT) and 2 O.R. Sick, 1 Officer 2nd Lieut J.C.GOADBY - 13th London Regt.- and 2 O.R. Reinforcements.

29th   Usual work on posts, trenches and wire.
           Patrol from "B" Company - strength 1 Officer and 10 O.R. from J.6.5. down CAMBRAI ROAD. No enemy seen or heard.

                                   Lieut Colonel
                        Commdg. 1/Queens' Westminster Rifles

Place	Date	Hour	Summary of Events and Information	Remarks and references to Appendices

1917.
Octr. 29th (Continued). Patrol from "C" Company – strength 1 Officer and 10 O.R. and Lewis Gun under 2nd Lieut STITT from K.7.2. to "CLOVER PATCH"
   A party of the enemy strength about 40 was encountered. The patrol opened fire with Lewis Guns and rifles. The enemy replied with Machine Gun and rifles but fired high. Our patrol exhausted its Lewis Gun ammunition and then withdrew to our lines. No casualties were sustained. The enemy are believed to have suffered casualties.
   Casualties 2 O.R. Sick 10 O.R. Reinforcements.

30th. Usual work on posts, trenches and wire.
   A patrol from "A" Company strength 1 Officer and 30 O.R. left K.7.2. for the "CLOVER PATCH" No enemy seen or heard. On the return journey about 200 yards in front of K.7.4., 8 dead Germans were found. They had evidently been there some time.
   Casualties 1 O.R. Sick.

31st. Usual work on posts trenches and wire.
   Two patrols – one to ruined house and one down DEMICOURT – GRAINCOURT ROAD to examine enemy's outpost wire. No enemy seen or heard.
   The Battalion should have been relieved by Q.V.R. but the relief was postponed for one day.
   Casualties 1 O.R. Other Causes.

	Offrs.	O.R.
Strength on Septr 30th	41	770.
ADD.	6	120.
	47	890.
LESS	9	79
	38	811.

P.W.Glasier
Lieut-Colonel.
Commanding 1/16th Battn THE LONDON REGIMENT.
(1st Queens Westminster Rifles).

Confidential

9A 36

169/56

WAR DIARY

1/16th London Regt

November 1917

35807. W16879/M1879 500,000 3/17 R.T. (1074) Forms/W3091/3   Army Form W.3091.

Cover for Documents.

Nature of Enclosures.

Notes, or Letters written.

To. H.Qrs. 56th Div.
Bm 332

Attached Amendment
to War Diary for
November of 1/5th
8th D.W.R.
is forwarded,
please.

John W Dowland
Capt
for D. m. 169 Inf Bde

11.12.17

WAR DIARY or INTELLIGENCE SUMMARY

Army Form C. 2118.

1917.
Novr. 1st.
 Usual work on Trenches, Posts and Wire. The Battalion was relieved in the evening by the 1st. Q.V.R. and proceeded to the Camp at LEBUCQUIERE in Divisional Reserve.
 Casualties:- 1 O.R. Reinforcement.

2nd.
 Cleaning up. Companies practised in Tests in efficiency in different weapons.
 Casualties:- 1 O.R. Sick. 9 O.R. Reinforcements.

3rd.
 Training and Tests for Specialists and rank & file. The Third anniversary of the Battalion landing in France was celebated by a Smoking Concert given by the Sergeants Mess in the Recreation Hut at LEBUCQUIERE. The BOW BELLS Concert Paty assisted. The Battalion was addressed by the C.O. on parade.
 Casualties:- 3 O.R. Sick. 11 O.R. Reinforcements.

4th.
 Trainng and efficiency Tests continued.
 Casualties:- 3 O.R. Sick. 2 O.R. Reinforcements.

5th.
 Training and efficiency Tests continued.
 Casualties:- 5 O.R. Sick. 2 O.R. Reinforcements.

6th.
 Training and efficiency Tests continued.
 Casualties:- 5 O.R. Sick. 1 O.R. Other Causes. 6 O.R. Reinf.

7th.
 Training and efficiency Tests continued.
 Casualties:- 2 O.R. Reinforcements.

8th.
 Training and efficiency Tests continued. The Battalion relieved the 1st. Q.V.R. in the line in the evening. Companies were disposed as follows. RIGHT B Coy. CENTRE C Coy. LEFT A. Coy. In support D Coy.
 Casualties:- 1 O.R. Wounded. 6 O.R. Sick. 1 O.R. Other Causes.

9th.
 Usual work on Trenches and Posts. The CAMBRAI Road was reconnoitred by 2nd. Lieut. G.A.N. LOWNDES.
 Casualties:- 2 O.R. Sick. 3 O.R. Reinforcements.

10th.
 Usual work on Posts and Trenches. Usual patrols, no enemy seen or heard.
 Casualties:- 2 O.R. Sick. 1 O.R. Other Causes. 1 Offr. 2nd. Lieut. O.A.M. EATON 13th. Lon. Regt. & 2 O.R. Reinforcements.

11th.
 Usual work on Posts and Trenches. Usual Patrols, no enemy seen or heard.
 Casualties:- NIL.

12th.
 Usual Work on Posts and Trenches. Usual patrols, no enemy seen or heard.
 Casualties:- 2 O.R. Sick. 1 O.R. Reinforcements.

13th.
 Usual work on Trenches and Posts. A BANGALORE TORPEDO was exploded by a party under 2nd. Lieut. J.P.D. KENNEDY under the enemy's outpost wire near the DEMICOURT--GRAINCOURT Road. It did not appear to effect the enemy he did not reply in any way. Orders received that there was to be no further patrolling outside our own wire except wire patrols.
 Casualties:- 18 O.R. Reinforcements.

Lieut Colonel
Commdg. 1/ Queens' Westminster Rifles

Place	Date	Hour

1917.
Novr. 14th.
　　Usual working parties. No patrols sent out.
　　Casualties :- 4 O.R. Sick.
15th.
　　Usual working parties. No patrols sent out.
　　Casualties :- 1 O.R. Wounded. 2 O.R. Sick. 2 O.R.
　　Other Causes. 4 O.R. Reinforcements.
16th.
　　Usual work on Posts and trenches. The Battalion was
　　relieved by the 1st.Q.V.R. and went out to Brigade
　　Reserve at LEBUCQUIERE. B & C Coys. returned with
　　the Battalion. A Coy remained in support to the Q.V.R.
　　in the reserve line on the RIGHT Sub-Sector. D Coy.
　　remained in support to the 2nd.LONDONS at SOLE Support Trench
　　on the LEFT Sub-Sector :-
　　Casualties:-   NIL.
17th.
　　All Companies employed on working parties.
　　Casualties :- 13 O.R. Reinforcements.
18th.
　　All Companies employed on working parties.
　　Casualties :- 2 O.R. Sick. 2 O.R.Reinforcements.
19th.
　　All Companies employed on working parties.
　　Casualties :- 4 O.R. Sick. 2 OR. 4 Reinforcements
20th.
　　The Battalion less 2 Companies in the Intermediate
　　Line standing by in Billets. At 3 p.m. orders were
　　received to move up and take over the line from the
　　DEMICOURT-GRAINCOURT Road.(K.7.2.) to (K.1.1.) the
　　DEMICOURT-MOEUVRES Road with H.Q. at TROUT, relieving the
　　Q.V.R. The whole Battalion was in by 8 p.m.
　　Casualties :- 2 O.R. Sick. 1 O.R.Other Causes. 4 O.R.
　　Reinforcements.
21st.
　　At 2 p.m. orders were received to attack TADPOLE COPSE
　　(ref.map.FRANCE 57 C.) D.18.a. and information was given
　　to us that MOEUVRES was in our hands, but that the
　　BOURSIES-MOEUVRES Road was covered by heavy machine gun
　　fire. It was therefore decided to approach up the DEMICOURT
　　MOEUVRES Road--A & D Companies were still in the intermediate
　　line and they were ordered to move up at once. As the majority
　　of B & C Coys. were working clearing away wire off the road
　　it was not until 4.30 p.m. that they moved off- B Coy.
　　leading in two lines of sections followed by C Coy. in the
　　same formation-A & D Coys. arrived shortly afterwards
　　and A Coy. moved up after the two leading Coys. D Coy.
　　remaining in Support with Battalion H.Q. at K.1.c.40.25.
　　At 7 p.m. a message was received from B Coy. to the effect that
　　the road was swept by M.G. from the HINDENBURG LINE and that
　　he had suffered casualties. This was reported by wire to
　　Brigade and orders were then received to return to the main
　　CAMBRAI Road and then go up this road and enter the
　　HINDENBURG LINE at E.26.c.3.2. and E.26.c.65.30 and work
　　up until clear of the front held by the 109th.Brigade,
　　and then to continue and work up to TADPOLE COPSE--
　　This was cancelled and eventually the 3 Coys.were ordered
　　back to our old line between K.1.c.40.25. and the CAMBRAI
　　Road and rations and water were issued.
　　Casualties :-3 O.R.Killed. 7 O.R. Wounded. 2 O.R.Sick
　　2 O.R. Died of Wounds.

P.H.Glasier Lieut Colonel
Commdg. 1/ Queens' Westminster Rifles

WAR DIARY or INTELLIGENCE SUMMARY

(Erase heading not required.)

Place	Date	Hour	Summary of Events and Information	Remarks and references to Appendices

1917.
Novr. 22nd.

At 2.30 a.m. Operation Orders were received to attack TADPOLE COPSE (D.18.d.) at 11 a.m. the next morning entering the HINDENBURG LINE by the C.T. running from E.25.b.8.4. to E.20.b.4.4. - Verbal Orders were given to the Coy. Commanders to assemble by 6.30 in this C.T. and German Outpost Line in E.25.b. & E.26.c. - A Coy. were ordered to attack up the second line of the system and B the first line, with half C Coy attached to each Company to relieve sentries over dug-outs & C.T. & clear them. D Coy. was instructed to move up and clear the Outpost Line and get touch with the other Coys. at E.19.a.4.8. in the HINDENBURG LINE. The L.R.B. were ordered to support the Battalion, moving behind them. The Battalion was to move under a barrage, moving at the rate of 100 yds. in 5 minutes. C Coy was late in assembling with the result that about 6.30 there was heavy hostile shelling and M.G.fire. which however only cost that Coy one casualty.

At Zero hour (11 a.m.) our guns put down a heavy barrage across the HINDENBURG LINE and on MOEUVRES which went forward as laid down-- this barrage got some way ahead of our men but owing to the uncertainty of the position of the troops it was impossible to bring it back.

At 12.30 p.m. a runner came with a request for more bombs and the news that our men had passed the BOURSIES-MOEUVRES Road and were using german bombs. At this time a forward H.Q. was established at the old enemy barrier on the CAMBRAI Road at K.1.b.8.7. Bombs were sent forward and a dump established at E.19.c.35.15. Large quantities of bombs were taken forward by parties of the Q.V.R. By 5.25 A,B & C Coys were in TADPOLE COPSE & at 4.30 p.m. D Coy was at E.19.a.6.6.

During the night our dispositions were as follows.
B Coy.- D.18.d.3.6.to D.18.d.5.7. ½ C Coy--D.18.d.3.6. to E.19.a.3.8.-- A Coy E.13.c.3.6. to E.13.c.5.3.
From this point we had patrols out continually to E.19.b.2.6. where we got into touch with the L.R.B. On our LEFT we were in touch with the LONDON SCOTTISH who held, back to the old British Front Line.

Casualties :- 5 O.R. Killed. 5 O.R. Wounded. 2 O.R. Sick.
1 O.R. Other Causes.

23rd.

Before dawn the LONDON SCOTTISH relieved a portion of the position held by us so that our left rested on about D.18.d.6.9. The LONDON SCOTTISH continued to push up the HINDENBURG LINE. several times during the day they were assisted by our men with supplies of bombs and parties of our men carried up bombs during the day from the German Outpost Line.

Casualties :- 1 O.R. Killed. 7 O.R. Wounded. 1 O.R. Sick
1 O.R. Reinforcement.

24th.

The Regt. was relieved early in the morning by the LONDON SCOTTISH and 2nd. LONDON REGT. and went back to the old British front line between the BOURSIES-MOEUVRES Road and the C.T. junction at D.29.c.85.35. with H.Q. & 1 Coy. at WHITING J.5.c.6.5.- C Coy. did not return till 12.30 p.m. as being caught by the daylight they had to come a long way round through the HINDENBURG LINE across the CAMBRAI Road in order to get out-- in the evening A B & D Coys were on a working party digging a C.T. from

P.H.Glasier Lieut Colonel
Commdg. 1/ Queens' Westminster Rifles

1917.
Novr.24th.(Contd)
J.5.b.3.4. forward to D.30.a.95.70. They dug for 3 hours.
Casualties :- 1 Officer Wounded 2nd.Lieut.W.H.ORMISTON.
13th.Lon.Regt.Att.1 Officer Lieut & Q.M.E.W.JACKSON and
3 O.R.Sick. 1 O.R. Other Causes. 2 O.R. Reinforcements.

25th.
A quiet day;in the evening the Battalion continued digging
the C.T. commenced the previous night.
Casualties :- 2 O.R. Wounded.

26th.
The day was quiet;in the evening the Battalion relieved
the L.R.B. in the Brigade RIGHT Sub-Sector, with our RIGHT
at E.20 a. 15.15 & our left at E.19.a.3.5. B Coy on the
right C Coy in the centre,holding up SWAN LANE C.T. to the
block at E.19.b.9.5. D Coy on the Left A Coy insupport.
It snowed for a considerable time during the night.
Casualties :- 2 O.R.Wounded.1 O.R. Sick. 2 O.R.Other Causes.

27th.
Intermittent hostile shelling,work on trenches and clearing
wire.
Casualties :- 1 Officer, Capt A.J.M.GORDON & 1 O.R.Killed
6 O.R. Wounded. 4 O.R. Sick. 4 O.R. Reinforcements.

28th.
Fairly quiet day; work on clearing trenches and improving
trenches- party digging in outpost line near Battalion
H.Q.
Casualties :-3 O.R. Wounded. 1 Officer,2nd.Lieut.H.A.KILBURN
and 2.O.R.Sick. 4 O.R. Reinforcements. 13th Lon Regt

29th.
Enemy shelled outpost line and round Battalion H.Q. at
E.25.a.9.5. between 1p.m. and 4 p.m. Work on trenches
and clearing up sap at E.19.d.2.7. which was full of
wire.
The night was very quiet.
Casualties :-1 O.R. Killed. 9 O.R. Wounded. 5 O.R.Sick
1 O.R. Died of Wounds. 1 Officer,2nd.Lieut.G.L.LLOYD
9th.Lon.Regt Att.& 24 O.R. Missing. 1 O.R. Reinforcement.

30th.
At about 8.4.a.m. our observers near Battalion H.Q.reported
that the enemy were leaving MOEUVRES in large numbers;
further observation revealed the fact that although they
were leaving MOEUVRES others appeared to be entering
and enormous numbers of troops were moving EAST through
QUARRY WOOD thence towards BOURLON. Heavy artillery fire
opened on our ≠ trenches at 10.15 which increased until
about 10.45 when under a barrage of trench mortars the
enemy attacked down SWAN LANE and down the BOURSIES--
MOEUVRES Road and over the top between the two points--
the great width of the Trenches prevented much cover being
obtained against the T.M.barrage. A stiff fight commenced
of which it is impossible to give details,and although we
managed to beat the enemy back over the top-they penetrated
on our right from the road mentioned above and along the
trench on our left and although at 1.15 we still had a footing
in our front line. The position was critical and we had
asked for reinforcements. By 2 p.m. we were holding the
support line and the two C.Ts with a block in each close up
to the front line

Lieut Colonel
Commdg. 1' Queens' Westminster Rifles

Place	Date	Hour

1917.
Novr.30th.(Contd)

At 3.30 p.m. an urgent wire was sent for reinforcements as our line was giving way and again at 4.10 p.m.-- after this time although there was a considerable amount of bombing at the blocks things became quieter and by 6.30 p.m. except for machine gun fire all was quiet. At 6.30 p.m. the Battalion was reinforced by one company of the Q.V.R. who relieved our men in the C.T.s--later 2 Coys of the L.R.B. arrived and relieved our men in a position of the support line and another company commenced digging themselves in in the old German Outpost Line--during the day a continuous stream of messages arrived to the effect that our guns were firing short and they continued to do so although urgent messages were sent back. Our A.A.Guns appeared to have been put out of action as they took no notice of large numbers of enemy aircraft which patrolled our lines almost at will during the day. Orders that the Battalion would be relieved by the L.R.B. were received about 8.30-- The Battalion was clear of the trenches by 1 a.m. having waited until the C.O. of that Battalion was satisfied the position was secure. Wagons were provided to take the Battalion back to COKE CAMP, LEBUCQUIERE. Owing to a barrage across the Cambrai Road only the Signallers, Runners &c were able to reach them, the remainder of the Battalion marched back.
Casualties :- 2 Officers, 2nd.Lieut J.H.M.HOOPER & 2nd.Lieut.T.CAUDWELL and 21 Other Ranks Killed.
2 Officers, Capt W.G.ORR/& 2nd.Lieut.H.K.MOULTON 18th Lon 10th.Lon.
and 66 O.R. Wounded. 1 O.R. Died of Wounds. 1 Officer 2nd.Lieut.G.L.LLOYD 9th.Lon. and 24 O.R. Missing 1 O.R. Reinforcement.

	Offrs.	O.R.
Strength on 31st.October 1917	38	811
Add.	1	95
	39	906
Less.	9	242
	30	664

P.M.Glasier
Lieut Colonel
Commdg. 1/ Queens' Westminster Rifles

WAR DIARY or INTELLIGENCE SUMMARY

Army Form C. 2118.

1st Battn Queens Westminster Rifles.

A M E N D M E N T.

- to -

W A R   D I A R Y.

for month of November 1917.

1917.
Novr. 22nd.

During the operations on this day, 3 Machine Guns, 1 Trench Mortar, and 75 Prisoners were captured by the Battalion.

PhGlasier.

Lieut-Colonel.
Commanding 1st Queens Westminster Rifles.

Army Form W.3091.

Cover for Documents.

Nature of Enclosures.

CONFIDENTIAL

WAR DIARY

1/16th LONDON REGT. (Q.W.R.)

DECEMBER 1917.

Notes, or Letters written.

WAR DIARY or INTELLIGENCE SUMMARY

Place	Date	Hour	Summary of Events and Information	Remarks and references to Appendices
			1917.	

Decr 1st. Battn rested and bathed. Casualties 1 O.R. Sick 1 O.R. Other Causes 8 O.R. Reinforcements.

2nd Remainder of Battn bathed. Battn moved to Camp near BAPAUME where tents had to be put up. Casualties 2 O.R. Sick, 1 O.R. Other Causes, 4 O.R. Reinforcements.

3rd. Struck camp and moved off 9 a.m. to FREMICOURT where we entrained for BEAUMETZ LES LOGES which we reached about 2 p.m. and marched to BERNAVILLE, where Battn was billetted in barns and huts. Casualties 3 O.R. Sick.

4th. C.O's inspection in the morning - continued cleaning and refit-ting. Parade in the afternoon for address by the B.G.C., in which he congratulated the Battn on its work during the recent operations. Casualties 3 O.R. Sick.

5th. Left BERNEVILLE 1 a.m. and proceeded by route march via WARLUS - DUISANS to MAROEUIL where Battn was billetted in barns, huts and dug-outs. Casualties 1 O.R. Reinforcement.

6th. Carried on refitting and reorganization. Parade all Battn Duties at Retreat for the first time for several months. Casualties 4 O.R. Sick.

7th. Battn refitting and reorganizing. RED LINE reconnoitred by Commanding Officer, Company Commanders and Int. Officer during the morning. Casualties 2 O.R. Sick.

8th. Battn left MAROEUIL at 9.15 a.m. and marched to ECURIE WOOD CAMP via ANZIN ST AUBIN where men were billetted in huts. Casualties 2 Officers Sick (Major J.Q. HENRIQUES and 2nd Lieut R.A. BASSHAM).

9th. Ordinary training carried out from 9 a.m. to 1 p.m. Casualties 2 O.R. Wounded (Gas) 3 O.R. Sick, 1 O.R. Other Causes.

10th. Ordinary training from 9 a.m. to 1 p.m. Casualties 1 O.R. Wounded (Gas) 2 O.R. Sick, 1 O.R. Other Causes.

11th. As for 10th. Casualties 4 O.R. Wounded (Gas) 6 O.R. Sick.

12th Front Line and forward Battn H.Q. reconnoitred by Commanding Officer and Adjutant. Usual training carried out by Companies. Casualties 2 O.R. Sick.

13th. Front Line reconnoitred by Company Commanders, Works and Intelligence Officers. Usual training by Companies. Casualties 5 O.R. Sick, 24 O.R. Reinforcements.

S.R. Savill
Captain.
Commanding 1st Queens Westminster Rif

1917.

Decr 14th. Battn left ECURIE CAMP at 10.30 a.m. and proceeded as a Battn to ROUNDHAY CAMP which was reached at 12.15 p.m. Battn had dinner there and proceeded at 1.15 p.m. by Companies to relieve 2nd LONDON REGT in the front line system. Last Company passed RED LINE before 2.30 p.m. Relief complete by 4.30 p.m. Batt-tn front was I.1.c.1.8.(Sheet OPPY (3) and 51.b.N.W.) Casualties 1 O.R. Wounded 1 O.R. Sick, 5 O.R. reinforcements

15th. Situation Quiet. Enemy's chief activity T.Ms and M.Gs. Work started on new firebay in INVICTA C.T. Casualties 4 O.R. Sick, 1 O.R. Reinforcements.

16th. Situation Quiet. 2 men killed in WATER POST by 15 cm shell, one of three direct hits on trench. Orders received for relief by 31st Divn on 18/12/17. Work on new firebay continued.
Casualties 2 O.R. Killed, 1 O.R. Wounded, 6 O.R. Sick, 3 O.R. Other Causes, 23 O.R. Reinforcements.

17th. Situation Quiet. Orders for relief by 31st Div cancel-led. Weather cold with considerable fall of snow during the morning. Enemy M.Gs active during evening and night. Casualties 2 O.R. Sick, 1 Officer Other Causes (2nd Lieut J.P.D. KENNEDY, 18th London Regiment to M.G. School, GRANTHAM) 3 O.R. Reinforcements

18th. Situation Quiet - weather frosty. Hostile artillery fire confined to ARRAS - GAVRELLE ROAD Our artillery retaliated on enemy T.M. emplacement for fire on TOWY POST. E.A. brought down by Lewis Gun fire. Crashed in enemy's lines directly East of TOWY POST. Casualties 7 O.R. Sick.

19th. Situation very quiet. No enemy artillery or T.M. fire. Enemy's lines obscured during greater part of day. Hard frost all day. Between 7 p.m. and 9 p.m. our artillery fired bursts on enemy post just North of GAVRELLE POST, one shell apparently hitting Listening Post. Casualties 4 O.R. Sick, 4 Officers Reinforcements from Reserve Battn.
    2nd Lieut H.W. THOMPSON.
      "   J.E.S. GOLDING.
      "   L.G. SPECK.
      "   S.L. MANN.

20th. Battn relieved in front line by 2nd LONDON REGT. Relief complete by 11.20 a.m. "A" and "D" Companies moved to RED LINE (Support), "B" and "C" Companies moved to ROUNDHAY CAMP where they were bil-letted in shelters and unfinished huts. Frost continued all day. Casualties 3 O.R. Sick, 1 O.R. Other Causes, 1 O.R. Reinforcement.

Captain.
Commanding 1st Queens Westminster Rifles

1917.

Decr 21st. All Companies worked for some hours on collecting salvage in area 100 yards East and West of RED LINE. Owing to mist this work was done in daylight.
Casualties 1 O.R. Sick, 2 O.R. Reinforcements.

22nd. Work on collecting of salvage continued. Battn bathed during the day at the Baths near CHANTECLER SIDINGS. Frost still severe. Casualties 4 O.R. Sick, 3 O.R. Reinforcements.

23rd. Two Companies in RED LINE worked for 2nd LONDON REGT. Two Companies at ROUNDHAY CAMP rested.
Information received that all recommendations for MILITARY MEDALS for CAMBRAI attack and counter attack had been passed. Number of MILITARY MEDALS altogether received was 16. Frost continued. Casualties 2 O.R. Sick

24th. Battn relieved 2nd LONDON REGT in Right Sub-Sector. Relief complete by 12.15 p.m.
"A" Company in TOWY POST.
"D"   "   " GAVRELLE and WATER POSTS.
"C"   "   " NAVAL TRENCH.
"B"   "   " RED LINE.
Situation very quiet. Frost continued.
Casualties 1 Officer (2nd Lieut W.H. GATFIELD) and 4 O.R. Sick, 4 O.R. Reinforcements.

25th. Situation very quiet. Our Machine Guns and artillery a little more active than usual, during on tracks and H.Qs. Thaw in morning - snow during the evening. Casualties 2 O.R. Sick, 23 O.R. Reinforcements.

26th. Situation on front very quiet. Our M.Gs again active during evening. Enemy aeroplanes active over our lines during afternoon. Considerable fall of snow during night of 25/26th. Casualties 1 O.R. Sick.

27th. Situation very quiet. Slight enemy artillery during afternoon on NAVAL LINE and ARRAS - GAVRELLE ROAD. B.G.C. went round TOWY POST during afternoon. Snow still on ground.
Casualties 1 Officer (2nd Lieut T.J.M. VAN DER LINDE, 9th London Regt) Wounded, 6 O.R. Sick, 3 O.R. Reinforcements.

28th. Situation quiet. A few gas shells on junction of NAVAL TRENCH and ARRAS - GAVRELLE ROAD at 1.30 p.m. Battn relieved by the 2nd LONDON REGT. Relief complete by 4.30 p.m. Battn moved to AUBREY CAMP (ARRAS - SOUCHEZ ROAD) where Bat-tn was billetted in huts.
Casualties 4 O.R. Reinforcements.

Captain.
Commanding 1st Queens Westminster Rifles.

1917.
Decr 29th.   Battn cleaned up - kit inspections etc.
             Casualties 4 O.R. Sick, 1 Officer (2nd Lieut R.A.
             BASSHAM) from Hospital.

30th.   Church Parades and resting.
             Casualties 1 O.R. Sick, 2 O.R. Reinforcements.

31st.   Battn carried out general training from 9.30 a.m.
             to 1.30 p.m. Preparations for relieving in line on
             1st January.
             Casualties 4 O.R. Sick, 1 Officer, Capt S.R. SAVILL, M.C.
             from Senior Officers' Course and 5 O.R. Reinforcements.

	Officers.	O.R.
Strength on 30.11.17.	30	664.
ADD.	6	113.
	36	777.
LESS.	6	84.
Strength on 31.12.17.	30	693.

S. R. Savill
Captain.
Commanding 1st Queens Westminster Rifles.

35807. W16879/M1879 500,000 3/17 R.T. (1074) Forms W3091/3   Army Form W.3091.

Cover for Documents.

Nature of Enclosures.

<u>Confidential</u>

War Diary

of

1/16th Bn The London Regt.

for month of

January 1918.

Notes, or Letters written.

WAR DIARY or INTELLIGENCE SUMMARY

(Erase heading not required.)

Place	Date	Hour	Summary of Events and Information	Remarks and references to Appendices

1918.

Jan. 1st. Battalion proceeded at 6 a.m. to GAVRELLE SECTOR (Front Line). Casualties 7 O.R. Reinforcements.

2nd. Quiet day in trenches - very hard frost.
Casualties 1 O.R. Sick.

3rd. Battalion relieved by the 1/4th LONDON REGIMENT and proceeded by Light Railway to MAROEUIL, arriving at about 7 p.m.
Casualties 1 O.R. Sick, 3 O.R. Reinforcements.

4th. Battalion cleaned up etc.
Casualties 2 O.R. Sick, 2 O.R. Other Causes, 3 O.R. Reinforcements.

5th. Battalion moved to CAUCOURT by rail from MAROEUIL to SAVY, thence by road to CAUCOURT, arriving about 12.30 p.m. Battalion billetted in huts and barns.
Casualties 4 O.R. Sick, 1 Officer (2nd Lieut W.E.S. JOTCHAM, 19th LONDON REGIMENT, Posted 169th T.M.B.) 2 O.R. Reinforcements.

6th. Battalion rested and cleaned up. No Church Parade could be arranged.
Casualties 2 O.R. Sick, 35 O.R. Reinforcements.

7th. Training carried out individually by Companies during morning, finishing up with a Battalion Parade for Battn Drill.
Casualties 1 O.R. Sick, 4 O.R. Reinforcements.

8th. Very heavy snow interfered with training. Companies carried out route marches in the morning and cleared snow from the roads in the village in the afternoon.
Casualties NIL.

9th. The whole Battalion employed all day in clearing snow drifts from the roads between the villages.
Casualties 2 O.R. Sick.

10th. Training was again interfered with by the weather. Rifles and Respirators were inspected and Companies did Physical Training, elementary musketry and gas drill.
Casualties 4 O.R. Sick, 2 O.R. Other Causes, 16 O.R. Reinforcements.

11th. Battalion bathed and carried out Brigade Tests.
Casualties 5 O.R. Sick, 22 O.R. Reinforcements.

12th. Company training in the morning. The Commanding Officer and Quartermaster attended Divisional Conference on "Economy" and "Social conditions after the War"
The first and part of the second rounds of the Inter-platoon football competition were played off in the afternoon.
Casualties 3 O.R. Sick, 2 O.R. Other Causes, 4 O.R. Reinforcements.

P.H.Glasier
Lieut Colonel
Commdg. 1/ Queens' Westminster Rifles

Army Form C. 2118.

WAR DIARY or INTELLIGENCE SUMMARY

Place	Date	Hour	Summary of Events and Information	Remarks and references to Appendices

1918.

Jan. 13th. Church Parade Service in the morning. Rev. CRISFORD preached farewell sermon. The second round of the inter-platoon football was completed in the afternoon. The first and second rounds of rounder competition were played off.
Casualties 6 O.R. Sick, 1 O.R. Other Causes.

14th. Companies fired qualifying practices on the range in the morning and Lewis Guns in the afternoon. One semi-final of the football tournament was played.
Casualties 7 O.R. Sick.

15th. Battalion competition to select Platoon to represent Battalion in the Brigade Competition. Heavy rain prevented Battn Drill as previously arranged.
Battn held Christmas dinner and Concert in the evening.
Casualties 1 O.R. Sick, 2 O.R. Other Causes, 1 O.R. Reinforcements.

16th. Training programme cancelled by reason of rain. Rain ceased later and Battn went for route march. Rain fell again however and the Battn got very wet.
In the afternoon, Officers attended lecture on Fire Direction and Control, by Brigade Musketry Instructor.
Lieut F.E. SMITH, QuarterMaster reported for duty from 5th Res. Battn BEDFORD REGT.
Casualties 3 O.R. Sick, 1 Officer and 3 O.R. Reinforcements.

17th. Range practices, originally arranged were cancelled owing to the weather. Steady rain all day.
"B" and "C" Companies moved to HERMIN to make room for Divisional Artillery.
Lieut-Colonel P.M. GLASIER, D.S.O. returned from leave.
Casualties 2 O.R. Sick, 1 O.R. Other Causes, 1 O.R. Reinforcement.

18th. Company training in the morning. In the afternoon Brigade Platoon Competion. No. 12 Platoon was entered and gained second place in the Brigade.
Casualties 1 O.R. Sick; 10 O.R. Reinforcements.

19th. "C" Company fired on Range, which was badly water-logged. Only rapid could be carried out owing to state of ground. Other Companies Brigade Tests.
Casualties 4 O.R. Sick.

20th. Church Parade. Battalion beat 1/Q.V.R. 20 - NIL in Rugby Football Match. "C" Company moved to forward area for attachment to 185th Tunnelling Company.
Casualties 1 Officer (2nd Lieut O.A.M. EATON, 23rd LONDON REGIMENT) and 3 O.R. Sick, 3 O.R. Reinforcements.

P.M. Glasier
Lieut Colonel
Commdg. 1/ Queens' Westminster Rifles

Army Form C. 2118.

Place	Date	Hour

1918.

Jan. 21st. "B" Company fired Rapid and Lewis Gun Practices on Range. "A" and "D" Companies bathed and did Company training. No clean clothing available.
Casualties 2 O.R. Sick, 1 O.R. Reinforcements.

22nd. Box Respirator Test in tear gas combined with route march. "B" Company bathed, no clean clothing could be obtained. Casualties 5 O.R. Reinforcements. Men had to remain verminous.

23rd. Platoon competition to select Platoon to represent Battn in Corps Competition.
Result:- No. 2 Platoon, 1st, No. 6 Platoon, 2nd, No. 13 Platoon, 3rd, "C" Company did not compete.
Casualties 5 O.R. Sick.

24th. Battalion moved to forward area for wiring under XIII Corps R.E. Battalion H.Q. TRAFALGAR CAMP, "B" and "D" Companies, ROCLINCOURT, "A" Company in GREEN LINE behind BAILLEUL. "C" Company remained attached to 185th Tunnelling Company.
Casualties 2 O.R. Sick, 1 Officer, (2nd Lieut W.H. GATFIELD) from Hospital.

25th. Battn (less "C" Company) rendez-vous CHANTECLER DUMP 9.30 a.m. to meet R.E. Work for 4 hours.
Casualties 2 O.R. Sick, 1 O.R. Reinforcement.

26th As for 25th.
Casualties 3 O.R. Sick, 2 O.R. Other Causes.

27th Battn continued wiring under R.Es as/for two previous days.
Casualties 2 O.R. Sick, 3 O.R. Reinforcements.

28th Wiring under REs continued. All Company Officers less 1 per Company watched Corps Competition.
Casualties 2 O.R. Reinforcements.

29th Wiring as usual. No. 2 Platoon (A Company) proceeded by train from ECURIE - AUBIGNY and from AUBIGNY to FREVILLERS to take part in Brigade A.R.A. competition on 30th.
Casualties NIL.

30th. Wiring as usual. No. 2 Platoon won Brigade A.R.A. competition at FREVILLERS. Casualties 1 O.R. Other Causes 1 O.R. Reinforcement.

31st. Wiring as usual. Casualties 1 Officer (2nd Lieut L.G. SPECK) Sick and 3 O.R., 14 O.R. Reinforcements.

P.H.Glasier.
Lieut Colonel
Commdg. 1/ Queens' Westminster Rifles

1918.
January 31st
(Contd).

SUMMARY OF BATTALION STRENGTH.

	Offrs.	O.R.
Strength on 31.12.17.	28	693.
Add.	2	141.
	30	834.
Less.	3	90.
Strength on 31.1.18.	27	744.

P.M.Glasier.
Lieut-Colonel.
Commanding 1st Queens Westminster Rifles.

Army Form W.3091.

Cover for Documents.

SECRET

Nature of Enclosures.

WAR DIARY

16th LONDON REGIMENT

(Q.W.R).

FEBRUARY 1918.

Notes, or Letters written.

Army Form C. 2118.

WAR DIARY
or
INTELLIGENCE SUMMARY
(Erase heading not required.)

Instructions regarding War Diaries and Intelligence Summaries are contained in F. S. Regs., Part II. and the Staff Manual respectively. Title Pages will be prepared in manuscript.

Place	Date	Hour	Summary of Events and Information	Remarks and references to Appendices
In the Field	1918. Feb. 1st.		Battalion marched to EGURIE RAILHEAD, entrained there at 2 p.m. and proceeded to TINCQUES from where they marched to billets at FREVILLERS. Men in barns etc. Part of the Draft of 12 Officers and 250 O.R. from Q.V.R. joined Battn. Casualties 2 OWR. Sick, 1 O.R. Other Causes, 12 Officers and 261 Other Ranks Reinforcements.	
"	2nd.		Battalion cleaned up. Kit inspections etc. Draft inspected and posted to Companies. Casualties 2 O.R. Sick 4 O.R. Reinforcements.	
"	3rd		Working parties worked in shifts on markers trench at range 0,30,b. No parade services held. Men rested and bathed. Casualties 7 O.R. Sick, 2 O.R. Other Causes, 3 O.R. Reinforcements.	
"	4th.		"B" Company and sybdicates from other Companies carried out Brigade Scheme in conjunction with L.R.B. and 169th Machine Gun Company. Other Companies carried out ordinary training. Casualties 2 O.R. Sick, 1 O.R. Other Causes, 4 O.R. Reinforcements.	
"	5th.		Flagged attack carried out by "A" "B" & "D" Companies followed by march past in columns and close column of platoons. "C" Company on range. Casualties 2 O.R. Sick, 7 O.R. Other Causes, 10 O.R. Reinforcement.	
"	6th.		Commanding Officer, 1 Officer per Company and A/Adjutant left Brigade H.Q. on lorry at 9 a.m. for ROUNDHAY CAMP and from there visited GAVRELLE SECTOR pending relief, returning to FREVILLERS about 6.30 p.m. Companies held private parades. No. 2 Platoon won Divisional A.R.A. Competition. Casualties 2 Officers (2nd Lieuts C.A.F. KNAPP & F.L. CHAMBERLIN, 21st LONDON REGIMENT) and 17 O.R. Reinforcements.	
"	7th.		Battalion paraded and moved off at 9.15 a.m. for SAVY, entraining there for MAROEUIL from which place it marched to ST AUBIN. Casualties 3 O.R. Sick, 2 O.R. Other Causes, 16 O.R. Reinforcements.	
"	8th.		Battalion entrained at ST AUBIN at 4 p.m. and went to CHANTECLER siding marching from there to the front line (TOWY POST) relieving the 2/4th Duke of Wellingtons Regt - "B" Company in TOWY and GAVRELLE POSTS - "A" Company WATER POST & NAVAL LINE, "C" Company NAVAL & RED LINES "D" Company in DITCH POST. Relief complete by 11 p.m. Casualties 11 O.R. Sick, 1 Officer	

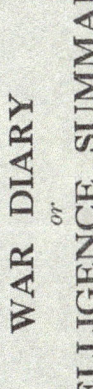

Lieut Colonel
Commdg. 1/ Queens' Westminster Rifles

2449 Wt. W14957/M90 750,000 1/16 J.B.C. & A. Forms/C.2118/12.

Army Form C. 2118.

WAR DIARY
or
INTELLIGENCE SUMMARY

(Erase heading not required.)

Instructions regarding War Diaries and Intelligence Summaries are contained in F. S. Regs., Part II. and the Staff Manual respectively. Title Pages will be prepared in manuscript.

Place	Date	Hour	Summary of Events and Information	Remarks and references to Appendices
In the Field, 1918.	Feb 8th (Contd).		(2nd Lieut K.PALMER, 22nd LONDON REGT. transferred to R.E., 3 Officers (2nd Lieut O.A.M. EATON from Hospital, 2nd Lieuts C.G.WARREN & F.L. HITCHINGS, 21st LONDON REGIMENT) & 1 O.R. Reinforcements.	
	Feb.	9th.	Situation very quiet. Work on cleaning up trenches carried out at night. Casualties 5 O.R Sick, 1 O.R. Reinforcement.	
	"	10th.	Enemy's attitude was quiet. Work was continued on TOWY ALLEY where most of mud was cleared from trench. Visibility was good all day. Casualties 2 O.R. Wounded, 3 O.R. Sick.	
	"	11th.	Enemy artillery and machine guns unusually quiet on forward area. Considerable movement in enemy lines all day. Work on TOWY ALLEY continued. Casualties 2 O.R. Sick, 5 O.R. Other Causes, 5 O.R. Reinforcements.	
	"	12th.	Situation quiet during day. At 7.15 p.m. and again at 8.10. p.m. enemy bombarded. TOWY ALLEY (E. of NAVAL LINE), DITCH POST and RED LINE with Yellow Cross gas shells. There were no casualties. Casualties 3 O.R. Sick, 7 O.R. Reinforcements.	
	"	13th.	Battalion relieved by 2nd LONDON REGIMENT and moved as follows:- "A" & "B" Companies to ROUNDHAY CAMP with Battn H.Q. "C" & "D" Companies to RED LINE. Relief complete 8.15 p.m. Casualties 3 O.R. Sick, 1 O.R. Reinforcement.	
	"	14th.	Battalion rested and cleaned. "B" Company supplied working party on making huts splinter proof, also some working parties supplied for R.E. Casualties 2 O.R. Sick, 1 O.R. Other Causes, 1 O.R. Reinforcement.	
	"	15th.	1 Officer (2nd Lieut E.W.G.MALCOLM) and 75 O.R. attached to R.Es. for work on mined dug-outs. Work on huts continued. Casualties 2 O.R. Sick, 44 O.R. Other Causes, 1 O.R. Reinforcements.	
	"	16th.	Enemy showed unusual artillery and aircraft activity probably owing to clear frosty weather. Work continued on improving and cleaning camp. Casualties 5 O.R. Sick, 4 O.R. Reinforcements.	

Lieut Colonel
Commdg. 1/ Queens' Westminster Rifles

Army Form C. 2118.

WAR DIARY
or
INTELLIGENCE SUMMARY
(Erase heading not required.)

Instructions regarding War Diaries and Intelligence Summaries are contained in F.S. Regs., Part II. and the Staff Manual respectively. Title Pages will be prepared in manuscript.

Place	Date	Hour	Summary of Events and Information	Remarks and references to Appendices
In the Field	1918. Feb. 17th.		Battalion relieved at ROUNDHAY CAMP and moved to ST AUBIN by Light Railway, leaving CHANTECLER at 6 p.m. Casualties 2 O.R. Sick, 2 O.R. Reinforcements.	
"	18th.		Battalion cleaned up and rested in the morning. At 3 p.m. practice parade for G.O.C's inspection held. Casualties 1 Officer (2nd Lieut E.W.THOMPSON) and 10 O.R. Sick, 7 O.R. Reinforcements.	
"	19th.		At 11 a.m. Battalion was inspected by G.O.C., 56th Division. After inspecting Battalion G.O.C. gave an address complimenting the Battalion on its success at CAMBRAI. Casualties 1 Officer (Lieut C.E.MOY, M.C.) & 1 O.R. Reinforcement.	
"	20th.		Specialist training of Lewis Gunners and Observers carried out. Also training on B.F. Course and Drill ground. Casualties 1 Officer (2nd Lieut R.A.BASSHAM) and 13 O.R. Sick, 1 O.R. Reinforcement.	
"	21st.		Battalion relieved 1st L.R.B. in GAVRELLE SECTOR. Entrained ST AUBIN 11.30 a.m. for CHANTECLER "A" Company to TOWY POST. - "B" Company to DITCH POST. - "C" Company to WATER POST & NAVAL (N) "D" Company to NAVAL SOUTH and RED LINEN. Relief complete by 3.30 p.m. Situation very quiet. Casualties 6 O.R. Sick, 59 O.R. Reinforcements.	
"	22nd.		Work on maintenance of trenches and by night making of knife rests in TOWY POST. Enemy shelled RED LINE and NORTHUMBERLAND AVENUE heavily during night 21/22nd. Casualties 4 O.R. Sick, 2 O.R. Other Causes, 2 O.R. Reinforcements.	
"	23rd.		Work on trenches, making and putting out of knife rests in front of WILLIE TRENCH and putting up a double apron to north of COLOUR TRENCH. Situation very quiet (all arms). Casualties 1 Officer (Capt F.M.E.M.WHITBY, M.C.) and 3 O.R. Sick, 1 O.R. Other Causes.	
"	24th.		Enemy's attitude was generally quiet. Patrols went up DITCH and CHICO TRENCH to GAVRELLE ROAD but saw no enemy. Usual work on knife rests and other wire continued and covering party supplied for CHESHIRE REGIMENT. Casualties 3 O.R. Sick, 3 O.R. Other Causes, 4 O.R. Reinforcements.	

Lieut Colonel
Commdg. 1/ Queens' Westminster Rifles

Army Form C. 2118.

WAR DIARY
or
INTELLIGENCE SUMMARY

(Erase heading not required.)

Instructions regarding War Diaries and Intelligence Summaries are contained in F. S. Regs., Part II and the Staff Manual respectively. Title Pages will be prepared in manuscript.

Place	Date	Hour	Summary of Events and Information	Remarks and references to Appendices
In the Field.	1918. Feb. 25th.		Enemy's attitude was again quiet. Patrols went up DITCH and to GAVRELLE ROAD. Covering party for men putting out knife rests was fired on by what appeared to be a covering party of the enemy's. 1 Corporal was killed and the covering party withdrew. Casualties 1 O.R. Killed. 4 O.R. Sick.	
"	26th.		BAILLEUL - WILLERVAL LINE shelled with 5.9's nearly all day. Otherwise everything was quiet and patrols near GAVRELLE ROAD had nothing to report. Casualties 3 O.R. Wounded, 4 O.R. Sick, 3 O.R. Reinforcements.	
"	27th.		Battalion relieved by 2nd LONDON REGIMENT - "A" "C" & "D" Companies moved to ROUNDHAY CAMP. "B" Company remained in the BAILLEUL WILLERVAL LINE. In the evening Brigade wired that from information received from German deserter hostile attack expected at GHELUVELT at dawn on morning of 28th. Battalion was ordered to be ready to move off at ½ hours notice. Casualties 2 O.R. Sick, 2 O.R. Reinforcements.	
"	28th.		Orders received to "Stand Down" All Companies working on reserve lines of defence and improvements to camp. Casualties 4 O.R. Sick.	

	Officers & Other Ranks.
Strength on 31.1.18.	27 744.
ADD.	19 408.
	46 1,152.
LESS	4 177.
Strength on 28.2.18.	42 972.

Ph Mastin
Lieut-Colonel.
Commanding 1st Battn QUEENS WESTMINSTER RIFLES

SECRET.  Copy No. 10

1st Battn QUEENS WESTMINSTER RIFLES.

OPERATION ORDER, No. G.13.

7th February 1918.

RELIEF.

The Battn will relieve the 2nd/4th Bn DUKE OF WELLINGTONS Regt in the RIGHT SUB-SECTOR tomorrow evening Feb.8th.

The L.R.B. will be on the Left, and a Battn of the GUARDS Division on the Right of the Battalion.

DISPOSITIONS.

1 Sergeant and 11 men of "B" Coy Q.W.R. (to include 1 S.B. and 1 Signaller) will relieve a similar party of "D" Coy 2/4th D.ofW.Regt in GAVRELLE POST.

"B" Company Q.W.R. will relieve "D" Company 2/4th D.ofW.Regt in TOWY POST.

2 Officers, 3 Lewis Gun Sections and 1 Rfn Section of "A" Coy Q.W.R. will relieve "B" Coy 2/4th D.ofW.Regt in WATER POST

Remainder of "A" Coy Q.W.R. will relieve the remainder of "B" Coy 2/4th D.ofW.Regt in NAVAL NORTH TRENCH.

2 Platoons of "C" Company Q.W.R. will relieve 2 Pltns of "A" Coy 2/4th D.ofW.Regt in NAVAL SOUTH TRENCH.

2 Platoons of "C" Coy Q.W.R. will relieve 2 Pltns of "A" Company 2/4th D.ofW.Regt in the RED LINE.

"D" Company Q.W.R. will relieve "C" Coy 2/4th D.ofW. Regt in DITCH POST.

MOVE.

The Battalion will parade in the road with its head at Battn H.Q. facing EAST in the order "B", "A", "C", H.Q., & "D" Companies at 3.15 p.m.

O.C. "B" Company will arrange to have the garrison of GAVRELLE POST at the head of his Company.

Sergt MABBITT,M.M. will detail 1 Signaller to report to O.C. "B" Company on parade at 3.15 p.m. for duty in GAVRELLE POST.

The Battalion will entrain at ST AUBIN, Light Railway Station at 4 p.m. and proceed by Light Railway to CHANTECLER.

On detraining at CHANTECLER the Battn will immediately fall in in the following order:-

P.T.O.

"B" Company's garrison of GAVRELLE POST.
" " " " TOWY POST.
"A" " " " WATER POST.
" " " " NORTH NAVAL TRENCH.
"C" " " " SOUTH NAVAL TRENCH.
Battalion H.Q.
"D" Company's garrison of DITCH POST.
"C" " " " RED LINE.

O.C. Companies will have their garrisons told off before leaving billets.

The Battalion will move off from CHANTECLER via the new track and the GAVRELLE ROAD to the front line by Platoons at 50 yards interval.

4. ENTRAINING & DETRAINING OFFICER.
----------- 2nd Lieut A.B. RUSSELL will act as entraining and detraining Officer.

5. GUIDES.
------- Battalion Guides will be at the Detraining Point on arrival of Battn
The following guides for the garrisons of posts will be at the junction of the GAVRELLE ROAD and TOWY ALLEY at 6 p.m.

1 Guide for each of GAVRELLE, TOWY and WATER POSTS.
1 " " " " NAVAL NORTH & SOUTH TRENCHES.
1 " " DITCH POST.
1 " " BATTN H.Q.

6. ADVANCE PARTY.
---------- 1 Officer from each of "B", "C", & "D" Companies, R.S.M., 4 C.S.Ms, Sergt ASHDOWN, Sergt MACREADY, Sergt HABBITT, M.M. - Corpl HILL and 4 Observers (to be detailed by the I.O.) will proceed under the orders of the Senior Officer on parade, entraining at ST AUBIN, Light Railway Station at 9 a.m. Guides will meet this party at CHANTECLER SIDING.

7. LEWIS GUNS.
----------- Lewis Guns will be taken on the limbers to the junction of GAVRELLE ROAD and TOWY ALLEY.
Each O.C. Company will detail 1 N.C.O. and 2 men to accompany their limbers.
They will unload the guns etc at the point mentioned above and will have them ready for their Companies to pick up as they pass. They must be unloaded by 8 p.m.

- 3 -

8. **TRANSPORT.** The Transport Sergeant will arrange for 2 G.S. Wagons to report to the Orderly Room at 12 noon to pick up Officers valises and H.Q. Stores to be taken to the Q.M. Stores.

He will also arrange for the 4 Lewis Gun Limbers to report to their Companies during the morning and 1 limber and the Maltese Cart to report to H.Q. at 2 p.m.

The Lewis Gun Limbers will report as mentioned in para 7 above and must arrive at their destination by 5.45 p.m.

Rations will be sent up tomorrow night on limbers as during last tour.

Those of "A" & "B" Companies & H.Q. to the junction of the GAVRELLE ROAD and the NAVAL LINE.

Those of "C" and "D" Companies to the junction of the GAVRELLE ROAD and the RED LINE.

The Maltese Cart and Limber for H.Q. mentioned above will proceed with the ration limbers of "A", "B" & H.Q. Coys.

9. **WATER.** Water for all Companies except "D" Company will be drawn from WATER POST. Petrol Tins will be taken over as Trench Stores.

The Transport Sergeant will arrange to take 1 full water cart and 15 full Petrol Tins to O.C. "D" Coy with his rations.

10. **RATION PARTIES.** O.C. "C" Company will detail a party of 16 men to carry rations from the dump to "B" Company. They will be "standing by" ready to carry immediately on the arrival of the ration limbers. All other Companies will carry their own rations.

11. **COOKS.** Sergt CROSSINGHAM will detail the necessary cooks to proceed to the line with their Companies.

12. **PIONEERS.** Sergt BRICKELL will detail 1 N.C.O. and 2 Pioneers to proceed to the line with the H.Q. Company.

13. **BUGLERS.** Sergt LETHERN will detail 2 Canteen Buglers to proceed to the line with the H.Q. Company to take over the Canteen.

He will also detail 1 N.C.O. and 10 Buglers to report to the Area Commandant, ST CATHERINE at 9 a.m. tomorrow morning and daily until further orders for work on roads.

P.T.O.

BLANKETS.
---------- Blankets rolled in bundles of ten and tied TIGHTLY with string will be stacked in the shed in front of Battn H.Q. by 8 a.m.

OFFICERS VALISES.
------------------- Officers Valises will be stacked outside Battn H.Q. by 12 noon.

OFFICERS MESS BASKETS.
----------------------- All Company Mess Baskets etc will be carried on the Company Lewis Gun Limbers or Ration Limbers.

MAPS, CODE NAMES, etc.
----------------------- All Maps, Air Photos and Defence Schemes will be taken over and receipts given. Copies of those receipts will be forwarded to Orderly Room. Code Names in use by the 2/4th D.of Ws. will be taken over and a list forwarded to this office.
All schemes of work in hand and proposed will be taken over

WORK.
------ Any necessary work on firesteps etc. and cleaning up trenches will be carried out by Companies in their own Sectors tomorrow night.

RELIEF COMPLETE.
----------------- Relief Complete will be wired by the Code Word "TIME" and also sent by Runner.

                                                        N.T. THURSTON.
                                                          Capt & L/Adjt.
                                  1st Queens Westminster Rifles.

DISTRIBUTION.
1. Commanding Officer.   9. 169th Infantry Brigade.
2. 2nd in Command.   10. 2/4th D. of W. Regt.
3. Adjutant.   11. Transport Sergeant.
4. File.   12. R.S.M.
5 - 8. All O.C. Companies.   13. Sergt BRICKELL.
                14. Sergt CROSSINGHAM.
                15.   "   LETHERN.

169th Inf.Bde.
56th Div.

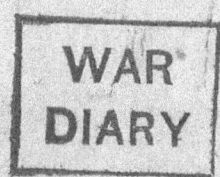

16th BATTN. THE LONDON REGIMENT.
(1st Queen's Westminster Rifles).

M A R C H

1 9 1 8

Attached:-

Narrative of Operations
28th March.

Army Form C. 2118.

WAR DIARY
or
INTELLIGENCE SUMMARY

(Erase heading not required.)

Instructions regarding War Diaries and Intelligence Summaries are contained in F. S. Regs., Part II. and the Staff Manual respectively. Title Pages will be prepared in manuscript.

Place	Date	Hour	Summary of Events and Information	Remarks and references to Appendices
In the Field.	1918 March 1st.	-	All Companies worked on various work in RED LINE, TOWY ALLEY and ROUNDHAY CAMP. Some men bathed. Casualties 1 Officer (2nd Lieut E.C.HAYES) to England for 6 months, 6 O.R. Sick. Reinforcements 6 O.R., Capt H.S.PRICE, M.C. brought on strength vide D.R.O.	
	2nd.		Some work done during day. All night working parties cancelled. Battn moved off from Camp at 8 p.m. and took up battle positions in PONT DU JOUR - THELUS LINE, returning to camp at 11 p.m. Casualties 5 O.R. Sick, 1 O.R. Other Causes, 4 O.R. Reinforcements.	
	3rd.		All usual working parties. RED LINE just North of sector occupied by Company of Support Battalion was heavily shelled with small calibre gas shells during night 3/4th. MILL POST was heavily bombarded during night 3/4th. Casualties 4 O.R. Sick, 2 O.R. Reinforcements.	
	4th.		Usual working parties day and night. Nothing unusual happened. Casualties 1 Officer struck off strength (2nd Lieut F.R.WILSON, 15th LONDON REGT) medically boarded whilst on short leave, and 5 O.R. Sick.	
	5th.		During the morning the Commanding Officer, 2 Officers from "A", "C" and "D" Companies and Signal officer reconnoitred Eastern end of ST CATHERINE SWITCH. Battalion relieved at ROUNDHAY CAMP by 1/2nd LONDON REGIMENT and proceeded by Light Railway to ST AUBIN, last train arriving at 8 p.m. Casualties 3 O.R. Sick, 1 O.R. Other Causes, 2 O.R. Reinforcements.	
	6th.		Companies (less Lewis Gunners and Snipers) and H.Q. Details worked on splinter-proofing huts and transport lines and in ST AUBIN. Casualties 3 O.R. Sick, 2 O.R. Reinforcements.	
	7th.		Companies (less Lewis Gunners and Snipers) and H.Q. Details continued work as on 6th inst. Lewis Gunners and Snipers, specialist training during morning. Casualties 1 O.R. Sick.	
	8th.		Work as on 6th and 7th inst. Lewis Gunners and Snipers fired on MAROEUIL RANGE during morning. Casualties 4 O.R. Sick, 22 O.R. Reinforcements.	

Commdg. 1/ Queens' Westminster Rifles
Lieut Colonel

Army Form C. 2118.

WAR DIARY
or
INTELLIGENCE SUMMARY
(Erase heading not required.)

Instructions regarding War Diaries and Intelligence Summaries are contained in F. S. Regs., Part II. and the Staff Manual respectively. Title Pages will be prepared in manuscript.

Place	Date	Hour	Summary of Events and Information	Remarks and references to Appendices
In the Field.	1918. March 9th.	—	Battalion co-operated with 185th Infantry Brigade in a practice counter-attack with contact patrols. Battalion paraded at 10-45 a.m. and moved to L.6.a. (Ref MAROEUIL MAP 1/20,000), where it remained in reserve until 2-30 p.m.; when it moved up to occupy trenches just South of ARRAS BETHUNE ROAD (A.14.c. and 20.a.). At 3.30 p.m. Battalion started moving back to ST AUBIN. Casualties 4 O.R. Sick.	
	10th.		No working parties found. Church parade service at 10-30 a.m. followed by Holy Communion in Church Army Hut. Casualties 4 O.R. Sick, 2 O.R. Other Causes, 1 O.R. Reinforcements.	
	11th.		Battalion relieved the 1st Battn LONDON RIFLE BRIGADE in the RED LINE, leaving ST AUBIN by Light Railway at 8 a.m. Much Gas on TOWY ALLEY near RED LINE, mixed with a few H.E. Shells - otherwise situation quiet. Casualties 7 O.R. Wounded, 1 O.R. Other Causes, 6 O.R. Reinforcements.	FRONT LINE
	12th.		Our artillery was active. Enemy again gassed RED LINE and DITCH POST area. Warning issued that attack expected on morning of 13th inst between ARRAS and CAMBRAI and possibly on this Sector. Patrols ordered to lie out all night in front of our wire. Casualties 13 O.R. Wounded, 5 O.R. Sick, 29 O.R. Other Causes (28 O.R. to M.G. BATTN).	
	13th.		All night (12/13th) our artillery was extraordinarily active firing chiefly on sector on our right. Enemy retaliation negligible. Battalion "stood to" in battle positions at 5 a.m. No attack attempted by the enemy. Our patrols heard and saw enemy wiring in front of CHINK C.T., but could not engage them owing to our artillery driving them in. During the day M.T.Ms. fired on enemy front line wire at CARP, CHAFF and CHINK. Enemy retaliated during evening with H.T.M. on GAVRELLE VILLAGE. At 9-10 p.m. listening post reported a noise as of a tractor or tank in C.26. Orders issued for same precautions to be taken as on preceding night. Patrols also as for night before. Casualties 3 O.R. Wounded, 1 O.R. Sick, 5 O.R. Reinforcements.	
	14th.		During night 13/14th our artillery very active on counter scheme. M.Gs were also fired into gaps in enemy wire. M.T.Ms fired on CHINK and CHAFF. A patrol which went out during night 14/15th failed to reach enemy wire owing to darkness and broken state of ground. BAILLEUL - WILLERVAL LINE and DITCH POST were shelled with gas at frequent intervals. Slight	

(signed) Mylam
Lieut Colonel
Commdg. 1/ Queens' Westminster Rifles

WAR DIARY
or
INTELLIGENCE SUMMARY

(Erase heading not required.)

Army Form C. 2118.

Place	Date	Hour	Summary of Events and Information	Remarks and references to Appendices
In the Field.	1918. March 14th. (Contd)	—	enemy T.M. activity on TOWY POST and GAVRELLE. Battalion "stood to" at 5 a.m. Casualties 6 O.R. Wounded, 1 O.R. Sick, 1 O.R. Other Causes, 1 O.R. Reinforcements.	
	15th.		Battalion again "stood to " at 5 a.m. Artillery active during night and by day fired on wire at CHAFF and CHINK, Artillery fired short during night on TOWY POST and unoccupied portion of WILLIE TRENCH and WILLIE SUPPORT. Patrol of L.R.B. Officer and 8 (Q.W.R) Other Ranks went out at 9 p.m. Enemy wire at CHAFF examined and reported cut. Line laid out from our wire to gap. Enemy T.M. fired on COLOUR TRENCH during evening. Casualties 4 O.R. Wounded, 6 O.R.. Sick, 1 Officer (Capt F.E.WHITBY,M.C.) from Hospital and 4 O.R. Reinforcements.	
	16th.		Artillery again active during night. Battalion "stood to" at 5 a.m. During day 4.5" Hows continued to cut enemy wire. M.T.Ms dropped a round in TOWY POST, killing 2 men. L.R.B. attempted a raid on enemy lines at junction of CHAFF C.T. and GAVRELLE TRENCH (Ref OPPY Sheet (3) C.2.5. Zero hour 10 p.m. Raiding party found gap in enemy's wire very small, only a few being able to get through it. 6 Germans were killed. Raiders had 13 O.R. wounded, all of which were brought in. Enemy's retaliation for raid very small. Artillery again fired short on TOWY POST just before Zero Hour for raid. A good barrage, however, was put down for the raid. Casualties 2 O.R. Killed, 6 O.R. Wounded, 4 O.R. Sick, 2 O.R. Reinforcements.	
	17th.		The day was quiet, no gas shelling taking place on the BAILLEUL WILLERVAL LINE. Enemy working party dispersed in C.27 by 4.5" Hows, early in morning. Casualties 7 O.R. Wounded, 4 O.R. Sick, 2 O.R. Reinforcements.	
	18th.		Battalion relieved in the line by 1/2nd LONDON REGIMENT, moving from the line to ROUNDHAY CAMP. Relief was exceptionally quiet. Casualties 19 O.R. Wounded, 2 O.R. Sick, 3 O.R. Other Causes, 1 O.R. Reinforcements.	
	19th.		Battalion rested in the morning. "A" Company bathed and working parties worked during the afternoon and at night on RED LINE and NAVAL LINE. Casualties/4 O.R. Wounded, 2 O.R. Sick, 2 O.R. Other Causes, 45 O.R. Reinforcements.	

J.H.Tann
Lieut Colonel
Commdg. 1/Queens' Westminster Rifles

Army Form C. 2118.

WAR DIARY
or
INTELLIGENCE SUMMARY

(Erase heading not required.)

Instructions regarding War Diaries and Intelligence Summaries are contained in F.S. Regs., Part II. and the Staff Manual respectively. Title Pages will be prepared in manuscript.

Place	Date	Hour	Summary of Events and Information	Remarks and references to Appendices
In the Field.	1918. March 20th.	—	Lewis Gun training carried on. Usual work. Situation fairly quiet. Warning order for relief by 62nd Division issued. Casualties 4 O.R. Wounded, 4 O.R. Sick, 1 Officer (Hon Lieut and Q.M. F.E. SMITH) to England in exchange, 1 O.R. Other Causes.	
	21st.		In the early morning severe artillery activity on our front and to the south. Enemy offensive started south of MONCHY. Usual Lewis Gun training. Warning order for Divisional relief cancelled. Casualties 12 O.R. Wounded, 2 O.R. Sick, 4 O.R. Reinforcements.	
	22nd.		Considerable artillery activity during night. During the day artillery was fairly active chiefly to the south. Lewis Gun training carried out. All working parties cancelled. During the day Canadian officers of 2nd CANADIAN DIVISION came to look round camp and the positions. Warning order for relief by this Division were issued. Platoon of "A" Company returned from Corps M. & R. Camp early in the morning. Casualties 32 O.R. Wounded, 3 O.R. Sick, 1 Officer (2nd Lieut J.E. GOLDING) Medically Boarded whilst on leave, 2 O.R. Reinforcements.	
	23rd.		Warning order for relief cancelled. Usual Lewis Gun training and work in the camp. Low flying enemy aeroplane fired on by anti-aircraft Lewis Gun Battery. Casualties 2 officers (2nd Lieut E.W.G.MALCOLM, and C.G.WARREN) and 1 O.R. Sick, 7 O.R. Reinforcements.	
	24th.		Battalion warned to be ready to relieve the 2nd LONDON REGIMENT in GAVRELLE SECTOR on 25/3/18. Preparations for same made. Valley just W. of railway cutting was lightly shelled during the afternoon. Also considerable artillery activity could be heard south of ARRAS. During the night 23/24th a prisoner was captured by the L.R.B. near MILL POST. Casualties 3 O.R. Sick, 5 O.R. Reinforcements.	
	25th.		Battalion relieved the 1/2nd LONDON REGIMENT in the Right sub-sector during day. Relief was quiet. Dispositions were as follows:— "A" Company — WATER POST and NAVAL LINE. "B" " — TOWY POST. "C" " — RED LINE (South of TOWY ALLEY) "D" " — CASTLEFORD, PELICAN, THAMES POSTS etc.	

(signed)
Lieut Colonel
Commdg. 1/ Queens Westminster Rifles

Army Form C. 2118.

WAR DIARY
or
INTELLIGENCE SUMMARY
(Erase heading not required.)

Instructions regarding War Diaries and Intelligence Summaries are contained in F. S. Regs., Part II. and the Staff Manual respectively. Title Pages will be prepared in manuscript.

Place	Date	Hour	Summary of Events and Information	Remarks and references to Appendices
In the Field	1918. March 25th (Contd).		When relieving garrison for GAVRELLE POST went out from TOWY POST after dusk it found the old garrison (2nd LONDON REGIMENT) all missing or killed. 2 Bodies were found at the bottom of steps of dug-out and there were signs of a struggle in the dug-out. Many stick bombs were found in the trench near the Post. Patrols were at once pushed through the village from West and South West in the hope of finding enemy in the village. None, however, were found. Strong patrol lay out in front of village. From information received from prisoner captured by the L.R.B. it appeared very likely that enemy would attack on morning of 26th with right flank of attack on OPPY. WITH OBJECT OF PUSHING FORWARD ABOUT 4 miles AND THEN SWINGING RIGHT BEHIND VIMY RIDGE. It was decided that KEILLAR POST was tactically a better place for Battalion H.Q. than junction of NAVAL TRENCH and TOWY ALLEY. Headquarters were therefore moved to KEILLAR POST during the night 25/26th only a few signallers being left at the old Battn H.Q. Casualties 11 O.R. Wounded, 1 O.R. Reinforcement.	
	26th.		During the night and early morning our heavy and field artillery bombarded enemy's positions East of GAVRELLE very heavily. Early in the morning of 26th a party of 40 to 50 enemy were seen to approach our wire. They were fired on by Rifles and Lewis Guns and dispersed, 2 wounded men being seen carried away. Later a further party of 3 were dispersed. A Battalion was seen moving N.E. behind FRESNES at 8-45 p.m. No attack developed in morning and day passed quietly. Orders were received during the afternoon for three raids to be carried out simultaneously that night, 1 by L.R.B. up CUP TRENCH, 1 by 2nd LONDONS on CHAFF C.T. and by this Battalion on CHINK C.T. Zero Hour to be 10.30 p.m. 4.5" and 6" Hows fired on wire in front of these trenches until late in the evening. 6" Mortars were found to be firing too inaccurately to be used for cutting wire. 2nd Lieut V.G. RAYMER (9th London Regiment) and a Platoon of "A" Company were detailed as the Raiding Party. Programme of Raid was arranged, as follows:- 8-30 p.m. Food provided for Raiding Party in NAVAL TRENCH. 9-30 p.m. Raiding Party to leave NAVAL. 10-0 p.m. Raiding Party to assemble at head of TOWY C.T. in WILLIE TRENCH. 10-20 p.m. Raiding party to form up near our wire. 10-24 p.m. L.T.Ms to fire on enemy wire and trenches in vicinity of raid area for 6 minutes. 10-30 p.m. Raiding Party to advance towards CHINK. No time was laid down for duration of raid.	

Commdg. 1/ Queens Westminster Rifles
Lieut Colonel

WAR DIARY
or
INTELLIGENCE SUMMARY
(Erase heading not required.)

Instructions regarding War Diaries and Intelligence Summaries are contained in F.S. Regs., Part II. and the Staff Manual respectively. Title Pages will be prepared in manuscript.

Place	Date	Hour	Summary of Events and Information	Remarks and references to Appendices
In the Field.	1918. March 26th.	—	The programme up to 10-20 p.m. was carried out but owing to 2nd LONDONS raiding party being late in arriving Zero Hour was postponed to 10-55 p.m. At Zero the party advanced towards CHINK (route previously reconnoitred by 2nd Lieut V.G. RAYNER). Party was in two waves. 1st wave stopped 50 yards from enemy wire, as many enemy were seen in their trenches and on the parapets of their trenches. Raiding party were seen and several Granatenwerfer were fired on them. Commands were heard after which enemy apparently loaded their rifles and opened fire. 3 Men ran out from main trench into small sap where they fired Very Lights. Another man running out to enemy's inner belt of wire and firing lights from there. Enemy were seen to be between the inner and outer belt of wire by the Sergeant, who got through outer belt. No distinct gap was found in wire. Party lay up in NO MANS LAND for 1½ hours, after which they returned. The total casualties amounted to 1 Killed and 1 Wounded. Neither of other two raids were successful, many Germans being found in the trenches in both cases. Casualties 1 O.R. Killed, 2 O.R. Wounded, 4 O.R. Sick, 4 O.R. Reinforcements.	
	27th.		Enemy's lines were again heavily bombarded during early morning, for which no retaliation followed. During the day C.O. and Company Commanders of Battn of 167th Inf, Bde reconnoitred sector previous to taking over following day. Movement in front of sector was considerably above normal during the morning. Many small carrying parties being seen in front of FRESNES. Also many low flying planes crossed our lines during the day. During morning Commanding Officer had instructions to have all ammunition cleared from forward posts and NAVAL LINE preparatory to a withdrawal from there totake place that night. This order was cancelled in early afternoon and orders were issued for Company in RED LINE to take over NAVAL LINE as far as BELVOIR ALLEY, owing to the extensions northwards of the Brigade front. This change was effected during the early part of the night, the 2nd LONDON REGIMENT taking over the RED LINE from "C" Company. New dispositions examined by C.O. late that night Casualties 3 O.R. Sick.	
	28th.		Ref. Sheet MAROEUIL 1/20,000 In the night, 27/28th the Battalion extended its front, northwards to just South of BELVOIR ALLEY, "C" Company moving up from the BAILLEUL - WILLERVAL LINE. The Battalion was then distributed as follows:-	

Sgd.
Lieut Colonel
Commdg. 1/ Queens' Westminster Rifles

WAR DIARY
or
INTELLIGENCE SUMMARY

(Erase heading not required.)

Instructions regarding War Diaries and Intelligence Summaries are contained in F.S. Regs., Part II. and the Staff Manual respectively. Title Pages will be prepared in manuscript.

Place	Date	Hour	Summary of Events and Information	Remarks and references to Appendices
In the Field.	1918. March. 28th (contd).	-	~~Briefed~~ as follows:— "B" COMPANY. (Capt G.A.N.LOWNDES) in TOWY POST and GAVRELLE POST (2nd Lieut L.W. FRIEND). "A" COMPANY. (2nd Lieut H.T. HARPER) in WATER POST (2nd Lieut W.A. STILLWELL) and NAVAL TRENCH (South)(2nd Lieut V.G. RAYMOR). "C" COMPANY. (Capt R.L.WHITTLE) in NAVAL TRENCH (North) (2nd Lieut F.A.CHALBERLIN), PELICAN and THAMES POSTS (2nd Lieut O.A.M.EATON). "D" COMPANY. (2nd Lieut F.W.RUSSELL) in NAVAL TRENCH (Central)(2nd Lieut C.H.RAVEN) and KEILLAR POST (2nd Lieut F. FISHER) and CASTLEFORD POST. At 3 a.m. the enemy barrage fell on NAVAL LINE and Posts in rear. At 5-45 a.m. it also came down on the front line. The barrage was continuous until 7-15 a.m., when the enemy attack developed. As an impending attack was obvious, the garrison of GAVRELLE POST had, by this time, withdrawn to TOWY POST. The enemy at once obtained a footing in WILLIE TRENCH, the garrison having become very depleted by the bombardment. The strong point round Company H.Q. was then manned and a very stiff fight continued. By this time the enemy had penetrated GAVRELLE and the undefended portions on both flanks of TOWY POST and had obtained a footing in TOWY ALLEY in rear. The garrison still held out and the enemy seeing this worked up TOWY ALLEY towards TOWY POST. During this time heavy fire from Vickers and Lewis Guns and rifles was brought to bear on the enemy. He was in large numbers in WILLIE SUPPORT, bombing towards the Post. The POST still held out. The garrison had by this time been driven into a very small area and had used practically the whole of the Company reserve of bombs. Sufficient, however, had been put aside to enable them to bomb down TOWY ALLEY. Capt G.A.N. LOWNDES, 2nd Lieuts L.W. FRIEND and J.C.B.PRINCE and 25 Other Ranks succeeded in reaching the NAVAL LINE, which they reinforced. By this time the garrison of WATER POST had also fallen back, owing to the fact that the enemy had come through GAVRELLE in great numbers and completely outflanked them. The enemy advanced in great numbers through GAVRELLE and also entered the NAVAL LINE North of BELVOIR ALLEY. Accordingly our flank was swung back to run along THAMES ALLEY (including THAMES POST) and thence along NAVAL LINE. Although the enemy advanced continuously in lines of men shoulder to shoulder, the NAVAL LINE put up a spirited resistance, inflicting numerous casualties on the enemy, and remained intact until enemy penetrated our right flank ("A" Post). A Battalion of the LANCASHIRE FUSILIERS on our right were driven out of HUMID TRENCH and the vicinity and fell back over the open to TOWY ALLEY and the BAILLEUL WILLERVAL LINE. Instructions were then issued for the	

[signature]
Lieut Colonel
Commdg. 1/ Queens Westminster Rifles

WAR DIARY or INTELLIGENCE SUMMARY

(Erase heading not required.)

Place	Date	Hour	Summary of Events and Information	Remarks and references to Appendices
In the Field.	1918. March 28th. (Contd)	—	garrison of NAVAL LINE, South of TOWY ALLEY to swing back and form a defensive flank in TOWY ALLEY. While this was being carried out, the block in front of junction of TOWY and NAVAL was blown down by our own artillery. The enemy who, up to now, had been kept well in check, swarmed into NAVAL TRENCH, surrounded and either killed or captured the remainder of the garrison between the GAVRELLE ROAD and the South. At about the same time our block on the extreme left of the trench, which had put up a very fine fight was forced back and the enemy linked up all along the NAVAL LINE. The enemy was held by bombing blocks in THAMES and TOWY ALLEYS near their junctions with the NAVAL LINE. The enemy then advanced over the open ground North of THAMES, between THAMES and TOWY, and South of TOWY ALLEY. The resistance now centred on THAMES, PELICAN and KEILLAR POSTS. All the surviving men from the trench in front and Battalion Headquarters manned the berms sump pits, and firesteps of both O.Ts. By degrees the enemy encircled THAMES and KEILLAR POSTS, our men contesting every yard of ground and falling slowly back to the BAILLEUL-WILLERVAL LINE and at 11 o'clock, the position was as follows:— Our men had reinforced the 2nd LONDONS in the BAILLEUL WILLERVAL LINE and bombing blocks were established and held in THAMES and TOWY ALLEYS - 300 yards East of BAILLEUL WILLERVAL LINE. Castleford POST was still intact. From 11 a.m. the situation was comparatively quiet, except for desultory shelling and movement by small parties of the enemy, who, however, did not attempt any organized attack. About 6-30 p.m. orders were received that the Commanding Officers of the Brigade would divide the Brigade frontage so that it could be held according to the strength of the Battalions. This Battalion took over from the Light Railway (the approximate Brigade Southern Boundary) in touch with the ESSEX REGIMENT of the 4th Division, to the GAVRELLE ROAD, in touch with the 2nd LONDON REGIMENT, also holding CASTLEFORD POST and the block East of it. This latter was evacuated under orders during the night and about 100 yards of THAMES C.T. was filled in from about 50 yards in front of our wire eastwards. Similar action was taken in TOWY ALLEY. The Battalion was relieved early in the morning of the 29th by the 8th Battn MIDDLESEX REGIMENT, relief being complete by 5 a.m. The Battalion was withdrawn to ROUNDHAY CAMP. The artillery barrage was weak and the short shooting, with which the Battalion had been worried during the preceding days and during the last tour in trenches was maintained. After a barrage had been asked for East of the NAVAL LINE, and during a critical part of the action, although the R.A. was warned of the block in TOWY ALLEY, and asked to keep at least 300 yards up the trench, messages were received that our guns were knocking out more of our own men than the enemy's.	

Commdg. 1/ Queens' Westminster Rifles
Lieut Colonel

WAR DIARY
or
INTELLIGENCE SUMMARY

(Erase heading not required.)

Instructions regarding War Diaries and Intelligence Summaries are contained in F.S. Regs, Part II. and the Staff Manual respectively. Title Pages will be prepared in manuscript.

Place	Date	Hour	Summary of Events and Information	Remarks and references to Appendices
In the Field.	1918. March. 28th. (Contd).	(a)	The Machine Guns were of the greatest assistance and liason was maintained throughout. The outstanding features of the fight were:— The spirited defence put up by "B" Company in TOWY POST and their subsequent withdrawal after they had undoubtedly checked the first rush of the enemy and broken up that portion of his attack.	
		(b)	The defence of the NAVAL LINE against heavy enemy attacks and under a terrible bombardment, until both flanks were turned and it was impossible to maintain such a large frontage. The success of the communication from TOWY POST is attributed to the action of Lance Corporal SAMUELS and the Signallers with him, who remained at their instruments after the Post had been captured. These men are unfortunately "Missing". Casualties 18 O.R. Killed, 3 Officers (Capt: G.A.N.LOWNDES and 2nd Lieut H.T.HARPER and 2nd Lieut F.A.CHAMBERLIN, 21st LONDON REGIMENT) and 56 O.R. Wounded, 1 Officer, (2nd Lieut F.W.RUSSELL) Wounded at Duty, 8 O.R. Wounded and Missing, 2 Officers (2nd Lieut I.d'A.S.STITT and 2nd Lieut G.H.RAVEN, 9th London Regt and 143 Other Ranks Missing, also Lieut R.B.RHETT (M.O.R.C) U.S.A. - Missing, and 1 O.R. Reinforcement.	
	29th.		Battalion arrived at ROUNDHAY CAMP at 6-50 a.m., rested until 1-30 p.m. Battalion then reorganised into two Companies. Officers at Transport Lines took place of Company Officers who had been through the fight, the last mentioned going to the Transport Lines. Casualties 1 O.R. Wounded, 1 O.R. Sick, 12 O.R. Reinforcements.	
	30th.		Battalion moved off by Platoons from ROUNDHAY CAMP at 9 a.m. for ST AUBIN. Previous to the move and during it several light shrapnel shells burst over the camp. Later H.E. replaced the shrapnel. Battalion arrived at ST AUBIN at 10-45 a.m., when orders were received to proceed to OTTAWA CAMP, near MONT ST ELOI. At 11 a.m. a Draft of 321 Other Ranks joined the Battalion. At 12-30 p.m. the Battalion left ST AUBIN for MONT ST ELOI. The draft marched in rear of the Battalion. On arrival at MONT ST ELOI, the Canadian Battalion in possession of the camp turned out their band and played to the men of this Battalion until the Canadians were clear of the camp.	

Commdg. 1/ Queens Westminster Rifles
Lieut. Colonel

WAR DIARY
or
INTELLIGENCE SUMMARY

(Erase heading not required.)

Place	Date	Hour	Summary of Events and Information	Remarks and references to Appendices
In the Field.	1918. March 30th (Cont'd)		Draft was divided amongst Companies and general re-organisation started. Casualties 2 O.R. Wounded, 2 O.R. Sick, 326 O.R. Reinforcements.	

	31st.		Easter Service for men of all Christian denominations held in Y.M.C.A. Hut by Revrd. TEMPLE at 10-30 a.m. Re-organisation of Battalion continued. Casualties – NIL.
			
			S U M M A R Y
			– of –
			STRENGTH of BATTALION.
			
			                        Officers. Other Ranks.
			Strength on 28-2-18 42 972.
			         ADD. 2 473.
			                     44 1,445.
			         LESS. 11 495.
			                     33 950.	

Lieut-Colonel.
Commanding 1st Battn QUEENS WESTMINSTER RIFLES.

HQ 169 IB.   1402 1/4/18

Herewith report on the action of this Batt'n on the 28th March 1918 – I regret that I am unable to give more exact times & that the account is somewhat disjointed but I hope that with this & the information supplied by me during the action – you will have all the details you require.

P H Glasier Lt Col.
Com'dg 1st QW Rifles

1st April 1918.

N A R R A T I V E
- of -
OPERATIONS on the 28th March 1918.

MAROEUIL Sh 1/20,000

On the night of the 27/28th, the Battalion extended its front northwards to just South of BELVOIR ALLEY, "C" Company moving up from the BAILLEUL-WILLERVAL LINE. The Battalion was then distributed as follows:-

"B" Company (Capt G.A.N.LOWNDES) in TOWY and GAVRELLE POSTS (2nd Lieut L.W. FRIEND)
"A" Company (2nd Lieut H.T. HARPER) in WATER POST (2nd Lieut W.A.STILLWELL) and NAVAL TRENCH (South) (2nd Lieut V.G.RAYNOR)
"C" Company (Capt R.L.WHITTLE) in NAVAL TRENCH (North) (2nd Lieut F.A.CHAMBERLIN) PELICAN and THAMES POSTS (2nd Lieut O.A.M.EATON).
"D" Company (2nd Lieut F.W.RUSSELL) in NAVAL TRENCH (Central)(2nd Lieut C.H.RAVEN) and KEILLAR (2nd Lieut F. FISHER) and CASTLEFORD POST.

At 3 a.m. the enemy barrage fell on NAVAL LINE AND POSTS in rear. At 5-45 a.m. it also came down on the front line. The barrage was continuous until 7-15 a.m., when the enemy attack developed. As an impending attack was obvious, the garrison of GAVRELLE POST had by this time withdrawn to TOWY POST. The enemy at once obtained a footing in WILLIE TRENCH, the garrison having become very much depleted by the bombardment. The strong point round Company H.Q. was then manned and a very stiff fight continued.

By this time the enemy had penetrated GAVRELLE and the undefended portions on both flanks of TOWY POST and had obtained a footing in TOWY ALLEY in rear. The garrison still held out and the enemy seeing this worked up TOWY ALLEY towards TOWY POST.

During this time heavy fire from Vickers and Lewis Guns and Rifles was brought to bear on the enemy.

He was in large numbers in WILLIE SUPPORT, bombing towards the Post. The Post STILL HELD OUT. The small garrison by this time had been driven into a very small area and had used up practically the whole of the Company reserve of bombs. Sufficient, however, had been put aside to enable them to bomb their way down TOWY ALLEY.

Capt. G.A.N. LOWNDES, 2nd Lieuts L.W. FRIEND and J.C.B. PRINCE, with 25 ORs succeeded in reaching the NAVAL LINE, which they reinforced.

By this time the garrison of WATER POST had also fallen back, owing to the fact that the enemy had come through GAVRELLE in large numbers and completely outflanked them.

The enemy advanced in great numbers through GAVRELLE and also entered the NAVAL LINE North of BELVOIR ALLEY. Accordingly our flank was swung back to run along THAMES ALLEY (including THAMES POST) and thence along the NAVAL LINE.

Although the enemy advanced continuously in lines of men shoulder to shoulder, the NAVAL LINE put up a spirited resistance, inflicting numerous casualties on the enemy and remained in tact until the enemy penetrated our right flank ("A" Post).

A Battalion of the LANCASHIRE FUSILIERS on our Right were driven out of "HUMID" Trench and the vicinity and fell back over the open to TOWY ALLEY and the BAILLEUL - WILLERVAL LINE. Instructions were then issued for the garrison of NAVAL LINE, South of TOWY ALLEY to swing back and form a defensive flank in TOWY ALLEY. While this was being carried out the block in front of the junction of TOWY and NAVAL was blown down by our own artillery. The enemy who, up to now, had been kept well in check, swarmed into the NAVAL LINE, surrounded and either captured or killed the remainder of the garrison between GAVRELLE ROAD and the South.

At about the same time our block on the extreme left of the trench and which had put up a very fine resistance, was forced back and the enemy linked up all the way along the NAVAL LINE. The enemy was held by bombing blocks in THAMES and TOWY ALLEYS near their junctions with the NAVAL LINE.

The enemy then advanced over the open ground North of THAMES, between THAMES and TOWY, and South of TOWY ALLEY. The resistance now centred on THAMES, PELICAN and KEILLAR POSTS. All the surviving men from the trench in front and Battalion Headquarters manned the berms, sump pits and firesteps of both C.Ts. By degrees the enemy encircled THAMES and KEILLAR POSTS, our men contesting every yard of ground and falling slowly back to the BAILLEUL WILLERVAL LINE and at 11 o'clock the position was as follows:- Our men had reinforced the 2nd LONDONS in the BAILLEUL WILLERVAL LINE and bombing blocks were established and held in THAMES and TOWY ALLEYS - 300 yards East of the BAILLEUL WILLERVAL LINE. Castleford Post was still in-tact.

From 11 a.m. onwards the situation was comparatively quiet except for desultory shelling and movement by small parties of the enemy, who, however, did not attempt any organized attack.

About 6-30 p.m. orders were received that the Commanding Officers of the Brigade would divide the Brigade frontage so that it could be held according to the strength of the Battalions. This Battalion took over from the light railway, the approximate Brigade Southern Boundary, in touch with the ESSEX REGIMENT of the 4th Division to the GAVRELLE ROAD in touch with the 2nd LONDON REGIMENT, also holding CASTLEFORD POST and the block East of it. This latter was evacuated under orders during the night and about 100 yards of THAMES C.T. was filled in from about 30 yards beyond our wire eastwards

- 4 -

Similar action was taken in TOWY ALLEY.

The Battalion was relieved early in the morning by the 8th Battn MIDDLESEX REGIMENT, relief being complete by 5 a.m. The Battalion was withdrawn to ROUNDHAY CAMP.

The Artillery Barrage was weak and the short shooting with which the Battalion had been worried during the preceding days and during the last tour in trenches was maintained. After a barrage had been asked for East of the NAVAL LINE and during a critical part of the action, although the R.A. was warned of the block in TOWY ALLEY and asked to keep at least 300 yards up the trench - messages were received that our own guns were knocking out more of our own men than the enemy's.

The Machine Guns were of the greatest assistance and liason was maintained throughout.

The outstanding features of the fight were (a) The spirited defence put up by "B" Company in TOWY POST and their subsequent withdrawal after they had undoubtedly checked the first rush of the enemy and broken up that portion of his attack (b) The defence of the NAVAL LINE against heavy enemy attacks and under a terrible bombardment until both flanks were turned and it was impossible to maintain such a large frontage.

I attribute the success of the communication from TOWY POST to the action of Lance Corporal SAMUELS and the Signallers with him who remained at their instruments after the POST had been captured, and, I regret to say, these men are missing.

I was ably supported by my Adjutant and Company Commanders, who, throughout the action, shewed great initiative.

Lieut Colonel
Commdg, 1/ Queens Westminster Rifles

169th Brigade
56th Division.

(Queen's Westminsters)

1/16th BATTALION

THE LONDON REGIMENT

APRIL 1918.

Army Form C. 2118.

WAR DIARY
or
INTELLIGENCE SUMMARY
(Erase heading not required.)

Instructions regarding War Diaries and Intelligence Summaries are contained in F.S. Regs., Part II. and the Staff Manual respectively. Title Pages will be prepared in manuscript.

Place	Date	Hour	Summary of Events and Information	Remarks and references to Appendices
In the Field.	1918. April 1st.	—	Battalion was inspected by the Commanding Officer at 12 noon. The Draft was inspected by the Medical Officer during the day. Two performances were given by the "BOW BELLS" in the Theatre in the Camp. Each performance was free. Casualties 2 O.R. Sick, 2 O.R. Other Causes, 14 O.R. Reinforcements.	
	2nd.		Specialist training was carried out during the morning. Reorganization of Companies carried on. Casualties 2 O.R. Sick, Reinforcements 2 officers (2nd Lieuts E.W.G.MALCOLM and C.G.WARREN from Hospital) and 3 O.R.	
	3rd.		All available men paraded at 9 a.m. and proceeded to ARRAS - ST POL ROAD to dig HAUTES - AVESNES SWITCH. Battalion returned at 3-30 p.m. Casualties 1 O.R. Wounded, 2 Officers Sick (2nd Lieut C.A.F.KNAPP, 2nd Lieut J.C.B.PRINCE) and 1 O.R. Reinforcement 1 O.R.	
	4th.		400 men (95 per Company and 20 H.Q.) again paraded at 9 a.m. for work on HAUTES - AVESNES SWITCH. All Lewis Gunners trained during morning under L.G.O. "C" Company Lewis Gunners fired on range during the afternoon. Casualties 5 O.R. Sick, 1 O.R. Other Causes, 1 O.R. Reinforcement.	
	5th.		400 men again provided for work on HAUTES - AVESNES SWITCH. Lewis Gunners trained in the morning. Casualties 4 O.R. Sick, Reinforcements 1 Officer (Hon Lieut & Q.M. JACKSON E.W.N) & 9 O.R.	
	6th.		Company and specialist training carried out near camp during morning. Flagged attack executed by "D" Company. Bugle Band proceeded by lorry to Corps H.Q. in early afternoon to take part in Band Competition in which it took 2nd Prize (£20) - 1st Prize (£40) won by 1/7th Battn Middlesex Regt. Casualties NIL.	
	7th.		Parade Service in Y.M.C.A. Hut for C. of E's at 11-30 a.m. Service conducted by Assistant Chaplain General. Casualties 1 O.R. Wounded, 1 O.R. Sick, 1 officer (2nd Lieut C.E.MOY, MC) to 169th T.M.B.	
	8th.		Battalion left MONT ST ELOI by march route at 2-30 p.m. and proceeded to DAINVILLE where Companies were billetted in houses and bivouacs, Battalion H.Q. being in Chateau near Church. Battalion relieved was 15th Canadian Battalion,	

Commdg. 1/ Queens' Westminster Rifles
Lieut Colonel

Army Form C. 2118.

WAR DIARY
or
INTELLIGENCE SUMMARY

(Erase heading not required.)

Instructions regarding War Diaries and Intelligence Summaries are contained in F.S. Regs., Part II. and the Staff Manual respectively. Title Pages will be prepared in manuscript.

Place	Date	Hour	Summary of Events and Information	Remarks and references to Appendices
In the Field.	April 8th (Contd)		Casualties 2 O.R. Sick.	
	9th.		Enemy shelled DAINVILLE with H.V.Gun at intervals during day also with 5.9's. Weather was misty but dry. Battalion "stood to" ready to move at 5 minutes notice at 5-30 a.m. Stand down at 7 a.m. No working parties found or training carried out. BLANGY RESERVE LINE reconnoitred by C.O. and Company Commanders in morning. Casualties 3 O.R. Wounded, 20 O.R. Sick, 11 O.R. Reinforcements.	
	10th.		At 2-30 a.m. "D" Company Officers' Mess had a direct hit by H.V. shell, 3 Officers, 1 Sergeant and 2 men wounded. Shelling was continuous throughout the night, being particularly heavy between 4-30 a.m. and 5-30 a.m. Shelling continued until 11-20 a.m., after which time day was quiet. No working parties or training. Route of possible counter attack from BLANGY RESERVE LINE reconnoitred by C.O. and Company representatives. Casualties 3 Officers (2nd Lieuts F.W.RUSSELL, F. FISHER, and E.W.G.MALCOLM) and 3 O.R. Wounded, 9 O.R. Reinforcements Sick, 2 O.R. Reinforcements.	
	11th.		Day was comparatively quiet. All companies carried out Lewis Gun training under Company arrangements during morning. "C" Company moved to edge of wood on DAINVILLE - WARLUS ROAD, where they went under canvas. Notice of the award of 12 Military Medals to N.C.Os and Men of the Battn received. RONVILLE CAVES reconnoitred by 2 Officers, Casualties 1 O.R. Wounded, 5 O.R. Sick.	
	12th.		Day was quiet. Battalion provided 450 men for work on DAINVILLE SWITCH. Otherwise nothing of importance to report. Casualties 8 O.R. Sick, Reinforcements 12 O.Rs.	
	13th.		Same working party provided. Day was very quiet. RONVILLE CAVES reconnoitred and arrangements made for relief. Work for night 14/15th inst reconnoitred. Casualties 1 O.R. Sick, 3 Offrs (Capt H.S.PRICE, MC, 2nd Lieut T.J.HUDSON, & E.C.HAYES) Other Causes, 3 O.R. Reinforcements.	
	14th.		Day again quiet. In the evening Battalion relieved 1st Battn LONDON REGTMENT in RONVILLE CAVES. Guides met Companies at entrance to ARRAS and lead them to LEWIS BARRACKS, where they entered sewer and proceeded underground to CAVES. At 9 p.m. Battalion proceeded for work on FICHEUX SWITCH returning by 2 a.m. (under 512th R.E. Company). Casualties 1 O.R. Killed, 5 O.R. Sick, 3 O.R. Other Causes, 2 O.R. Reinforcements.	

[signed] Lieut Colonel
Commdg. 1/ Queens' Westminster Rifles

Army Form C. 2118.

WAR DIARY
or
INTELLIGENCE SUMMARY

(Erase heading not required.)

Instructions regarding War Diaries and Intelligence Summaries are contained in F. S. Regs., Part II. and the Staff Manual respectively. Title Pages will be prepared in manuscript.

Place	Date	Hour	Summary of Events and Information	Remarks and references to Appendices
In the Field.	April 15th.	—	Battalion rested all day and proceeded out on same working party as previous night at 8 p.m. 40 men also being provided for work under CHESHIRE REGT at same time. Battalion "stood to" at 5 a.m. Day was quiet. Battle positions in old front line reconnoitred. Casualties 3 O.R. Reinforcements.	
	16th.		Battalion rested during the day. Party of Battalion (Less H.Q. Details and 40 O.R.) worked on trench in front of BLANGY TRENCH from 8 p.m. till 2 a.m. 49 O.R. "A" Company worked under CHESHIRE REGT. Day was quiet. Casualties 1 O.R. Sick, 1 O.R. Other Causes.	
	17th.		Battalion again rested by day and worked by night for R.Es. C.O. and 4 Company Commanders and Intelligence Officer reconnoitred right sub-sector of front line during afternoon. Casualties 2 O.R. Sick, 3 O.R. Reinforcements.	
	18th.		Part of Battalion bathed in ARRAS. 200 men provided for work during day but did not work during night. 2nd in Command visited LONDON SCOTTISH in the line previous to relief. Casualties 1 O.R. Wounded, 4 O.R. Sick, 19 O.R. Reinforcements.	
	19th.		Battalion rested during day. Raid carried out in early morning by LONDON SCOTTISH. Battn was ready to move off by Companies from RONVILLE CAVES at 8 p.m. to relieve the LONDON SCOTTISH but was ordered to "stand by" owing to S.O.S. going up on our front. This was result of counter-attack on LONDON SCOTTISH. Battalion eventually moved off at 10-30 p.m. and relief was complete by 2-30 a.m. 20/4/18. Dispositions "D" Company - Right Front Company. "C" " - Left Front Company. "A" " - Left Support Company. "B" " - Right Support Company. Casualties 7 O.R. Sick, 1 O.R. Other Causes, 1 Officer (2nd Lieut H.T.HARPER) and 1 O.R. Reinforcements.	
	20th.		Day was very quiet. Only wire and visiting patrols went out at night. Nothing of importance happened on the front. Casualties 1 Officer (2nd Lieut F.A.HITCHINGS) and 1 O.R. Wounded, 3 O.R. Sick.	

Lieut Colonel
Commdg. 1/ Queens Westminster Rifles

Army Form C. 2118.

WAR DIARY
or
INTELLIGENCE SUMMARY

(Erase heading not required.)

Instructions regarding War Diaries and Intelligence Summaries are contained in F. S. Regs., Part II. and the Staff Manual respectively. Title Pages will be prepared in manuscript.

Place	Date	Hour	Summary of Events and Information	Remarks and references to Appendices
In the Field.	April 21st	—	Our artillery was very active indeed but enemy was generally quiet. Enemy planes were extraordinarily active, flying in large formation and twice very low over our lines. Patrol went out from Right outpost to locate enemy Machine Gun suspected at N.8.c.7.1. (51.b.S.W.), but did not succeed. Another patrol left our left outpost and proceeded along trench running N.E. through N.8.a., but was challenged after advancing about 160 yards, when they returned to our post and fired Lewis Gun towards point where challenged. Casualties 2 O.R. Wounded 8 O.R. Sick, 2 O.R. Other Causes, 4 O.R. Reinforcements.	
	22nd.		At 4 a.m. enemy heavily bombarded our lines for 1 hour. After 12 noon enemy artillery became quieter. Our artillery was active all day. During night 22/23rd dispositions were changed to the following:- Right Front Company "C" Company. Centre " " "B" " Left " " "D" " Support " "A" " Night Wire patrol went out on left company front and a patrol which was advancing towards N.8.a.35.80. was forced to return owing to a barrage being put down by our artillery. Casualties 2 O.R. Killed, 5 O.R. Wounded, 5 O.R. Sick.	
	23rd.		Our artillery was again very active all day, but enemy was unusually quiet. An enemy aeroplane was brought down by our A.A. Lewis Gun at 4-20 p.m. Night. Patrols went out to Sunken Road at N.8.c.8.1. Strong enemy patrol was seen but no encounter took place. Casualties 3 O.R. Sick.	
	24th.		Our artillery was again active all day and put down a heavy barrage on enemy's lines in support of raid by 2nd LONDONS. Enemy's artillery quiet until 9.20 p.m. when he put down a light barrage on parts of our line, obtaining direct hit on one entrance of H.Q. dug-out. Night. A large patrol of 1 Officer and 30 O.R. went out from N.8.c.1.3. (Right outpost) to reconnoitre listening post at N.8.c.65.10. but found enemy had pushed forward his outpost some 100 yards and had two new M.G. positions. Casualties 10.O.R. Wounded, 2 O.R. Reinforcements.	
	25th.		Enemy's artillery exceptionally quiet but ours again very active. Day was misty and	

Signed J. Maynes
Lieut Colonel
Commdg. 1/ Queens Westminster Rifles

Army Form C. 2118.

WAR DIARY
or
INTELLIGENCE SUMMARY

(Erase heading not required.)

Instructions regarding War Diaries and Intelligence Summaries are contained in F. S. Regs, Part II. and the Staff Manual respectively. Title Pages will be prepared in manuscript.

Place	Date	Hour	Summary of Events and Information	Remarks and references to Appendices
In the Field.	April 25th	(Contd).	aeroplane activity was practically NIL. Night. Patrol of 1 officer and 10 O.R. went out to verify information obtained by patrol of previous night, but no enemy movement could be seen or heard and owing to light and state of the ground, movement was slow and required information was not obtained. Casualties 1 O.R. wounded, 5 O.R. Sick, Reinforcements 12 officers (Lieuts J.J.WESTMORELAND & R.R.GALKIN, 2nd Lieuts G.W.AVENS, A.J.PHILIP, A.E.CLAPHAM, W.F.D.YOUNG, O.W.ANDERSON, A.H.CHAPLIN, O.R.JACOMB, C. SHEPPARD, H.T.GALBRAITH, F.R.A.DANSEY).	
	26th.		Day was very quiet, our artillery being less active. Night. A patrol of 1 officer (2nd Lieut V.G.RAYNOR) and 15 O.R. left our lines at 12 midnight at N,8.c.05.30. (Right outpost) and proceeded in diamond formation along North side of trench running E.S.E. towards N.8.c.70.05. till within 100 yards of Sunken Road, when they extended and advanced 25 yards. A man then jumped up in front of them and ran to road. Patrol then advanced 15 yards and then heard sounds and saw 30 enemy with a Machine Gun advancing in line towards our lines on South side of trench. Our men fired on them at 20 yards range and observed some hits and then withdrew 100 yards, crossed the trench and waited for enemy. The next thing seen or heard of enemy was M.G. fire directed from the North side of trench. Our patrol then withdrew to our lines and the enemy bombed along O.T. towards our lines. Our casualties were 1 man missing. A small patrol also left our lines at midnight at N.8.a.0.5. and went along North side of trench running to N.8.a.35.80. until halfway across track when voices were heard. They withdrew to ourside of track and two lights were fired towards them from N.8.a.35.80. after a short wait patrol returned to our lines. Casualties 2 O.R. Wounded, 1 O.R. Missing, 1 officer (Capt H.S. PRICE, MC) and 2 O.R. Reinforcements.	
	27th.		Day was again very quiet, our artillery only firing bursts during evening "stand to". A sniper claimed a hit at 6 a.m. Patrols went out at night but no important information was gained and no enemy encountered. Casualties 1 officer (2nd Lieut O.A.M.EATON) Sick.	
	28th.		Day was very quiet. Company Commanders from KENSINGTONS reconnoitred line in morning and advance party arrived about 5-30 p.m. Battalion relieved by KENSINGTONS during the evening first Company of KENSINGTONS passing over BEAURAINS – TILLOY Road at 8-45 p.m. Relief complete 12-47 a.m.	

[signed] Phylours
Lieut Colonel
Commdg. 1/ Queens' Westminster Rifles

Army Form C. 2118.

WAR DIARY
or
INTELLIGENCE SUMMARY

(Erase heading not required.)

Place	Date	Hour	Summary of Events and Information	Remarks and references to Appendices
In the Field.	April 28th	(Contd)	Casualties 1 Officer (2nd Lieut A.C.BROOKE) and 2 O.R. Sick, 2 O.R. Reinforcements.	
	29th		On relief Battalion marched back to BERNEVILLE about 3-45 a.m. Companies billetted in huts. During day only bathing resting and cleaning up carried out. Casualties 1 O.R. Sick.	

	30th		Specialist and company training carried on during the morning. C.O. inspected "A" Company at 10 a.m. Casualties 2 O.R. Sick,/5 O.R. Reinforcements.
			
			                      Offrs. O.R.
			 Strength on 31-3-18. 33 950.
			 ADD. 17 119.
			                           50 1069.
			 LESS. 11 148.
			 Strength on 30-4-18. 39 921.
			
			                       [signature]
			                               Lieut-Colonel.
			 Commanding 1st Battn QUEENS WESTMINSTER RIFLES.	

Army Form W.3091.

Cover for Documents.

WAR DIARY

Nature of Enclosures.

CONFIDENTIAL

1/16th London Regt (QWR)

MAY 1918.

Notes, or Letters written.

Army Form C. 2118.

WAR DIARY
or
INTELLIGENCE SUMMARY

(Erase heading not required.)

Instructions regarding War Diaries and Intelligence
Summaries are contained in F. S. Regs., Part II.
and the Staff Manual respectively. Title Pages
will be prepared in manuscript.

Place	Date	Hour	Summary of Events and Information	Remarks and references to Appendices
In the Field.	1918 May 1st		"A" and "B" Companies left BERNEVILLE at 12.25 p.m. for ST.SAUVEUR CAVES, where they came under orders of 167 Infantry Brigade. Commanding officer inspected "C" Company at 2.30 p.m. "C" Company fired on range during morning. "D" Company carried out specialist training. Casualties, 6 other ranks sick, 6 other ranks Other causes, 2 other ranks Reinforcements.	
	2nd		"D" Company fired on range during morning and was inspected by the Commanding Officer at 2.30 p.m. "C" Company carried out specialist training. Divisional Band played in camp during evening. Casualties, 1 officer (Lieut.J.J.WESTMORELAND) and 7 other ranks Sick, 2 other ranks Other causes, 1 officer (2Lieut.A.C.BROOKE) and 2 other ranks Reinforcements.	
	3rd		Headquarter details, "C" and "D" Companies, snipers and poor shots of "C" Company on range in morning, specialist training also carried out. Football match during afternoon against Brigade Headquarters. Result, 2-1 in our favour. Casualties, 13 other ranks Sick, 5 other ranks Reinforcements.	
	4th		Battalion relieved 1/8th Middlesex Regiment in support in left sector in support, "A" and "B" Companies relieving from the CAVES, leaving them at 7.30 p.m. and "C" and "D" Companies and Headquarter details meeting guides on CAMBRAI ROAD at 7.50 p.m. Relief complete 9.30 p.m. Dispositions. "A" Company in dugout behind BLANGY SUPPORT just north of CAMBRAI ROAD. "B" Company, "C" Company and "D" Company were left, centre, and right companies respectively in BLANGY TRENCH from RAILWAY (G.24) to (G.36 b 35.00) Headquarters on CAMBRAI ROAD at G.29 d 94.40. Casualties, 10 other ranks Sick, 1 other rank Reinforcement.	
	5th		Day was quiet. Fairly heavy mist during early morning. ARRAS CEMETERY shelled with 5.9" shells from 4 p.m. to 6.30 p.m. Two hostile aircraft over our lines for about 25 minutes during evening. Some working parties found during day. Casualties, 1 other rank Wounded, 10 other ranks Sick.	
	6th		Day was again quiet, except for fairly consistent shelling with of ARRAS CEMETERY with 8" How. H.E. and 5.9" shrapnel. "A" and "D" Companies worked for forward battalions during night 5/6th and	

2449 Wt. W14957/M90 750,000 1/16 J.B.C. & A. Forms/C.2118/12.

Phayoun

Lieut.Colonel, Commanding
1st Battalion, QUEENS WESTMINSTER RIFLES

Army Form C. 2118

WAR DIARY
or
INTELLIGENCE SUMMARY
(Erase heading not required.)

Instructions regarding War Diaries and Intelligence Summaries are contained in F.S. Regs., Part II. and the Staff Manual respectively. Title Pages will be prepared in manuscript.

Place	Date	Hour	Summary of Events and Information	Remarks and references to Appendices
In the Field.	1918 May 6th (cont)		"B" and "C" Companies for R.E. during day. The Commanding Officer reconnoitred route to left line Battalion Headquarters. Casualties, 1 other rank Sick, 1 officer (Captain J.B.BABER,M.C.) Reinforcement.	
	7th		Work as on previous day. Day again quiet. Casualties, 6 other ranks Sick, 9 other ranks Reinforcements	
	8th		Work as usual. Enemy was exceptionally quiet during the whole day. Casualties, 5 other ranks Sick 2 officers (2nd Lieut. F.W.RUSSELL,M.C. and 2nd Lieut. O.A.N.EATOM) and 18 other ranks Reinforcements.	
	9th		As on previous 3 days. Casualties, 9 other ranks Sick, 1 other rank Other causes, 1 other rank Reinforcement.	
	10th		At "stand to" an inter-company relief was carried out, the dispositions then becoming as follows; "A"Company, Left front company, "B"Company, Support company at disposal of Officer Commanding 1st London Rifle Brigade, "C"Company, Right Front Company at disposal of Officer Commanding 1/2nd London Regiment, "D"Company, Centre Front Company. Usual work carried out. Day was quiet. Casualties, 1 other rank Killed, 3 other ranks Wounded, 2 other ranks Sick.	
	11th		Enemy again quiet except for slight shelling of ARRAS and CAMBRAI ROAD. Usual working parties by day and night. Brigadier General Commanding inspected system held by Battalion at 10 a.m. Commanding Officer reconnoitred 1/2nd London Regiment's front (Right Sub Sector) Casualties, 1 other rank Wounded, 5 other ranks Sick.	

Lieut.Colonel,Commanding
1st Battalion,QUEENS WESTMINSTER RIFLES.

Army Form C. 2118.

WAR DIARY
or
INTELLIGENCE SUMMARY
(Erase heading not required.)

Instructions regarding War Diaries and Intelligence Summaries are contained in F.S. Regs., Part II. and the Staff Manual respectively. Title Pages will be prepared in manuscript.

Place	Date	Hour	Summary of Events and Information	Remarks and references to Appendices
In the Field. 1918	May 12th.		Day was exceptionally clear and aerial activity abnormal, especially during evening, but except for occasional shelling of CAMBRAI ROAD during day and heavy shelling of ARRAS during evening and early part of night, period was quiet. Battalion provided usual working parties. Casualties; 4 other ranks Sick, 1 officer (Lieut. C.E.MOY,M.C.) other causes, 5 other ranks other causes.	
	13th		Weather changed to cold and rain, which fell for some hours at intervals during the day. Usual bursts of fire directed against CAMBRAI ROAD. Battalion, less Lewis Gunners of two companies again found working parties for front line Battalions, and R.E. Casualties, 2 other ranks Wounded, 2 other ranks Sick.	
	14th		Day was again quiet except for usual slight shelling. Night of 14/15th "A" and "D" Companies carried wire for new belt being erected in front of ~~out~~ for ~~his~~ new trench in H27 a & b and on various small jobs Remainder of Battalion less nucleus of two companies working for R.E. 1 other rank Reinforcement. Casualties, 4 other ranks Wounded, 3 other ranks Sick, 1 other rank Reinforcement.	
	15th		Day was fine and hot, and was again quiet. Battalion less nucleus of two companies started digging of new trench in H27 a & b on night 15/16th. Parties were shelled with 77mm guns and trench mortars and rifle grenades (both H.E. and filled with gas) fell in vicinity of trench. Machine guns were also very active. Casualties, 6 other ranks Wounded, 1 other rank Sick.	

Phylaw.

Lieut.Colonel,Commanding,
1st Battalion, QUEENS WESTMINSTER RIFLES.

Army Form C. 2118.

WAR DIARY
or
INTELLIGENCE SUMMARY

(Erase heading not required.)

Instructions regarding War Diaries and Intelligence Summaries are contained in F. S. Regs., Part II. and the Staff Manual respectively. Title Pages will be prepared in manuscript.

Place	Date	Hour	Summary of Events and Information	Remarks and references to Appendices
In the Field	1918 May 16th		A German Albatross machine was driven down and crashed by 2 of our fighting machines near BOIS DE BOEUFS about 7 p.m. 3 parties of 26 men each dug our three posts in new trench. Remainder of Battalion did not work owing to gassing of previous night. Casualties, 2 other ranks killed, 8 other ranks Wounded, 15 other ranks Sick, 1 other rank Other causes, 39 other ranks Reinforcements.	
	17th		Usual quiet day. A 6" Mark VII shell fell near BLANGY SUPPORT and PELVES TRENCH at about 8.30 p.m. 3 Companies worked on new trench and one company for R.E. during night 17/18th Parties on new trench were not much troubled by the enemy. Casualties, 10 other ranks Sick.	
	18th		Commanding Officer visited TELEGRAPH HILL sector during morning to obtain all information available concerning enemies line preparatory to proposed raid. Work as for night 17/18th Casualties, 3 other ranks Sick, 3 other ranks Other causes.	
	19th		Day quiet. Enemy's guns slightly more active during evening. Work as on two previous nights Casualties, 1 other rank Wounded, 2 other ranks Sick, 1 other rank Reinforcement.	
	20th		Nothing unusual happened during day. Divisional General went round BLANGY SYSTEM during morning. Work as on previous nights. Casualties, 1 officer (2nd Lieut. W.T. GALBRAITH) sick, 1 other rank Reinforcement.	
	21st		Usual quiet day. Battalion was relieved during early night 21/22nd by 1st London Scottish and proceeded to billets in ARRAS where it became responsible for manning TELEGRAPH HILL SWITCH in case of attack. Relief was quiet and was complete before midnight. Casualties, 2 other ranks Reinforcements.	

Ph Mains.
Lieut-Colonel, Commanding
1st Battalion, QUEENS WESTMINSTER RIFLES.

Army Form C. 2118.

WAR DIARY
or
INTELLIGENCE SUMMARY

(Erase heading not required.)

Instructions regarding War Diaries and Intelligence Summaries are contained in F.S. Regs., Part II. and the Staff Manual respectively. Title Pages will be prepared in manuscript.

Place	Date	Hour	Summary of Events and Information	Remarks and references to Appendices
In the Field	1918 May 22nd		With the exception of a few odd parties working, Battalion rested until evening. Part of Battalion bathed. During night all available men dug and wired TILLOY RESERVE in front of DEVILS WOOD. 2 Lewis Gun limbers went with party in case ALARM should go while whole battalion was out. Everything was quiet. Casualties, 4 other ranks Sick, 2 other ranks other causes, 3 other ranks Reinforcements.	
	23rd		Everything as on 22nd May. Casualties, 1 other rank Wounded, 9 other ranks Sick.	
	24th		Day was wet but cleared up towards night. Battalion was relieved in ARRAS by 1st London Rifle Brigade, but proceeded up to TILLOY RESERVE and worked there, returning after work to DAINVILLE where men were mostly billetted along DOULLENS-ARRAS ROAD. Battalion arrived in DAINVILLE at 4 a.m. Casualties, 1 other rank Wounded, 1 other rank Sick, 1 other rank Reinforcement.	
	25th		Day fine. Whole day devoted to rest, cleaning up and disinfecting. Casualties, 2 other ranks Sick, 24 other ranks Reinforcements.	
	26th		Sunday. Day fine. Voluntary Services in the Y.M.C.A. in the morning. Parade Service in the afternoon conducted by Assistant Chaplain General, Colonel Blackburn. Casualties, 3 other ranks Sick, 1 other rank Reinforcement.	
	27th		"A" Company fired on the range in the morning. Specialist training from 11 a.m. to 1 p.m. "B" Company Lewis Gunners on the range in the afternoon. Casualties, 1 other rank Wounded, 3 other ranks Sick, 1 other rank Other causes, 1 other rank Reinforcement.	

Lieut.Colonel, Commanding

1st Battalion, QUEENS WESTMINSTER RIFLES.

Army Form C. 2118.

WAR DIARY
or
INTELLIGENCE SUMMARY

(Erase heading not required.)

Instructions regarding War Diaries and Intelligence Summaries are contained in F. S. Regs., Part II. and the Staff Manual respectively. Title Pages will be prepared in manuscript.

Place	Date	Hour	Summary of Events and Information	Remarks and references to Appendices
In the Field. 1918	May 28th		"B" Company on the range in the morning. Specialist training as yesterday. Lewis Gunners of "A" Company on the range in the afternoon. The "Bow Bells" gave a performance in the open near the village. Casualties, 2 other ranks Sick, 1 officer (Lieut. C. TABBERER) Other causes, 1 other rank Reinforcement.	
	29th		"C" and "D" Companies fired on the range in the morning. Specialist training as yesterday. Lewis Gunners of "C" Company fired on the range in the afternoon. A few shells fell in DAINVILLE during the evening. Another performance was given by the "Bow Bells". Casualties, 1 officer (2nd Lieut. A.B.RUSSELL) and 1 other rank Sick, 22 other ranks Reinforcements.	
	30th Night		The Battalion left DAINVILLE at 9.15 p.m. to relieve the 1st London Regiment in the TELEGRAPH HILL X sector. Relief was complete by 1.30 a.m. The usual quiet night. The companies were disposed as follows; "C", Right company, "B", Centre Company, "A", Left Company, "D" Company in reserve. Casualties, 4 other ranks Sick, 1 officer (2nd Lieut. W.T.GALBRAITH) Reinforcement	
	31st		The day was generally quiet. Casualties, 1 officer (2nd Lieut. W.T.GALBRAITH) sick, 1 other rank Reinforcement.	

	Officers	Other ranks
Strength on 30.4.1918	39	921
ADD	5	134
	44	1055
LESS	6	195
Strength on 30.5.1918	38	960

Phytaun

Lieut.Colonel, Commanding
1st Battalion, QUEENS WESTMINSTER RIFLES.

Army Form W.3091.

Cover for Documents.

WAR DIARY
Nature of Enclosures.

CONFIDENTIAL

10TH LONDON REGIMENT (P.W.R.)

JUNE, 1918

Notes, or Letters written.

Army Form C. 2118.

WAR DIARY
or
INTELLIGENCE SUMMARY.
(Erase heading not required.)

Instructions regarding War Diaries and Intelligence Summaries are contained in F. S. Regs., Part II. and the Staff Manual respectively. Title pages will be prepared in manuscript.

Place	Date	Hour	Summary of Events and Information	Remarks and references to Appendices
In the Field	1918. June 1st.		Slight shelling by 4.2's and 77 mm on Support Line during the day. At 9 p.m. a barrage was fired in support of a raid by the KENSINGTONS in the Left Brigade Sector. About 1 minute before our barrage commenced the enemy dropped a light barrage on HONEY LANE and TELEGRAPH SWITCH, lasting till about 10 p.m.	
			Casualties 2 O.R. Killed, 1 Officer (2nd Lieut C.W. ANDERSON) and 3 O.R. Wounded, 6 O.R. Sick.	
	2nd		About 9 p.m. the enemy obtained a direct hit on an artillery O.P. in CREST TRENCH, killing 3 men. At 11 p.m. the enemy put down a light barrage, soon after which an S.O.S. was sent up by the Battalion on our left. No infantry action followed. When the shelling commenced to die down the Commanding Officer (Lieut-Colonel P.M. GLASIER, D.S.O.) went up the stairs of the dug-out to look at the situation, and was killed by a direct hit on the entrance by a 4.2 shell.	
			At 12.45 a.m. a successful raid was carried out by the Canadians on our right, during which our front was slightly shelled. Major S.R. SAVILL, M.C. rejoined from the Nucleus Personnel and assumed command.	
			Casualties 1 Officer (Lieut-Colonel P.M. GLASIER, DSO) and 1 O.R. Killed, 2 O.R. Wounded, 2 O.R. Other Causes.	
	3rd.		The day was fairly quiet. Work on the trenches carried on and wiring at night. Our patrols active reconnoitring disused trenches and enemy positions opposite our Battn front.	
			Casualties 4 O.R. Wounded, 3 O.R. Sick, 4 O.R. Reinforcements.	
	4th.		Work on ammunition and maintenance of trenches carried out. TELEGRAPH HILL SWITCH shelled slightly during the morning.	
			During the night enemy's artillery was fairly active on TILLOY SUPPORT, CREST TRENCH and CAVALRY TRACK, used by ration limbers.	
			Considerable amount of individual movement observed in the enemy's lines. Low flying aeroplanes were very active over our front system. Our patrols reconnoitred AYR TRENCH DOUGLAS TRENCH and the SUNKEN ROAD in N.8.c.	
			Casualties 5 O.R. Sick, 1 O.R. Other Causes.	
	5th.		The day was very quiet. The night was spent on wiring and work on trenches. A good deal of movement was observed behind the enemy's lines.	

Army Form C. 2118.

WAR DIARY
OR
INTELLIGENCE SUMMARY.
(Erase heading not required.)

Instructions regarding War Diaries and Intelligence Summaries are contained in F. S. Regs., Part II. and the Staff Manual respectively. Title pages will be prepared in manuscript.

Place	Date	Hour	Summary of Events and Information	Remarks and references to Appendices
In the Field.	1918. June 5th. (Contd).		Casualties, 2 O.R. Wounded, 3 O.R. Sick, 22 O.R. Reinforcements.	
	6th.		At 1 a.m. several "blind" 6" shrapnel shells fell in our lines. DOUGLAS TRENCH again carefully reconnoitred. Work on trenches as yesterday. One of our patrols was forced to withdraw by the enemy's "sneezing" gas. Considerable individual movement observed; several in Full marching order seen. Casualties, 2 O.R. Sick.	
	7th.		The day was fairly quiet. L/Sergt NELSON of "D" Company with 3 O.R. who had been posted at N.8.a.3.0. during the night reconnoitred the dug-out shafts at N.8.a.3.0. and shallow trench running N.E. from DOUGLAS TRENCH by daylight. His report was of some considerable value in forming the plan for the proposed raid on AIRY WORK. Tractors and transport were heard in the direction of WANCOURT during the night. Casualties 1 O.R. Sick.	
	8th.		In the early morning two sticks with luminous paint on them facing the enemy were found in our wire. Enemy aircraft very active. The day was quiet and work was done improving occupied bays. At 9.45 p.m. the enemy bombarded our right and centre Companies continuing until about 10.15 p.m. At 9.50 p.m. we fired a protective barrage. The enemy bombardment was in support of a raid on the Canadians in NEUVILLE VITASSE. Casualties 1 O.R. Killed, 1 O.R. Sick, 1 O.R. Other Causes.	
	9th.		Slight shelling of trench junctions took place during the day. Work on occupied bays continued. Lewis Gun instruction and classes in the new No. 36 bomb were held. Considerable individual movement was observed. Casualties 4 O.R. Sick, 2 O.R. Reinforcements.	
	10th.		Very quiet. Work and instruction as yesterday. The proposed raid was cancelled by the Brigadier. At 1.30 p.m. a large hostile patrol approached one of our outposts. Precautions were taken but no action followed. Casualties 1 O.R. Sick.	

Army Form C. 2118.

WAR DIARY
or
INTELLIGENCE SUMMARY.
(Erase heading not required.)

Instructions regarding War Diaries and Intelligence Summaries are contained in F.S. Regs., Part II. and the Staff Manual respectively. Title pages will be prepared in manuscript.

Place	Date	Hour	Summary of Events and Information	Remarks and references to Appendices
In the Field.	1918. June 11th		Another very quiet day. Work and Instruction as yesterday. Considerable movement seen in enemy's lines. Casualties, 1 Officer (Capt B.L.MILES) and 2 O.R. Sick, 1 Officer (Capt H.F.GRIZELLE, M.C.) and 41 O.R. Reinforcements.	
	12th		At 3 p.m. a concentration on AIRY WORK was carried out in support of a raid by the L.R.B. on our left. 8 Minutes from zero elapsed before the enemy replied and then only a light barrage fell on our front. Slight activity during the night. Instruction in Lewis Gun and bombs carried out also wiring and deepening trenches. Casualties 1 O.R. Sick.	
	13th		At 2 a.m. NEUVILLE VITASSE was heavily bombarded with gas, in retaliation for which enemy shelled our front and reserve lines for about ¾ hour. The weather continued fine. Day very quiet. Instruction and work as yesterday. Casualties 1 O.R. Killed, 2 O.R. Wounded, 1 O.R. Sick, 1 O.R. Other Causes.	
	14th		At 1 a.m. our guns fired in support of a raid by the Canadians on our right. The enemy's barrage fell just outside our wire and at 1.8 a.m. in answer to a single orange light it lifted on to our front line. The barrage ceased at 1.35 a.m. little damage being done to our line. A hostile patrol of about 39 men approached our left outpost (N.7.b.95.50) at 1.45 a.m. The garrison opened fire and the enemy was seen to disperse and run back towards his own lines. Work on the maintenance of trenches and instruction continued. Casualties 2 O.R. Sick.	
	15th		Very quiet day. Work etc as yesterday. At 11 p.m. left outpost at N.7.b.95.50. heard enemy wiring and saw his covering party. They fired on the enemy who withdrew, no further sounds being heard during the night. At 10 p.m. 2 6" shells fell short at N.7.c.85.20. Casualties 1 O.R. Other Causes, 2 O.R. Reinforcements.	
	16th		At 7.30 a.m. an enemy plane was brought down in N.2.c. by an S.E.5. from a height of 10,000 feet. Again at about 9 a.m. a low flying E.A. was brought down by Lewis Gun and Machine Gun fire. It fell in N.14.c. Both our own and E.A. very active by day and night. At 11.20 p.m. 3 bombs were dropped near Battn H.Q.	

Army Form C. 2118.

WAR DIARY
or
INTELLIGENCE SUMMARY.
(Erase heading not required.)

Place	Date	Hour	Summary of Events and Information	Remarks and references to Appendices
In the Field	1918. June 16th (Contd).		A small enemy party seen by our outpost at N.7.b.95.50, was dispersed by rifle fire. Work and instruction as yesterday. Casualties 1 O.R. Wounded at duty, 2 O.R. Sick, 1 Officer, (2nd Lieut J.C.B.PRINCE) and 6 O.R. Reinforcements.	
	17th		The day was quiet. During the night the Battalion was relieved by the KENSINGTONS and proceeded to billets in DAINVILLE. The last Company arrived about 3.15 a.m. 18-6-18. "A", "C" and "D" Companies were accommodated along the ARRAS - DOULLENS ROAD and "B" Company in DAINVILLE Village. The Battalion while in reserve, was responsible for manning TELEGRAPH HILL SWITCH in case of alarm. Casualties 6 O.R. Killed, 1 O.R. Wounded, 4 O.R. Sick.	
	18th		Day spent in bathing and general cleaning up. Casualties 2 O.R. Reinforcements.	
	19th		Remainder of Battn bathed. Kit inspections, clothing parades and innoculations carried out. All day spent in interior economy. Casualties 3 O.R. Sick, 14 O.R. Reinforcements.	
	20th		All "D" Company Lewis Gunners available fired on the Range in the morning. "C" Company fired on the Range near the CITADEL at ARRAS. At 8 p.m. "A" and "B" Companies moved to billets in ARRAS for work under the C.R.E. Major WHITMORE was in command of the two Companies. Casualties 2 O.R. Sick, 1 O.R. Reinforcement.	
	21st.		"C" Company Lewis Gunners fired on the Range near DAINVILLE STATION in the morning. "D" Company fired on the "BUTTE DE TIR" rifle range at ARRAS. On the night 21/22nd "A" and "B" Companies were wiring East of DEVILS WOOD. 4 shells near the ARRAS - DOULLENS ROAD, South of DAINVILLE during the evening. Casualties 2 O.R. Sick, 1 O.R. Other Causes, 1 O.R. Reinforcement.	

Army Form C. 2118.

WAR DIARY
or
INTELLIGENCE SUMMARY.
(Erase heading not required.)

Instructions regarding War Diaries and Intelligence Summaries are contained in F. S. Regs., Part II. and the Staff Manual respectively. Title pages will be prepared in manuscript.

Place	Date	Hour	Summary of Events and Information	Remarks and references to Appendices
In the Field.	1918. June 22nd		"C" and "D" Companies relieved "A" and "B" Companies in ARRAS; "A" and "B" Companies then returned to DAINVILLE, arriving at 11.30 a.m. On the night 22/23rd "C" and "D" Companies worked on firebays in SCOTTISH AVENUE - Map reference G.29.d. and G.36.a. Casualties 2 O.R. Sick, 3 O.R. Reinforcements.	
	23rd		A parade service was held in the grounds of Battalion Headquarters at 10.45 a.m. In the afternoon a cricket match was played between Officers of Battn H.Q. and "A" and "B" Company and the Battn Signallers. During the night 23/24th, "C" and "D" Coys worked on a cable trench. Casualties 4 O.R. Sick, 1 Officer (Capt. B.L.MILES) Reinforcement.	
	24th.		"C" and "D" Companies returned to DAINVILLE, arriving at 4 a.m. "A" Company Lewis Gunners fired on the range, "B" Company fired on the rifle range "BUTTE DE TIR" near ARRAS. In the afternoon photographs of Officers and Companies were taken in billet grounds. Casualties 32 O.R. Reinforcements.	
	25th.		The Brigadier General inspected the Battalion by Companies. Casualties 1 O.R. Sick, 3 O.R. Reinforcements.	
	26th.		A lecture by the Divisional Educational Officer was given to Companies in the Lecture Hall, DAINVILLE. The Battalion relieved the 1/8th Middlesex Regt in the Left Sub-Sector. Companies moved off at 9 p.m. from Sugar Factory DAINVILLE. Relief was complete by 12.45 a.m. Dispositions as follows:— "D" Company on the left front in FEUCHY TRENCH and SUPPORT. "B" Company on Right in FEUCHY TRENCH and TILLOY TRENCH, and TILLOY SUPPORT. "C" Company in SUPPORT IN BATTERY VALLEY. "A" Company in Reserve in TILLOY TRENCH and TILLOY SUPPORT. The night was quiet. Casualties 1 O.R. Wounded, 4 O.R. Sick, 1 O.R. Other Causes.	
	27th		Very quiet day. Patrol of Lieut CALKIN and 10 O.R. examined old gun pits in NO MANS LAND, found them unoccupied. Casualties 1 O.R. Wounded, 1 O.R. Sick, 1 Officer (2nd Lieut V.H. KIRBY) to Base	

Army Form C. 2118.

WAR DIARY
or
INTELLIGENCE SUMMARY.
(Erase heading not required.)

Place	Date	Hour	Summary of Events and Information	Remarks and references to Appendices
In the Field	1918. June 27th (Contd.)		3 Officers (Major G.H.LAMBERT, 2nd Lieuts O.M.POWER and A.E.POLLARD) and 7 O.R. Reinforcements.	
	28th		Quiet all day. E.A. patrolling the line occasionally. The C.O., Lieut-Colonel S.R. SAVILL, M.C. left the trenches to proceed on leave. Command of the Battalion was taken over by Major J.B. WHITMORE. Casualties 2 O.R. Sick.	
	29th		Very quiet day. In the evening concentrated shoot by enemy with 5.9's on Railway on left of Battalion boundary. A patrol of 2nd Lieut V.G. RAYNOR and 10 O.R. reconnoitred old gun positions in NO MANS LAND. Enemy was wiring in these pits. Casualties 2 O.R. Sick.	
	30th		No further activity in Battalion Area. Casualties 2 O.R. Sick.	

	Officers	O.R.
Strength on 31st May 1918.	38	860.
ADD	6	145.
	44	1,005.
LESS	4	99.
STRENGTH on 30th June 1918.	40	906.

J.S. Whitmore Major.
Commanding 1st Battn QUEENS WESTMINSTER RIFLES.

Army Form W.3091.

Cover for Documents.

WAR DIARY

Nature of Enclosures.

Confidential

1/16th London Regt (QWR)

for month of

JULY, 1918

Notes, or Letters written.

Army Form C. 2118.

WAR DIARY
or
INTELLIGENCE SUMMARY.
(Erase heading not required.)

Instructions regarding War Diaries and Intelligence Summaries are contained in F.S. Regs., Part II. and the Staff Manual respectively. Title pages will be prepared in manuscript.

Place	Date	Hour	Summary of Events and Information	Remarks and references to Appendices
In the Field.	1918. July 1st.		After quiet night enemy put down a light barrage on our line from 5.15 a.m. to 5.30 a.m. This was repeated at same time in the evening. Quiet night. Casualties:- 3 O.R. Wounded, 1 O.R. Sick, 8 O.R. Reinforcements.	
	2nd.		The day was quiet. During the night the Battalion was relieved by the 1st Battn LONDON RIFLE BRIGADE and moved into Brigade Support in BLANGY SYSTEM, the last Company reporting in at 2.45 a.m. Casualties 1 O.R. Wounded, 2 O.R. Sick, 1 officer (2nd Lieut F.R.A. DANSEY) cross posted to 7th Battn LONDON REGIMENT, 4 Officers Reinforcements (2nd Lieut T.W.R.PROCTER 2nd Lieut J.A.N. WEBB from 21st Battn LONDON REGIMENT) 2nd Lieut B. WADE and 2nd Lieut W.E. TODD) taken on strength, being cross posted from 7th Battn LONDON REGIMENT.	
	3rd.		The Battalion working in relays day and night under the C.R.E. Casualties 1 O.R. Sick, 15 O.R. Reinforcements.	
	4th.		Battalion working under the C.R.E. "A" Company were relieved of their working parties and moved back to DAINVILLE for training. Casualties 1 O.R. Sick, 1 O.R. Reinforcements.	
	5th.		"B" "C" and "D" Companies working under C.R.E. - "A" Company training for Raid. Casualties 1 O.R. Wounded, 3 O.R. Sick, 1 O.R. Reinforcements.	
	6th.		"A" Company raid rehearsed. Inspected by Lieut -Colonel JACKSON, DSO, Acting Brigadier General Commanding. "B" "C" and "D" Company work under C.R.E. Casualties 1 O.R. Other Causes, 6 O.R. Reinforcements.	
	7th.		"A" Company Raid rehearsed. Inspected by G.O.C. Raid which was to have taken place on night 7/8th postponed for further rehearsal. Casualties 1 officer (2nd Lieut H.T.HARPER) Wounded and 14 O.R. Sick.	

V.R. Quill
Lieut-Colonel.
Commanding 1st Battn QUEENS WESTMINSTER RIFLES.

Army Form C. 2118.

WAR DIARY
or
INTELLIGENCE SUMMARY.
(Erase heading not required.)

Instructions regarding War Diaries and Intelligence Summaries are contained in F.S. Regs., Part II. and the Staff Manual respectively. Title pages will be prepared in manuscript.

Place	Date	Hour	Summary of Events and Information	Remarks and references to Appendices
In the Field.	1918. July 8th.	9 p.m. 9.50 p.m.	Raid rehearsed by "A" Company. "A" Company moved to assembly positions in the afternoon. Raiding party in position & Advanced Battn H.Q. established. Zero Hour - Artillery bombardment of two Minutes on Gun Pits to be raided. Raiding Party of 3 officers and 110 O.R. started 9.50 p.m. Raiding party returned at 10.25 p.m. having captured 3 prisoners and blown up gun pits and dug-outs. All returned to our lines. Copy of Brigade report of Raid attached. Casualties 11 O.R. Wounded (10 slightly), 1 O.R. Sick.	
	9th.		Morning preparation to relieve 1/2nd LONDON REGIMENT in Right Sub-Sector. Battalion relieved 1/2nd LONDON REGIMENT in the evening. Dispositions "C" and "B" Companies in front line. "A" and "D" Companies in Support. Relief complete by 1 a.m. Casualties 1 Officer (2nd Lieut C.G.WARREN) and 5 O.R. Sick, 13 O.R. Reinforcements.	
	10th.		Quiet day. During the night 2nd Lieut SHEPPARD took out a fighting patrol, but no enemy were encountered. Casualties 1 O.R. Sick, 1 O.R. Other Causes, 2 O.R. Reinforcements.	
	11th.		Quiet day during day. About 9.15 p.m. enemy put down light barrage on our line causing no damage. In the evening a fighting patrol under 2nd Lieut A.E.POLLARD. No enemy were encountered and patrol returned to our lines. Casualties 1 officer (2nd Lieut L.W. FRIEND) and 4 O.R. Sick, 1 O.R. Reinforcement.	
	12th.		Quiet day. Casualties 1 O.R. Killed, 1 Officer (2nd Lieut W.E.TODD) and 1 O.R. Sick, 10 O.R. Reinforcements.	
	13th.		Quiet day during the day. During the night "C" Company was relieved by two half companies of the 10 CANADIAN INFANTRY. After completion of relief "C" Company moved to No. 1 Camp WARLUS. Casualties 1 O.R. Sick.	

A.R. Sewell
Lieut-Colonel.
Commanding 1st Battn QUEEN'S WESTMINSTER RIFLES.

Army Form C. 2118.

WAR DIARY
or
INTELLIGENCE SUMMARY.
(Erase heading not required.)

Instructions regarding War Diaries and Intelligence Summaries are contained in F. S. Regs., Part II. and the Staff Manual respectively. Title pages will be prepared in manuscript.

Place	Date	Hour	Summary of Events and Information	Remarks and references to Appendices
In the Field	1918. July 14th.		Normally quiet day. During the night 14/15th "A" "B" and "D" Companies were relieved. "B" Company was relieved by One Company of 10th CANADIAN INFANTRY BATTALION. "A" and "D" Companies by two Companies of 20th CANADIAN INFANTRY BATTALION. Relief was complete by 2.15 a.m. Surplus Personnel moved from ARRAS to WARLUS. Casualties, 1 O.R. Wounded, 2 O.R. Sick.	
	15th.		After relief "A" "B" and "D" Companies and Battn H.Q. marched to No. 1 Camp WARLUS. Breakfasts were served there and Battn embussed at 7.30 a.m. and arrived at LA COMTE at 10.45a.m. Marched to a large field to wait until billets were cleared of outgoing Battalion. Lieut-Colonel S.R. SAVILL, M.C. reassumed command on return from leave. Casualties NIL.	
	16th.		General cleaning up and clothing parades. Casualties NIL.	
	17th.		Training commenced. Companies marched to "D" Training Area for training from 8.30 a.m. until 12.30 p.m. Afternoon - Recreational training. Casualties 6 O.R. Sick, 10 O.R. Reinforcements.	
	18th.		Training in morning on "D" Area from 8.30 a.m. to 12.30 p.m. Afternoon - Recreational Training. Casualties 2 O.R. Sick.	
	19th		Morning - All Companies trained on "D" Area from 8.30 a.m. until 1 p.m. Practices in open fighting. Flagged-attack. Afternoon - Recreational training. Casualties 20 O.R. Reinforcements.	
	20th.		Morning - Companies inspected by Commanding officer. Afternoon - Recreational Training - Company Sports etc. Casualties:- NIL.	

S R Savill
Lieut-Colonel.
Commanding 1st Battn QUEENS WESTMINSTER RIFLES.

Army Form C. 2118.

WAR DIARY
or
INTELLIGENCE SUMMARY.

(Erase heading not required.)

Instructions regarding War Diaries and Intelligence Summaries are contained in F.S. Regs., Part II. and the Staff Manual respectively. Title pages will be prepared in manuscript.

Place	Date	Hour	Summary of Events and Information	Remarks and references to Appendices
	1918.			
In the Field.	July 21st.		Morning – 11 a.m. Church of England Parade Service by the A.C.G. Colonel BLACKBURN DSO, MC. The Army Commander and Brigadier General Commanding were present at the service. Casualties 2 O.R. Sick, 1 Officer (2nd Lieut C.G.WARREN) and 6 O.R. Reinforcements.	
	22nd.		Morning – Company training and baths at ROCOURT. Recreation in afternoon. Casualties 3 O.R. Sick, 10 O.R. Reinforcements.	
	23rd.		Morning – Battalion attended a demonstration with Tracer Bullets. The demonstration consisted of collective fire and fire control of Lewis Guns and rifles using tracer bullets. Location "C" Training Area. Afternoon – Recreation. Casualties 1 O.R. Other Causes, 5 O.R. Reinforcements.	
	24th.		Company training on "D" Area. Casualties 3 O.R. Sick, 1 Officer (2nd Lieut L.W. FRI????D) from Hospital.	
	25th.		Morning – Tactical scheme for Officers. "B" Company carried out a rearguard action while Battalion withdrew from LA COMTE to "D" Training Area. Battalion had dinners on "D" Area. Afternoon – Attack practice by all Companies "D" Area. Battalion returned to billets at 4.30 p.m. Casualties 1 Officer (2nd Lieut A.C.BROOKE) transferred to M.G.C. 1 O.R. Other Causes, 4 O.R. Reinforcements.	
	26th.		Company training on "D" Area until 11 a.m. Battalion Drill and short address by Commanding Officer. Return to billets at 1 p.m. Afternoon – Recreational training. Evening 3 miles Cross country run. Casualties 1 O.R. other Causes 2 O.R. Reinforcements.	

O.R. Small
Lieut-Colonel.
Commanding 1st Battn QUEEN'S WESTMINSTER RIFLES.

Army Form C. 2118.

WAR DIARY
or
INTELLIGENCE SUMMARY.
(Erase heading not required.)

Place	Date	Hour	Summary of Events and Information	Remarks and references to Appendices
In the Field.	1918. July 27th.		Wet all day. Morning - Companies carried out kit inspections and Company training near billets. Casualties 3 O.R. Reinforcements.	
	28th.		Morning - Voluntary Church services in morning. Battalion Sports in afternoon and evening, on "D" Training Area. Battalion Championship won by Transport, Battn Headquarters second. Casualties 2 O.R. Reinforcements.	
	29th.		Morning - Brigade Scheme arranged. Scheme cancelled and warning order received that Battn would move the following day. Companies trained on ground near their billets. In evening orders received that Battn would move the following day to CAUCOURT. Casualties 1 O.R. Sick, 1 O.R. Other Causes. 7 O.R. Reinforcements.	
	30th.	11.30 a.m.	Morning - Battn moved off at 9.10 a.m. from LA COMTE and marched to CAUCOURT - arriving at 11.30 a.m. Afternoon - Companies paraded for foot inspection and gas drill. Casualties 5 O.R. Sick 2 O.R. Reinforcements.	
	31st.		Morning - Company training - Short route march by Companies. Recreation in afternoon. Orders received that Battn would relieve a Battn of the CANADIANS the following night. Casualties 1 O.R. Sick, 6 O.R. Reinforcements.	

```
                                          Offrs    O.R.
Strength on 30th June 1918.                40      906
                            ADD.            6      134.
                                           46    1,040.
                            LESS.           5       83.
Strength on 31st July 1918.                41      957.
                                          ====    =====
```

[signature]
Lieut-Colonel.
Commanding 1st Battn QUEEN'S WESTMINSTER RIFLES.

REPORT ON RAID CARRIED OUT ON 8th INSTANT
BY 1/16th LONDON REGT. (Q.W.R.)

STRENGTH OF RAIDING PARTY.

1 Company divided into 9 sections each of 1 N.C.O. and 9 riflemen, referred to hereafter as Sections 1 to 9.

OBJECTIVE.

Enemy Gunpits at H.27.d.49.99 to H.27.d.53.72.

PRELIMINARY RECONNAISSANCE & PRACTICE.

The objective was carefully studied by means of ground observation and by all officers and N.C.Os. forming part of the Raiding party. Valuable information was obtained from Artillery Officers of the 15th Divisional Artillery who had actually built these gunpits. All ranks made a very minute study of Air photographs taken at a low altitude. The actual objective was taped out and a trench used to represent the jumping off point. The actual assault was rehearsed several times both by day and by night.

ZERO HOUR.

Zero hour was 9.50 p.m. 8th instant. This hour was decided upon in the hope of surprising the enemy whilst in his dugouts and before he had taken up his night dispositions. This actually proved to be the case.

ASSEMBLY.

The assembly was carried out during the afternoon of the 8th instant in that portion of BROKEN LANE between H.27.b.2.5. and H.27.b.6.6.

OUR BARRAGE.

At Zero, Artillery and Light T.Ms. opened on objective at intense rate.
At Zero plus 2, Artillery lifted from objective and opened on protective lines, in which barrage smoke was freely used.
Light T.Ms. ceased at Zero plus 2.
Machine guns opened at Zero and continued on protective lines throughout the raid.
All ranks testify to the excellency of our barrage.

THE ASSAULT.

The routes to the objective are shown on the attached sketch Sections 1,4,5,6 & 8 left the trench together at Zero and halted 70 yards South of BROKEN LANE until Zero plus 2 when they continued forward at the double.
Sections 2,3 & 9 followed immediately behind.
Section 7 followed immediately behind after Section 3
Sections 1 and 2 proceeded in succession in single file down track running South from the second E in BROKEN LANE to South of BROKEN MILL, changed direction half left, opened into extended order and doubled to their respective objectives.
Section 3 in single file, followed with Lewis Gun immediately behind Section 2.
Section 7 followed immediately behind Section 3 in the same formation.
Sections 4,5,6 & 8 proceeded together in line of sections in file to their respective objectives.
Section 9 in file with Lewis Gun followed section 8.

Each section proceeded straight to its objective without difficulty and found all wire obstacles blown away.

Sections 1,2,4,5 & 6 arrived at the main objective within a few seconds of one another and found the gunpits almost unrecognisable on account of shell fire.

ACTION WHILST IN THE OBJECTIVE.

The Gunpits were quickly cleared, no opposition being met with. 3 prisoners and 1 Light Machine Gun were captured in the most Southern Gunpit.

As soon as the Raiding Party had arrived at its objective the enemy attempted to come out of the deep dugout known to exist in the gunpits. The first one to show himself was an officer who fired his revolver at our sentry. He aimed badly and was at once shot and a Mobile charge (12 lbs Amonal) was thrown after him. This duly exploded some way down the stairway of the dugout and effectively blew in the entrance.

The second entrance was found and this was also dealt with first by "P" Grenades and "M.S.K." Grenades and finally by a Mobile Charge.

The small ground shelters round the pits were found destroyed by our artillery, but the Gunpits themselves still afforded good cover and contained many rifles, steel helmets and grenades.

ENEMY ACTION.

(a) _Infantry._ No actual infantry encounter took place.
(b) _Artillery._ The enemy's artillery was very late in opening and was by no means heavy. Chief attention was paid to BATTERY VALLEY and to the FEUCHY SYSTEM*. During the raid an enemy 77 m.m Battery was quickly silenced by our artillery.
(c) _M.Gs._ At Zero plus 2 enemy M.Gs. opened rapid fire in the direction of BROKEN LANE from apparently ICELAND TRENCH. Their fire was however very erratic and high and the Raiding Party was not caused any inconvenience.

WITHDRAWAL.

15 minutes proved to be sufficient to complete the task allotted and the withdrawal was commenced at about Zero plus 20. The withdrawal was effected by runners from section to section and no visual signal was given until all Section Commanders had reported in, when a Red, Green and Yellow Rocket was fired to warn possible stragglers. Immediately this rocket was fired the enemy fired Red Rockets and Very Lights but his artillery and M.Gs. did not increase their rate of fire and at Zero plus 60 all enemy action on the forward area had ceased.

COMMUNICATIONS.

Raid H.Q. was connected to Advanced Battalion H.Q. by cable and by Power Buzzer. These means held until Zero plus 20 when the cable was cut in several places and the Power Buzzer hit.

CASUALTIES.

Ours. 11 O.R. wounded, 10 of which were very slight.

Enemy's. 3 O.R. captured. It is practically certain that the enemy's casualties were heavy. The dugout of which the entrances were well bombed and blown in, was a very large one and the prisoners stated that at the time of the raid, 2 Officers and between 50 and 60 O.R. were accommodated therein.

GENERAL.

At Zero plus Chinese raids were carried out on :-
(a) STONE DUMP
(b) AIRY WORK N.8.c & d.
In both these demonstrations smoke was freely used.

* between front and support lines.

(signed) T.G.McCarthy, Captain
Brigade Major
169th Infantry Brigade

Army Form W.3091.

Cover for Documents.

WAR DIARY
Nature of Enclosures.

Confidential

1/16th London Regt. (Civil)

for month of

AUGUST 1918.

Notes, or Letters written.

Army Form C. 2118.

WAR DIARY
INTELLIGENCE SUMMARY.

(Erase heading not required.)

Instructions regarding War Diaries and Intelligence
Summaries are contained in F. S. Regs., Part II.
and the Staff Manual respectively. Title pages
will be prepared in manuscript.

Place	Date	Hour	Summary of Events and Information	Remarks and references to Appendices
In the Field	1918 August 1st		Battalion entrained MINGOVAL at 2 p.m. on Light Railway. Long delay near SAVY when order of trains was mixed up, 1st train containing Commanding Officer and Regtl. Staff dropped back to last train but one.	
			Detrained 7.30 p.m. (1½ hours late) at DAINVILLE WOOD. Consequently considerable rush to fill waterbottles, have teas, stack packs and fall out Nucleus. Marched off 9 p.m. and relieved Coys 13th, and 2 Coys 16th CANADIAN INFANTRY in LEFT SUB-SECTOR, TELEGRAPH HILL. Officer i/c these 4 Coys knew practically nothing of Sector, as 2 Coys had only come in night before. Relief complete 2 a.m. Casualties :- 1 O.R. Sick.	2
	2nd.		Brigade say dispositions only temporary so no re-arrangement attempted, practically entirely scooped out bivouacs with no revetting, very bad. Men all turned out of their bivouacs which are considered dangerous. Rain nearly all day. Front Line knee deep with water. No Regtl. Aid Post, Battn. H.Q. in old Coy H.Q. in old Coy H.Q. Trenches all very dirty, masses of Salvage and bad latrines. "D" Coy in Front Line "B" and "C" Coys in Support "A" Coy in Reserve. Casualties :- 1 O.R. Wounded, 1 O.R. Other Causes.	
	3rd.		Heavy rain in morning. Trenches still very wet and muddy. Little done to improve accommodation as R.E. material not yet to hand. No gumboots available. Little shelling. Only Iron Rations issued (to affect turnover) Casualties :- 2 O.R. Sick.	
	4th.		Quiet day. No rain. Trenches drying up. Casualties :- 1 O.R. Sick.	

J. R. Smith
Lieut Colonel
Comndg 1/Queen's Westminster Rifles

Army Form C. 2118.

WAR DIARY
or
INTELLIGENCE SUMMARY.
(Erase heading not required.)

Instructions regarding War Diaries and Intelligence Summaries are contained in F. S. Regs., Part II. and the Staff Manual respectively. Title pages will be prepared in manuscript.

Place	Date	Hour	Summary of Events and Information	Remarks and references to Appendices
In the Field	1918 Aug.5th.		Quiet Day. Nucleus rejoined Battn. Personnel surplus to establishment despatched to Divisional Reception Camp. Casualties :- 4 O.R. Sick. 10 O.R. Reinforcements.	
	6th.		Quiet day.	
			Casualties :- 1 O.R. Wounded, 1 O.R. Sick.	
	7th.		Relieved by 1st Battn. London Rifle Brigade and moved into Brigade Reserve. Accommodated in trenches and Shelters in the BLANGY SYSTEM. Casualties :- 1 O.R. Wounded, 1 Offr. (2nd Lt. W.E. TODD) and 1 O.R. Reinforcements.	
	8th.		Battn. on Brigade working parties and cleaning up.	
			Casualties 1 O.R. Wounded, 1 O.R. Reinforcement.	
	9th.		Baths. Fired on Lewis Gun Range. On Brigade Working Parties. No personnel at Baths to work them so running of the Baths was done by bathing parties. No clean towels. Casualties :- 5 O.R. Sick.	
	10th.		Same as 9th instant. Casualties 3 O.R. Sick, 2 O.R. Reinforcements.	
	11th.		Same as 10th instant. B.G.C. held Conference on "Training" Casualties :- 1 O.R. Sick.	
	12th		Brigade Working parties. Revolver practice for Nos. 1 & 2 of Lewis Gun Teams. Battn. Team from 1st Army Musketry-Camp-returned. Competition reported won by Cyclists and Horse Gunners. Battn. Rep was top of 56 Div representatives	

J.R. Davis
Lieut Colonel
Commdg 1/ Queens Westminster Rifles

Army Form C. 2118.

WAR DIARY
or
INTELLIGENCE SUMMARY.
(Erase heading not required.)

Place	Date	Hour	Summary of Events and Information	Remarks and references to Appendices
In the Field	1918 Augt. 12th		Contd :- Infantry Battns. unable to compete with Units who live almost permanently in back Areas. O.C. 2nd. Battn 311 Infantry Regt. A.E.F. arrived to arrange details of forthcoming instructional attachment of his Battalion. Commanding Officer held Conference of Coy Commander's on organisation, the system of making self-contained and efficient Platoons, and new lines of training laid down by Inspector-General "Training"	
	13th		Casualties :- 7 O.R. Sick. 16 officers, 32 N.C.Os. 2/311th Infantry Regt. A.E.F. arrived for instructional attachment. Battn. relieved 2nd London Regt LEFT SUB-SECTOR, TELEGRAPH HILL SECTOR. "A" "B" "C" Coys in Line "D" Coy in Reserve. Application to run a Battn. Musketry Course for Platoons in Village behind lines not sanctioned by Brigade.	
			Casualties :- 1 O.R. Sick, 3 O.R. Reinforcements.	
	14th		Commanding Officer went to Demonstration in Training a Platoon under the direction of the Inspector-General "Training" Bus to take party did not arrive. Party eventually went by lorry arriving one hour late missing opening remarks and explanation by I.T. Supplies came into force a fair amount of stock was received. Battn. has practically been without these supplies for a fortnight. For first time since new rationing scheme of E.F.C. Personnel from A.E.F. returned to their Unit. All accommodation reconnoitred and Scheme arranged for reception of 16 Platoons A.E.F. on 16th instant. At 10.30 p.m. enemy raided post held by 1st KENSINGTON Battn. Immediately on our Left. A fair amount of the hostile barrage fell on "A" Coy Front. Warning Order received of Divisional Relief by 18th instant. Casualties :- 2 O.R. Sick, 1 Ofrr. (2nd Lt. W.A. STILLWELL) to R.A.F. England.	

R. Shuttle
Lieut Colonel
Commdg. 1 Queens' Westminster Rifles

Army Form C. 2118.

WAR DIARY
or
INTELLIGENCE SUMMARY.
(Erase heading not required.)

Instructions regarding War Diaries and Intelligence Summaries are contained in F. S. Regs., Part II. and the Staff Manual respectively. Title pages will be prepared in manuscript.

Place	Date	Hour	Summary of Events and Information	Remarks and references to Appendices
In the Field	1918 Augt. 15th		Attachment of A.E.F. and all details arranged during last 4 days washed out. Casualties :- 4 O.R. Sick, 10 O.R. Reinforcements.	
	16th.		Relieved by 6th CAMERON HIGHLANDERS, 15th Division. Bus Convoy of incoming Unit delayed and relief complete at 3 a.m. Proceeded to BERNEVILLE arriving 4.30 to 5.30 a.m. Casualties :- 1 O.R. Other Causes.	
	17th.		Entrained 10.30 a.m. and proceeded to LIENCOURT arriving at about 1 p.m. Casualties :- 4 O.R. Reinforcements.	
	18th.		Arrangements made for Training, Baths and improvements of billets. Kit inspections commenced. Warning Order received at midday that Battn. would move on 19th inst. Casualties :- 1 O.R. Sick.	
	19th.		Battn. embussed 9.30 a.m. 1000 yards from billets and debussed BERNEVILLE where dinners were served. Proceeded at 2 p.m. by march route to ARRAS where all Coys were billeted in COLLEGE COMMUNALE with cellar accommodation for about 100 men only. Gas and H.E. bombardment in the vicinity most of the night. Casualties :- 4 O.R. Reinforcements.	
	20th.		Various parties proceeded to work collecting ammunition under the orders of the D.A..Q.M.G. Order received about 11 a.m. to cancel all parties and stand by. Another Warning Order received 6 p.m. stating that Brigade Group would move at about 9 p.m. Order confirmed and Battn. marched to NOYELLE VION arriving 3.30 a.m. Casualties :- 1 O.R. Sick.	

J. R. Sewill
Lieut Colonel
Commdg. 1/ Queens' Westminster Rifles

Army Form C. 2118.

WAR DIARY
or
INTELLIGENCE SUMMARY.
(Erase heading not required.)

Instructions regarding War Diaries and Intelligence Summaries are contained in F.S. Regs., Part II. and the Staff Manual respectively. Title pages will be prepared in manuscript.

Place	Date	Hour	Summary of Events and Information	Remarks and references to Appendices
In the Field	1918 Augt. 21st		Commanding Officers' Conference at Brigade H.Q. 2.30 p.m. B.G.C. indicated training to be carried out while in the Area including co-operation with Tanks. 4 p.m. Order received that Brigade Group would move in the evening. Battn. moved at 9.15 p.m. to BAVINCOURT arriving at midnight. Casualties :- 3 O.R. Sick, 1 Offr., 2nd Lt. W.H. GRAHAM, and 5 O.R. Other Causes 5 O.R. Reinforcements.	
	22nd.		Commanding Officers' Conference at Brigade H.Q. in morning reference forthcoming operations. Nucleus and Surplus Personnel despatched. Packs and baggage dumped. Casualties :- 4 O.R. Sick.	
	23rd.		Bathed. Proceeded at 6.45 p.m. to BAILLEULVAL arriving 9 p.m. The road was blocked the whole way by Cavalry and Artillery. No traffic orders were apparently being obeyed and the Battalion was much delayed. Casualties :- 2 O.R. Sick, 8 O.R. Reinforcements.	

P R Smith
Lieut Colonel
Commdg. 1/Queens' Westminster Rifles

Army Form C. 2118.

WAR DIARY
or
INTELLIGENCE SUMMARY.
(Erase heading not required.)

Instructions regarding War Diaries and Intelligence Summaries are contained in F. S. Regs., Part II. and the Staff Manual respectively. Title pages will be prepared in manuscript.

Place	Date	Hour	Summary of Events and Information	Remarks and references to Appendices
In the Field	1918 Augt. 24th		Order received in the middle of the night to move. Battalion moved at 4.42 a.m. Roads practically completely blocked. Arrived at BLAIREVILLE 7 a.m. Drew battle equipment, water bottles, ammunition and rations. Proceeded at 1.30 p.m. to BOISLEUX AU MONT arriving at 2.30 p.m. when dinners were served. Proceeded at 5.45 p.m. to BOYELLES Reserve Trench arriving at 7.30 p.m. Unable to find out dispositions of any troops in front, where our front line ran or whether we were under observation. Heavy Shelling with Gas and H.E. during the night. Casualties 1 O.R. Killed, 1 O.R. Sick, 1 O.R. other Causes.	
	25th.		Found 8th MIDDLESEX and discovered that out troops held LEGER RESERVE W. of CROISILLES as a Front Line, whereas we had believed our troops to hold that Village. Warning Order received for probable attack on CROISILLES. Details provisionally arranged and reconnaissance made by Commanding Officer, Coy Commanders, and as many officers as possible. All men instructed in use of German Stick Grenades of which many were lying about. Casual Gas and H.E. Shelling. Casualties :- 10 O.R. Wounded.	
	26th.		Warning Order to relieve 8th MIDDLESEX in Front of CROISILLES at dusk received noon. Order received at 6 p.m. to at once take over roughly from 8th MIDDLESEX and pass right forward to "Mop up" CROISILLES for the London Rifle Brigade. Officers out reconnoitring and men drawing rations and water. Coys moved up as early as possible and were met by M.G. fire crossing the ridge behind our Front Line. Verbal Order received not to wait for L.R.B. but push on. "D" and "C" Coys advanced with 2 Platoons each in Front Line. All Platoons found wire impenetrable and CROISILLES Trench thickly held by M.Gs. They tried all night to get forward but without success. Before dawn established a Front Line back in CROISILLES Trench with Outposts in front.	
			Casualties :- 23 O.R. Wounded, 6 O.R. Sick.	

J. R. Smith
Lieut Colonel
Comnm'g 1 Queens Westminster Rifles

WAR DIARY
or
INTELLIGENCE SUMMARY.
(Erase heading not required.)

Army Form C. 2118.

Place	Date	Hour	Summary of Events and Information	Remarks and references to Appendices
In the Field	1918. Augt.27th	J.R.S	GUARDS Division attacked on our immediate right from LEGER Trench. Stopped by M.G. fire and driven back beyond their jumping off trench, leaving a big gap on our right. ~~Troops were relieved~~ Capt. F.E. WHITBY, M.C. and Lieut. CALKIN, our Coy Commanders in the Front Line. ~~Two officers~~ filled the gap partly with ~~troops~~ men from the GUARDS Divn., and partly by moving up their own Support Platoons. Order received 4 p.m. that Battn. would be relieved by LONDON SCOTTISH. LONDON SCOTTISH arrived and commenced taking over. Commanding Officer proceeded to Brigade H.Q. T.4.b. to take orders for next day. In middle of relief LONDON SCOTTISH relief cancelled and 8th MIDDLESEX sent up instead. Coys proceeded to T.4.b. where rations and water were drawn. Orders received to concentrate in T.6 d. Casualties :- 3 O.R. Killed, 2 offrs., 2nd Lt. O.M.POWER and Lieut. F.W. RUSSELL, and 17 O.R. Wounded, 8 O.R. Sick, 1 O.R. other Causes.	
	28th.		On arrival Coy Commanders' Conference and orders issued to proceed at 8.30 a.m. to assemble for attack at 12.30 p.m. with objectives :- First QUEEN LANE - JOVE LANE, Second :- TANK AVENUE and TANK SUPPORT. Battn. assembled as ordered with exception of "B" Coy whose assembly trench was already occupied by 9th KINGS (LIVERPOOL) Regt. 57th Divn. "B" Coy assembled in NELLIE AVENUE and BURG SUPPORT with orders to swing round at right angles to HINDENBURGH SYSTEM when jumping off. Great difficulty was experienced in moving up to assembly Area as the trenches were packed with troops. All ranks arrived dead beat after being on the move all night. The Battn. had practically been without an unbroken night's sleep since 12th inst., and had moved nearly every 24 hours during that period - generally by night. Assembly positions :- Right Coy ("A") NELLIE AVENUE (South) and BURG SUPPORT. Left Coy ("B") do. (North) Support Coy ("C") JANET LANE (South) Reserve Coy ("D") do. (North) Battn. H.Q. Junction of JANET RESERVE and BURG SUPPORT.	

J.R. Smith
Lieut Colonel
Commdg. 1/ Queens' Westminster Rifles

Army Form C. 2118.

WAR DIARY
or
INTELLIGENCE SUMMARY.
(Erase heading not required.)

Instructions regarding War Diaries and Intelligence Summaries are contained in F.S. Regs., Part II. and the Staff Manual respectively. Title pages will be prepared in manuscript.

Place	Date	Hour	Summary of Events and Information	Remarks and references to Appendices
In the Field	1918. Augt.28th		Contd :-	
			When our barrage lifted at ZERO all Companies left their trenches with dash.	
			Hostile M.Gs opened at once very heavily from GUARDIAN RESERVE and high ground U.13.d., U.19 & U.20, and casualties were very heavy.	
			"A" and "B" Coys found the wire between the trenches of the HINDENBURGH SYSTEM impenetrable; and the hostile M.Gs from the right, and the fact that the Artillery barrage was short on the right drove them over to the left.	
			"C" Coy lost 80% of its men and all its Officers straggling through the wire in front of their jumping off trench.	
			"D" Coy followed "A" and "B".	
			Battn. H.Q., owing to rising ground just in front of its assembly position, was not aware to what extent the attack had swung to the left although it was realised the tendency had been for one to move over in that direction.	
			Battn. H.Q. moved as previously arranged down BURG SUPPORT endeavouring to get in touch with the leading Coys.	
			After advancing 500 yds Battn. H.Q. was held up by hostile M.Gs from the KNUCKLE and the right flank. Enemy were encountered immediately ahead in BURG SUPPORT and bombing was in progress in TUNNEL Trench on the left, and known in Stafford St. Trench.	
			Messages were sent back that the System was not mopped up and help was asked for in order to push on and gain touch with the Leading Coys. This help was a long time in coming and Battn.H.Q. advanced as far as junction of LUMP LANE and BURG SUPPORT.	
			The L.R.B. Coys were all already committed - 2 on right flank round GUARDIAN RESERVE and neighbourhood and 2 had gone forward with our Coys.	
			2nd LONDON REGT (very weak) was bombing up TUNNEL Trench with its Battn. H.Q..	
			Finally 3 Platoons of 4th LONDON arrived and were sent up BURG SUPPORT. They made little progress and later came back and reported they could not drive back the enemy.	
			They were again sent up with instructions to move up and along KNUCKLE Trench. Meanwhile Coys of L.R.B. and KENSINGTONS had taken GUARDIAN RESERVE and held STRAY RESERVE up to STRAFFORD AVENUE. They had also rounded up a Machine Gun nest which had caused much trouble from the Right.	
			During this time "A" "B" and "D" Coys had gone right forward though off their objectives. Several Officers realising their direction was wrong were killed and wounded in trying to alter it.	
			These Companies arrived at HENDECOURT which on account of a very marked similarity in roads and trenches they mistook for BULLECOURT.	

J.R. Savill
Lieut. Colonel
Comndg. 1/ Queens' Westminster Rifles

Army Form C. 2118.

WAR DIARY
or
INTELLIGENCE SUMMARY.
(Erase heading not required.)

Place	Date	Hour	Summary of Events and Information	Remarks and references to Appendices
In the Field	1918 Augt. 28th	Contd	:- The only officers left, Capt. F.E. WHITBY, M.C., Lieut. C.R. JACOMB, and 2nd Lt. J.A.N. WEBB took forward all men of Q.W.R. *(crossed out)* to a line running U.17.a.6.2., U.17.a.6.6., U.11.d.O.O. This party was all in touch but had no touch on the flanks and were a long way in advance of 57th Divn. whose whereabouts were not known. They remained here from 2.15 p.m. to about 5.30 p.m. They were shot at from all sides and from the rear by M.Gs and Snipers and in front by a Field Gun with open sights. Capt. F.E. WHITBY, M.C. became a casualty but carried on. The party was now very weak and was gradually being annihilated. It was decided to gradually withdraw until touch could be found with other troops. The retirement was carried out very gradually indeed to CEMETERY AVENUE. Lieut. C.R. JACOMB (Capt. F.E. WHITBY, M.C.) had by this time gone to the rear) re-organised all troops in the trench holding a front on either side of the Sunken Road in U.10.d. L.R.B. on the right, Kings (Liverpool) in the Centre and Q.W.R. on the left with some small posts of the S. LANCS. REGT. on their left and Posts out on the Railway in front. Sergt. GILLETT E.W. with a small party established a protective right flank in trench running back to USHER TRENCH. *(incomplete)* Capt. F.E. WHITBY, M.C. reported to Brigade H.Q. on his way down that his party were in PELICAN Trench. During the night orders were received from Brigade that L.R.B. would assemble in PELICAN Trench, Q.W.R. in BORDERER LANE, GOG and MAGOG (Support to L.R.B.), 2nd LONDONS to mop for L.R.B. OBJECTIVE :- Trench Angle U.29.d.7.8. - RIPON LANE - SELBY LANE - unnamed trench to STAR FISH Trench and along this trench to N.23.d.9.3. ZERO at 1 p.m. At 12 midnight Sergt. BERRY W.R. was sent back by Lieut. C.R. JACOMB with a message stating that he had now ascertained that he was in front of HENDECOURT instead of BULLECOURT, and asking for orders and rations. Casualties :- 3 officers, Lieut. L.P. HARROW, D.C.M., 2nd. Lt. J.C. GOADBY, 2nd Lt. C.G. WARREN Killed, and 37 O.R. Killed. 8 Offrs. Capt. F.E. WHITBY, M.C. Lieut. R.R. CALKIN, Lieut. A.J. PHILIP, 2nd Lt. W. FRIEND, 2nd Lt. T.W. PROCTER, 2nd Lt. A.H. CHAPLIN, 2nd. Lt. B. WADE, 2nd. Lt. W.E. TODD and 99 O.R. Wounded. 17 O.R. Wounded and Missing, 6 O.R. Sick.	

J.R. Paris
Lieut Colonel
Commdg 1/Queens Westminster Rifles

WAR DIARY
or
INTELLIGENCE SUMMARY.

(Erase heading not required.)

Army Form C. 2118.

Place	Date	Hour	Summary of Events and Information	Remarks and references to Appendices
In the Field	1918 Augt. 29th		Sergt. BERRY W.R. arrived at Battn. H.Q. at 5.30 a.m.. The Commanding Officer was then making a reconnaissance to find out the dispositions of the enemy as his reconnaissance the previous evening had located the enemy in front of the line of KNUCKLE AVENUE, and it was not understood how the Battn. could assemble as ordered. It was found that the enemy had gone back from where he was encountered the previous evening. The 4th LONDONS however had not pushed on and they were told to do so by him at once. One Coy in TUNNEL was put in touch with another Coy in BURG SUPPORT and they were advised to work in conjunction with each other. On the Commanding Officer's return he was ordered by Brigade to fetch Lieut. C.R. JACOMB's party to the assembly area via TRIDENT ALLEY. Sergt. BERRY W.R. was sent with these instructions. Meanwhile Lieut. C.R. JACOMB met Capt. MEARNS, South LANCS REGT., who as Senior officer in the trench ordered the whole party to the rear as their trench was to be the jumping off trench for fresh troops assaulting that morning. Lieut. C.R. JACOMB withdrew as ordered and on his way down met Sergt. BERRY in CRUX Trench. It was too late for him now to move down TRIDENT ALLEY, and he accordingly continued down FAG. His men were dead tired with a great hunger and thirst. He accordingly gave them a short rest and issued rations and water. Meanwhile the remainder of the Battn. (H.Q. and a few details) assembled as ordered. Lieut. C.R. JACOMB's party were blocked by troops of 168th Infantry Brigade and was unable to arrive by Zero hour. The available men of the Battn. (Lieut. GATFIELD, 2nd Lt. POLLARD and 40 O.R.) went over as the SUPPORT COY to the only 2 available Coys of the L.R.B. For 500 yards the advance proceeded rapidly, when it slowed down from the Northern outskirts of BULLECOURT Northwards. The LONDON SCOTTISH on our right swung right into BULLECOURT leaving the L.R.B. in one line with Q.W.R. 50 yds in rear. The L.R.B. were held up at Saddle Trench by M.Gs and Snipers from U.22.d. From the start the Brigade had no touch with the left and Lieut. W.H. GATFIELD lead his party up to the left of the L.R.B. but was still unable to gain touch. Lewis Guns engaged the hostile M.Gs which were too strong and the Lewis Gunners suffered heavily.	

J.R. Savile
Lieut Colonel
Commdg 17 Queens Westminster Rifles

WAR DIARY
or
INTELLIGENCE SUMMARY.
(Erase heading not required.)

Army Form C. 2118.

Place	Date	Hour	Summary of Events and Information	Remarks and references to Appendices
In the Field	1918 Augt. 29th		Contd:-	
			The Reserve Coy LONDON SCOTTISH came up and Lieut. W.H. GATFIELD asked them to extend our left flank. This they were unable to do as their orders were to keep touch with their other Coys. Lieut. W.H. GATFIELD ordered an L.R.B. officer whom he then found, to extend Northwards from Saddler Lane towards Sap Head U.22.b.0.1. and to send a patrol along that Sap to get in touch with 57th Division.	
			LONDON SCOTTISH then occupied SADDLER TRENCH and Lieut. W.H. GATFIELD instructed the L.R.B. Officer to establish a Post along Trench leading to BUNNY HUG, and withdrew his own Platoon to immediate Support at U.23.c.3.5.	
			Lieut. W.H. GATFIELD then went to 2nd LONDONS who were in rear and instructed the officer i/c to establish various Posts in front. These Posts coincided very nearly to positions ordered to be occupied by Brigade later on.	
			Lieut. W.H. GATFIELD then found a M.G. officer and arranged with him to cover the left flank. Battn. H.Q. was persistently shelled in the afternoon by a British 6" How.	
			Casualties :- 2 O.R. Killed, 111 O.R. Wounded, 2 O.R. Died of Wounds, 3 O.R. Sick.	
	30th		Just before dawn the Brigade was relieved by 7th MIDDLESEX. Lieut. W.H. GATFIELD'S party returned through a very heavy barrage of Gas and H.E.	
			The Battn. moved back to LINCOLN RESERVE.	
			A roll call showed about 200 men present; our wastage from casualties and other causes since 24th inst being about 400 men.	
			Casualties :- 1 O.R. Killed, 1 O.R. Wounded, 2 O.R. Died of Wounds, 5 O.R. Sick.	

J R Sewill
Lieut Colonel
Commdg. 1/ Queens' Westminster Rifles

Army Form C. 2118.

WAR DIARY
or
INTELLIGENCE SUMMARY.

(Erase heading not required.)

Instructions regarding War Diaries and Intelligence Summaries are contained in F. S. Regs., Part II. and the Staff Manual respectively. Title pages will be prepared in manuscript.

Place	Date	Hour	Summary of Events and Information	Remarks and references to Appendices
In the Field	1918 Augt.31st		Battn. moved back to DINGO Trench BOISLEUX AU MONT at 1 p.m.	
			Casualties :- 1 O.R. Died of Wounds, 1 O.R. Sick.	
			Officers. O.R.	
			Strength on 31st July 1918 41 957	
			Add :- 1 47	
			42 1004	
			Less 15 427	
			Strength on 31st August 1918 27 577	
			P. R. Savill	
			Lieut-Colonel,	
			Commanding, 1st Queens Westminster Rifles.	

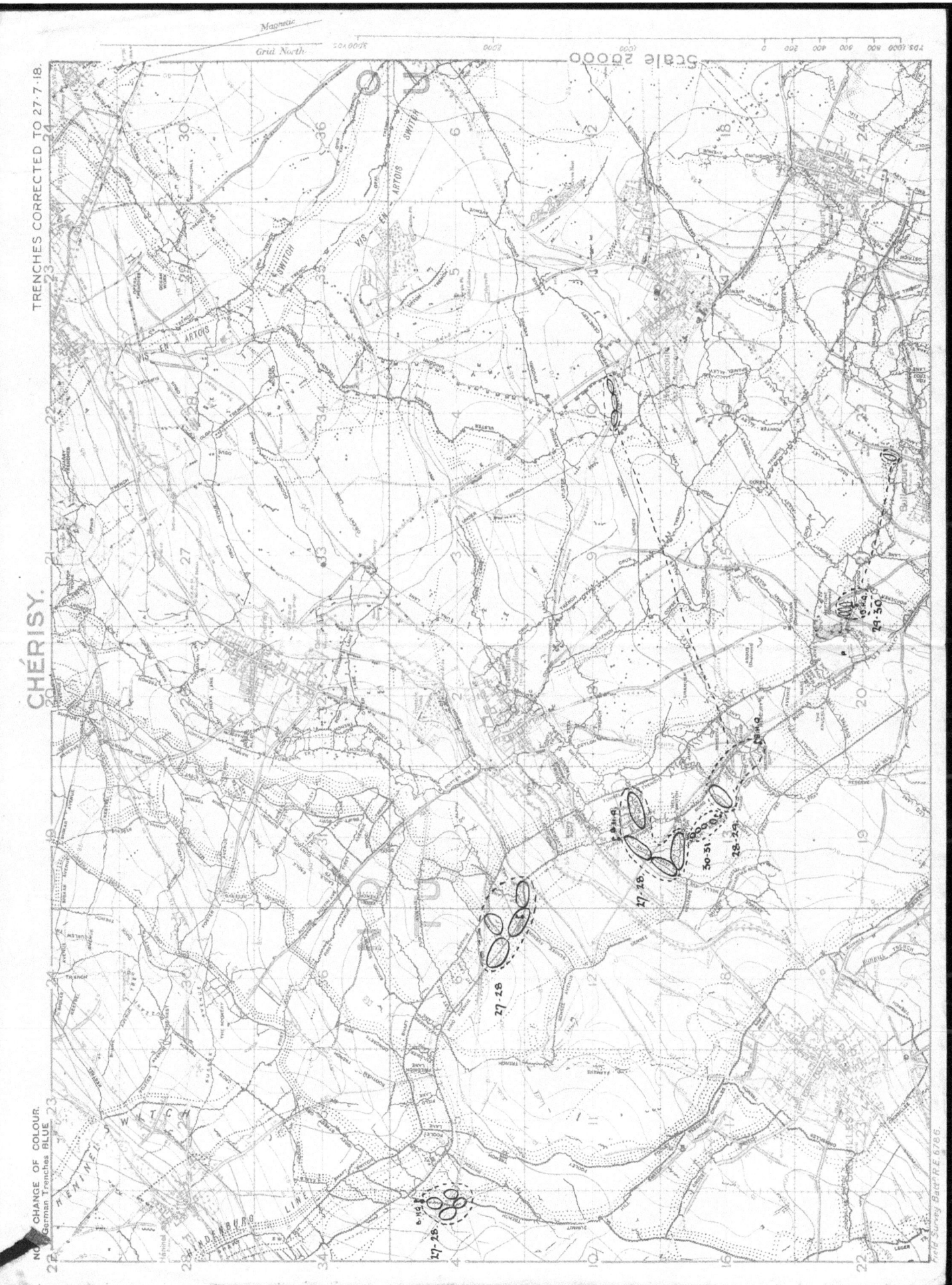

Reference Sketch on back.

To

1. My {Platoon / Company} has reached
   (Mark position on map or give map reference).
   and is consolidating.
      has consolidated.
      is ready to advance.

2. I am (not) in touch with   on right
       and (not) with   on left.

3. I am held up at   {by wire. / by M.G. fire. / by rifle fire.}

4. Enemy's artillery is firing on
                   from

5. I have sent forward patrols to

6. I estimate {my casualties at / my strength at}

7. I need   boxes S.A.A.
             Lewis gun drums
             Bombs
             Rifle Grenades
             Stokes Shells   (at once)
             Very Lights
             Ground Flares   (to-night)
             Stakes
             Coils wire
             Tins water
             Rations

8. I intend to

9. (General remarks on position and strength of enemy. Number of prisoners taken and identifications, if known).

Time   Name   Rank

Date   Platoon   Coy

                       Battalion

Strike out all that is not applicable and forward at once to Bn. H.Q.

(6392) Wt. W6192/P875 1,500,000 4/18 McA & W Ltd (E 2815) Forms W3091/4. Army Form W.3091.

Cover for Documents.

169/56

Confidential
_____
Nature of Enclosures.

War Diary
_____

1/16 London Regiment (QWR)

for month of

September 1918

_____
Notes, or Letters written.

Army Form C. 2118.

WAR DIARY
or
INTELLIGENCE SUMMARY.
(Erase heading not required.)

Instructions regarding War Diaries and Intelligence Summaries are contained in F. S. Regs., Part II. and the Staff Manual respectively. Title pages will be prepared in manuscript.

Place	Date	Hour	Summary of Events and Information	Remarks and references to Appendices
In the Field.	1/9/18.		Writing official account of recent fighting. Checking casualties and strengths. Bathed. Nucleus and Surplus rejoined. Casualties:- 1 O.R. Sick. 13 O.Rs. Reinforcements.	
	2/9/18.		Cleaning up. Commanding Officer addressed Battalion and passed comments made by G.O.C. and B.G.C. Casualties:- 1 O.R. Sick.	
	3/9/18.		Church Service arranged but washed out owing to weather. Casualties:- 3 O.Rs. Sick. 3 O.Rs. Reinforcements.	
	4/9/18.		Collecting Salvage. Lewis Gun instruction. Only able to man 7 Lewis Guns in the Battalion. Casualties:- 2 O.Rs. Sick. 1 Officer. Other Causes. Lieut. G. Chilton. to Bde. Int. Officer. 4 O.Rs. Reinforcements.	
	5/9/18.		Left Camp. 9-45.a.m. to relieve 52nd Division. Nucleus fallen out and baggage dumped. Arrived between BULLECOURT and HENDECOURT 1.10 p.m. Informed personally by Divisional Commander that relief was washed out. Ordered to have dinners and return to Camp. Started back 2.30p.m. arriving in Camp 6 p.m. Many men had new boots, heat and dust intense, frequent halts all day owing to congested traffic. Men all very tired. Nucleus rejoined. Casualties:- 4 O.Rs. Sick. 3 O.Rs. Reinforcements.	
	6/9/18.		Notified at 10 a.m. that Corps Commander wouldinspect Battalion at 11a.m. Corps Commander said "Goodbye" to Battalion, expressing appreciation of its work while in his Corps. Casualties:- 1 O.R. Sick. 1 Officer. 2nd Lt. G.W. AVENS, MM. AccdtL. Injury.	
	7/9/18.		Left Camp 4-25p.m. arrived in Reserve Brigade Area of 1st Division Front B.17,d. (Vigen-Artois) at 8.30 p.m. Reconnaisance of new Area by Commanding Officer. Casualties:- 2 O.Rs. Sick.	
	8/9/18.		Proceeded at 2.30 p.m. to take over from 1st Loyal North Lancs. (Brigade Reserve) in right Sector. Relief complete 4-15 p.m. Heavy rain on arrival and very little shelter for Other Ranks. Casualties. 1 O.R. Wounded. 4 O.Rs. Sick.	
	9/9/18.		Making accommodation, cleaning area and collecting salvage. Lewis Gun instruction for whole Battalion less Headquarters. Brigade boundary altered at Mid-day. New accommodation commenced within new boundaries. Casualties. 2 O.Rs. Sick.	

J.R. Sarill
Lieut Colonel.
Commanding 1st Battalion QUEEN'S WESTMINSTER RIFLES.

Army Form C. 2118.

WAR DIARY
or
INTELLIGENCE SUMMARY.
(Erase heading not required.)

Instructions regarding War Diaries and Intelligence Summaries are contained in F. S. Regs. Part II. and the Staff Manual respectively. Title pages will be prepared in manuscript.

Place	Date	Hour	Summary of Events and Information	Remarks and references to Appendices
In the Field.	10/9/18.		Cleaning up. Salvage. Burying and collecting dead men and horses. Lewis Gun Instruction. Casualties:- 2 O.Rs. Sick. 5 O.Rs. Other Causes. 23 O.Rs. Reinforcements.	
	11/9/18.		As on 10th. "A" and "B" Companies worked at night for Line Battalion. Casualties:- 1 O.R. Sick. 1 Officer. 2nd Lt. R.S. JACKSON to Town Major, Arras. 1 O.R. Reinforcement.	
	12/9/18.		-do- -do-	
	13/9/18.		Casualties. 2 O.Rs. Wounded. 1 O.R. Sick. "A","C", and "D" Companies worked under Line Battalion at night. Lewis Gun Instruction and salvage by day. Casualties. 1 O.R. Sick.	
	14/9/18.		"B" "C" and "D" Companies worked under Line Battalion. Casualties. 2 O.Rs. Wounded. 1 O.R. Sick. All available working under Brigade orders.	
	15/9/18.		Casualties:- 5 O.Rs. Sick. 1 O.R. Other Causes. 5 Officer Reinforcements. Capt. F.E. WHITBY, MC. 2nd Lt. H.F. SIMONDS. Lieut. J.H. WESTMORELAND. 2nd Lt. P.T. WORTHINGTON. 2nd Lt. H.J.D. TALLING.	
	16/9/18.		Relieved 2nd London Regiment in the Line. Relief Complete 11.30p.m. Thunderstorm and heavy rain. Bivouacs swamped. Casualties. 1 O.R. Sick.	
	17/9/18.		Fairly quiet day. Heavy shelling at night. Casualties:- 1 O.R. Killed. 2 O.Rs. Wounded. 2nd Lt. G.W. AVENS, MM. 1 Officer Reinforcements. 2nd Lt. G.H. LAMBERT. to England.	
	18/9/18.		Quiet day. Relieved by 1/7th Middlesex Regt. Returned to area around GUEMAPPE. Casualties. - 2 O.Rs. Killed. 5 O.Rs. Wounded. 1 O.R. Sick.	
	19/9/18.		Accommodated round old trenches. Inadequate accommodation for Other Ranks. Nucleus rejoined. Casualties:- 6 O.Rs. Sick. 32 O.Rs. Reinforcements.	
	20/9/18.		Baths allotted for morning. First two parties on arrival found baths not working and returned unwashed. Moved to Area. S.E. of VIS-en-ARTOIS. Casualties. 1 O.R. Sick. 1 O.R. Reinforcement.	
	21/9/18.		Platoon Commanders instructed in No. 23 Rifle Grenade. Platoon Commanders then instructed their Platoons. Casualties:- 2 O.Rs. Sick.	

Commdg. 1st /4th R. Lieut Colonel.

Army Form C. 2118.

WAR DIARY
or
INTELLIGENCE SUMMARY.

(Erase heading not required.)

Instructions regarding War Diaries and Intelligence Summaries are contained in F. S. Regs., Part II. and the Staff Manual respectively. Title pages will be prepared in manuscript.

Place	Date	Hour	Summary of Events and Information	Remarks and references to Appendices
In the Field.	22/9/18.		Church Parades. Newly arrived officers instructed in their duties. Rifle Grenade and Lewis Gun Training in afternoon. "A" Company, bathed. 8 Officer Reinforcements. T/Capt. W.C.M. MACRAE. 2nd Lt. F.H.B. MOORE. 2nd. Lt. A.A.W. RITCHINGS, MM. 2nd Lt. I.P. McEWAN. 2nd Lt. E. GOAKER. Lieut. J.B. MALTHOUSE. Lieut. J.A.A. SCOTT. 2nd Lt. G. DELAFORGE. Casualties. 1 O.R. Sick.	
	23/9/18.		Rifle Grenade and Lewis Gun training and Platoon Exercises. 1 Coy. work under Brigade. Casualties. 1 O.R. Other Causes.	
	24/9/18.		As for 23rd. Casualties. 7 O.Rs. Sick. 46 O.Rs. Reinforcements.	
	25/9/18.		As for 23rd. Casualties. 8 O.Rs. Sick.	

J.R. Sawny
Lieut Colonel.
Commanding 1st Battalion. QUEEN'S WESTMINSTER RIFLES.

Army Form C. 2118.

WAR DIARY
or
INTELLIGENCE SUMMARY.
(Erase heading not required.)

Instructions regarding War Diaries and Intelligence Summaries are contained in F. S. Regs., Part II. and the Staff Manual respectively. Title pages will be prepared in manuscript.

Place	Date	Hour	Summary of Events and Information	Remarks and references to Appendices
In the Field.	26/9/18.		Ref. Map Sheet. 51 B. S.E. and Order No. 73. Parts 1 and 11. Preparations for offensive operations. Moved forward to V.5.c. arriving at 9.30 p.m. Heavy rain during night. Fighting strength of Battalion. 15 Officers 318 O.Rs. Casualties. 1 O.R. Sick.	
	27/9/18.		Tea and porridge arrived oh Cooker fore-limbers at 3 a.m.. Rum issued. 5-20 a.m. CANADIAN CORPS attacked from SAINS-LEZ-MARQUION to ARRAS-CAMBRAI Road both inclusive. Fine morning. Men soon dry after wet night and very cheerful. 10-20 a.m. Moved forward to W.8.a. arriving at 11.15 a.m. The only casualties so far were caused by a shell which fell among "D" Company killing 1 man and wounding Sergt. TOOVEY (the Acting Company Sergeant Major) and 2 O.Rs. The Commanding Officer went forward to W.8.d.3-8- where he got in touch with O.C. 2nd LONDON Regt, Brigade Major and R.E. Officer detailed to prepare a crossing for the Battalion over the CANAL-du-NORD. Lieut. J.R. PLUNKETT who went forward to reconnoitre this crossing was wounded with his runner. 2nd Lt. A.E. CLAPHAM (attached 169th Infantry Brigade H.Q.) went forward in his place and reported that the R.E. were unable to approach the crossing owing to Machine Gun fire from the enemy who had not been cleared by the CANADIAN CORPS. At 1.10 p.m. information was received from Brigade that the crossing was clear. The Battalion moved forward (two companies) guided by 2 R.E. Officers and crossed the CANAL in single file by a path over the lock bridge at W.9.b.8-7- 2 Companies crossed 200 yards further South. The crossing which was held by a post of L.R.B. was under desultory Machine Gun fire from the enemy still in MARQUION and from the North. Hostile shelling was not very heavy and the Battalion was across the CANAL by 2 p.m. The Companies deployed on E, side of CANAL and formed up as laid down in Order No. 73, touch being gained with L.R.B. on the right. The Platoon of "C" Company on West of CANAL was unable to find 1st Battn. KENSINGTONS until 4 p.m. but advanced in line with "A" Company. Information was received that ZERO was postponed until 3.28 p.m. The CANADIAN troops (whom the Battalion was supposed to relieve at the jumping off line)	

J.R. Small
Lieut Colonel.
Commanding 1st. Battalion QUEEN'S WESTMINSTER RIFLES.

Army Form C. 2118.

WAR DIARY
or
INTELLIGENCE SUMMARY.
(Erase heading not required.)

Instructions regarding War Diaries and Intelligence Summaries are contained in F. S. Regs., Part II. and the Staff Manual respectively. Title pages will be prepared in manuscript.

Place	Date	Hour	Summary of Events and Information	Remarks and references to Appendices
In the Field.	27/9/18. Contd.		were not seen. The enemy occupied a line running E. and W. through Railway Bridge Q.4.c.3.-6- and opened fire with Machine Guns. The leading Companies had therefore to fight their way forward to their jumping off line unassisted by a barrage. This they did, "D" Company pushing forward and outflanking Machine Guns which were delaying the advance of "A" Company, on left. These Machine Guns were rushed and rounded up with about 30 prisoners. 1 Platoon of "A" Company on WEST bank of CANAL cleared several small groups. The leading Companies pressing back any hostile opposition reached the jumping off line in time to advance with our barrage. About 50 prisoners were taken before arrival on this line. From this point to the edge of SAUCHY CAUCHY the advance was uniformly successful. Our barrage was excellent and the troops kept well up to it. Such hostile shelling as there was fell in rear of our Companies. There was a moderate amount of Machine Gun fire but the shooting was poor. The enemy was mostly found in small trenches in the woods and along the tow-path of the CANAL. As our troops rushed each locality under the barrage, enture groups of Germans came out with their hands up. A large number of prisoners was made in two dugouts near the Cemetery Q.34.b.5.5. As our Platoons were of an average strength of 11 O.Rs., escorts could not be spared and the prisoners made their way to the rear at the greatest possible speed asking Officers they met if an escort could be provided. 2nd Lt. PRINCE, 9th LONDON attached,was killed by a Machine Gun while leading his Platoon from the jumping off line. CAPE WOOD was reached at 4.10 p.m. and the outskirts of the Village at 4.20 p.m. immediately South of SAUCHY CAUCHY at 5.40 p.m. Pear shaped Wood With the very weak strength of Companies it would have been difficult to clear the Village had the enemy put up a more spirited resistance. Our troops gained the Northern edge of the Village by 4.40 p.m. with practically no casualties. At this point very heavy hostile Machine Gun fire was opened by enemy from	

P.T. Newell
Lieut-Colonel,
Commanding, 1st QUEENS WESTMINSTER RIFLES.

Army Form C. 2118.

WAR DIARY
or
INTELLIGENCE SUMMARY.
(Erase heading not required.)

Instructions regarding War Diaries and Intelligence Summaries are contained in F.S. Regs., Part II. and the Staff Manual respectively. Title pages will be prepared in manuscript.

Place	Date	Hour	Summary of Events and Information	Remarks and references to Appendices
In the field	27/9/18 Contd:-		CANAL bank about Q.28.d.9.1. and from direction Q.29.c.a d. 2nd Lt. C. SHEPPARD was killed. There were Germans in the houses East of River AOACHE between ourselves and 2nd LONDONS Enemy sniped from rear in houses Q.35.a.3.7. The KENSINGTONS on the left were unable to clear up WEST bank of the CANAL and pressed forward round the West of the Bank. The enemy commenced to shell the village with Heavies. The Commanding Officer and 4 Company Commanders were all together and it was therefore easy to deal with the situation rapidly. "D" Company was ordered to send a Platoon to the right to clear out the Germans between ourselves and the 2nd LONDONS at Q.29.c.5.0. This they did. "C" Coy was ordered to clear the houses along the road running NORTH from Q.35.a.3.4 This they did collecting over 50 prisoners. "B" Coy was ordered to send 2 Platoons up the bank of the River AOACHE and 2 Platoons to work along the EAST bank of the CANAL. The two former Platoons were held up by Machine Gun fire. "D" Coy were ordered to reinforce them. 2nd Lt. G.M. AVENS M.C. (Commanding "D" Coy) reinforced and with great dash lead his own Company and 2 Platoons of "B" Coy forward in single file with direct enfilade Machine Gun fire from both flanks. The whole party charged the Railway Embankment Q.25.c. and d. in single file cheering. Although the enemy was holding the CANAL for 1000 yards in rear of them, and Lt. AVENS' party completely terrorised those on and around the Embankment who outnumbered him by nearly 2 to 1 and who surrendered at once. Meanwhile 2 Platoons of "B" Coy and 1 Platoon "A" Coy were endeavouring to advance up the CANAL bank. T/Capt. V.G.M. MacRAE, A.S.C. attached, was killed whilst most gallantly leading his men to the assault of a Machine Gun nest. No further progress was possible on the left flank as the enemy was in strength along the WEST bank of CANAL and maintained heavy M.G. fire. "A" Coy was ordered to hold a part of Q.25.d.9.5. and to send a Platoon back to cross the	

A.R.Smith
Lieut-Colonel,
Commanding, 1st WITHS WESTMINSTER RIFLES.

Army Form C. 2118.

WAR DIARY
or
INTELLIGENCE SUMMARY.
(Erase heading not required.)

Instructions regarding War Diaries and Intelligence Summaries are contained in F. S. Regs., Part II. and the Staff Manual respectively. Title pages will be prepared in manuscript.

Place	Date	Hour	Summary of Events and Information	Remarks and references to Appendices
In the Field	27/9/18 Contd:-		CANAL and mop up WEST bank. "B" Coy was ordered to send 2 platoons up the AGACHE and push on to the outpost line through "D" Coy. On their way up they engaged enemy along the EAST bank of CANAL with Lewis Guns killing twelve. "C" Coy (less 1 Platoon on WEST of CANAL) was ordered to reinforce "D" Coy who were under heavy Machine Gun fire from CANAL and OISY-le-VERGER, and who were now considerably embarrassed by the number of their prisoners. 2nd LONDONS had been held up by Machine Guns at Q.30.a.5.3 and Q.30.c.8.6., and consequently our right flank on the Railway Embankment was exposed. By 9 p.m. the position was as follows :- The Railway Embankment Q.23.c. and d. was held by "C" Coy (on right) "D" Coy (on left) Touch was gained via bridge Q.29.a.4.8 with KENSINGTONS who had cleared WEST bank of CANAL up to that point. "B" Coy were endeavouring to advance to Sunken Road Q.23 a.c. and b. but were held up by heavy Machine Gun fire and shelling. "A" Coy were ordered to withdraw into Reserve at about Q.29.c.1.3. Later 2nd Lt. A.W. RITCHINGS M.M. of "B" Coy (15th LONDON attached) with 12 O.Rs. worked his way up the CANAL bank to rush a Machine Gun nest on either side of the bridge at Q.23.a.6.1. His party was discovered and fired on at point blank range. The Officer, who was gallantly leading his men and 6 O.Rs. were killed, 3 O.Rs. wounded out of the party of 12. As a result of the days fighting the Battalion has accounted for a number of Germans in Killed and prisoners equal to its own fighting strength. 5 7.7; have captured & claimed as Trophies Many Machine Guns were captured or destroyed. 15 have already been claimed as trophies of War. Many more were thrown into the CANAL and into Ponds by the enemy. "D" Coy while holding an exposed position threw 4 heavy Machine Guns into the Canal lest a counter-attack should again leave them in the enemy's hands. Receipts were obtained for 4 Officers 242 O.Rs. Prisoners of War. An estimated number of 100 went down without escorts as no men were available for this duty.	Claimed as Trophies

J R Smith
Lieut-Colonel,
Commanding 1st QUEEN'S WESTMINSTER RIFLES.

Army Form C. 2118.

WAR DIARY
or
INTELLIGENCE SUMMARY.
(Erase heading not required.)

Instructions regarding War Diaries and Intelligence Summaries are contained in F. S. Regs., Part II. and the Staff Manual respectively. Title pages will be prepared in manuscript.

Place	Date	Hour	Summary of Events and Information	Remarks and references to Appendices
In the Field	27/9/18. Contd:-		Casualties :- 4 Officers, 16 O.Rs. Killed, 1 Offr. 47 O.R. wounded, 3 O.R. Sick. Killed :- Capt. W.C.M. MacRAE, 2nd Lt. J.C.B. PRINCE, 2nd Lt. C. SHEPPARD, 2nd Lt. A.A.W. RITCHINGS M.M. Wounded :- Lieut. J.R. Plunkett.	
	28/9/18.		Ref. Order No. 74. Before dawn 2nd LONDONS joined up with "C" Coy on Railway Embankment. KENSINGTONS captured MILL COPSE. "B" Coy secured Road Q.23.a.7.6. - Q.2.a.2.8 capturing German asleep and recovering a. wounded man of 2nd Lt. A.A.W. RITCHINGS' party who had been carried in and bandaged by the enemy. One Coy of 2nd LONDONS advanced at 10.30 a.m. and established posts at Q.12.c.5.4. - Q.11.d.5.3. - Q.11.d.3.6 without opposition. They were not required and finally "B" Coy advanced immediately in rear of them. withdrew to bivouacs in CANAL Bank Q.23.a.7.1. Remainder of day spent in collecting British dead and War Trophies. Casualties :- NIL.	
	29/9/18.		In Brigade Reserve. Cleared away dead and Salvage. Buried all Officers and O.R. Killed in Action 27th.	
	30/9/10.		Continued clearing Area.	

J R Paul
Lieut-Colonel,
Commanding, 1st QUEENS WESTMINSTER RIFLES.

WAR DIARY
or
INTELLIGENCE SUMMARY.
(Erase heading not required.)

Army Form C. 2118.

Place	Date	Hour	Summary of Events and Information	Remarks and references to Appendices
In the Field.	Contd.			
			Strength on 31st August, 1918.	
			Offrs. O.Rs.	
			27 577	
			Add. 15 125	
			42 702	
			Less. 9 151	
			Strength on 30th Sept. 1918. 33 551	
			J.R.Smith *(sgd.)*	
			Lieut Colonel.	
			Commanding 1st Battalion QUEEN'S WESTMINSTER RIFLES.	

VERY
SECRET.   Copy No. 8

1st QUEEN'S WESTMINSTER RIFLES.

ORDER No. 73.

Part 1.

Ref. Sheet. 51.B. S.E.   24th September, 1918.

1. **INFORMATION.**

    (a) L.R.B. are taking over Front Line from 56th Divisional Southern Boundary to ARRAS-CAMBRAI Road on night 25/26th inst.

    (b) Canadian Corps is shortly resuming operations towards CAMBRAI.
It will attack on a front W.4.c. X. to W.26.c. and secure BLUE LINE.

    (c) 11th Division and 169th Infantry Brigade. When the BLUE LINE is secured 11th Division and 169th Inf. Bde. pass through, relieve the 1st Canadian Division in BLUE LINE and attack in northerly direction. Boundary shown on Company Commanders maps.

    (d) 168th Infantry Brigade. 168th Inf. Bde. Cooperates on left of 169th Inf. Bde. by clearing the enemy from the WEST of the CANAL du NORD from about W.4.c.0.5. to MILL COPSE inclusive, advancing from South to North and keeping pace with the left of the 169th Infantry Brigade.

    (e) 167th Infantry Brigade. 167th Infantry Brigade is to have a Company about Q.10.c. or Q.16.a. with a light T.M. and 2 Vickers Guns ready to push Patrols out towards PALLEUL and the CANAL, if ordered, with the object of securing the causeway in Q.10.d. and of joining hands with 169th Infantry Brigade in Q.17.c.

    (f) General Plan of 169th Infantry Brigade attack.
169th Infantry Brigade will consist of 2 distinct attacks.

    RIGHT ATTACK. To be carried out by 2nd LONDON REGT. supported by L.R.B. less 2 Companies.
    LEFT ATTACK. To be carried out by Q.W.R.
Boundaries of these attacks are as follows:-

    2nd LONDONS Right Boundary. - Cross Roads at W.6.c.8.4. (inclusive), along the easternmost of the two trenches East of RAMILLI COPSE, through Q.36 Central to crossing of Road and Trench at Q.36.b.2.5.

    2nd LONDONS Left Boundary. - The AGACHE RIVER from W.5.a.3.3. to Q.29.c.4.3.

    Q.W.R. Right Boundary. - The AGACHE RIVER from W.4.d.3.7. to Q.29.c.4.3.

    Q.W.R. Left Boundary. - CANAL dur NORD both banks inclusive.

    O.C. L.R.B. will detail 1 Company to connect up these attacks by advancing between the two branches of the AGACHE RIVER as far North as their junction Q.29.a.4.2. This Company in addition to clearing any centres of resistance which may be met with in its area, will assist in the capture of SAUCHY LESTREE by firing on any enemy seen in the Western end of the village and by preventing movement between SAUCHY CAUCHY and SAUCHY LESTREE.

P.T.O.

-2-

  (g). **T.M. BARRAGE.** is being arranged by 169th Infantry Brigade with objective CANAL du NORD from W.4.c.9.3. to Q.35.a.7.0.

  (h). **Task of 2nd LONDONS.** The task of the 2nd LONDONS will be:-

(a). To clear all trenches of the MARQUION LINE, RAMZI COPSE, and to search the houses along the road in W.6.c. and to follow the barrage closely through the Q.36.c. Cemetery, KIDUNA COPSE and CEMETERY WOOD.
The prompt arrival of these troops in CEMETERY WOOD will enable them to move to the attack of the eastern portion of SAUCHY CAUCHY and so assist the attack of the Q.W.R.

(b). To clear thoroughly the whole of SAUCHY LESTREE including the buildings along the road in Q.35.c., to clear CHIS WOOD and thence to operate northwards against the eastern portion of SAUCHY CAUCHY.

  L.R.B. less 2 Companies follow the 2nd LONDONS in order to assist them if necessary.

2. INSTRUCTIONS.
     Detailed instructions will be issued later.

3. ACKNOWLEDGE.

                H.S. PRICE.
                Capt & Adjt.
            1st QUEENS WESTMINSTER RIFLES.

DISTRIBUTION.
1. Commanding Officer.
2/5. O.C. Companies.
6. 169th Infantry Brigade.
7. Lieut. MALTHOUSE.
8.   Plunkett.
9. File.

SECRET.   Copy. No. 8

1st QUEENS WESTMINSTER RIFLES.

Instructions No. 1. in connection with forthcoming
operations.

Ref. Map. Sheet. 51. B. S.E.   25th September. 1918.

1. **MOVE.**
    The Battalion will probably move forward to an assembly
area on evening of 25th inst. with a view to operations on 26th.

2. **BATTLE AMMUNITION.**
    The following will be drawn by Companies
from R.S.M. at 12 noon tomorrow.

   Per man. (50 Rounds S.A.A.
             (2 Mills. Grenades. No. 23.
             (1 Red Ground Flare.

   Per   (4 Rifle Grenades. No. 23.
   Company. (50 Rounds Very Pistol Ammunition.

3. **BAGGAGE.**
    The following will be stacked on the track onear
Battalion H.Q. at 2 p.m. Site will be selected by Major. WHITMORE,
who will detail an adequate guard.

   PACKS.   VALISES.
   BIVOUAC SHEETS. (receipts to be obtained from
   Sergt. BOWDIDGE.).
   Fighting Stores not required in Action.
   (including all Discharger cups for No. 36 R.Gs.)
   All other Stores not required.
   QUARTERMASTER will arrange to remove later.

4. **BATTLE ORDER.**
    Will be worn. O.C. Companies will ensure that
men deficient of necessary kit are completed at the expense of
the Nucleus, - especially Iron Rations and clean pair Socks.

5. **NUCLEUS.**
    On departure of the Battalion the Nucleus will clean
their Company areas and report to Major. WHITMORE on completion.

6. **FIGHTING STORES.**
    O.C. Companies will decide the number of
fighting Stores required by them. Any deficiency on that number
will be reported to Orderly Room forthwith.

7. **STRAGGLERS.**
    Stragglers Posts will be established at W. 8.b. 6.1.

8. **PRISONERS OF WAR.**
    As Companies are weak as few men as possible
should be employed as escorts to Prisoners of War. Prisoners of
War should if possible be handed over to any Unit who will accept
them, receipts being obtained and forwarded to Orderly Room later.

9. **TRANSPORT.**
    (a). 1 Limber per Company and Headquarters
         containing Water, Rations and Lewis Gun
         Equipment will accompany Battalion.

TRANSPORT. (Contd).

      (b).   Hot Tea will be sent to Assembly Area (probably
           V.6.a. and C.) at 4.30 a.m. in the foreparts
           of the Cookers.

      A Transport N.C.O. will accompany Battalion in the evening to be shown a suitable place and to guide Cookers up later.

                                                H.S. PRICE.
                                                Capt & Adjt.
                             1st QUEENS WESTMINSTER RIFLES.

DISTRIBUTION.

1. Commanding Officer.
2/5. O.C. Companies.
6. Major Whitmore.
7. Quartermaster.
8. Lieut Plunkett. - H.Q. Details.
9. File.

SECRET.   Copy No. 12

1st QUEENS WESTMINSTER RIFLES.

Order No. 73.

Part II.

Ref. Map Sheet. 51.b. N.E.   26th September, 1918.

1. **MOVES.**

   (a). From present area to assembly area V.8.c.
   H.Q. march off at 7.30 p.m. today. Companies
   follow in order D. A. C. B.
   ROUTE. Cross Roads P.31.c.0.1. - Cross Roads
   P.32.a.3.4. - P.33.c.6.1. - thence by track
   through factory V.4.b.
   INTERVALS.   100 yards between Platoons.
   LIMBERS.   Limbers will report to Companies at
   7 p.m., load up and meet respective Coy. H.Q.
   at Cross Roads. P.31.c.
   PARADES.   Companies will not form up before
   7 p.m.

   (b). Move from Assembly area to BLUE LINE.
   H.Q. march off PROBABLY Zero plus 4 hours.
   Companies will follow in order D. A. C. B.
   INTERVALS.   100 yards between Platoons.
   ROUTE.   By track to POINT "K" - W.8.d.3.8.
   (marked by board) - Crossing over CANAL W.9.b.
   8.8. - jumping off area.

2. **CROSSING OVER CANAL.** A bridge is being constructed at W.9.b.8.8.
   by the R.E.
        Lieut J.R. PLUNKETT with 3 runners will ascertain from
   R.E. at ZERO plus 4½ hours the progress being made with its
   construction. He will hand a report written by the R.E. to the
   Brigade Major. at Point "K" and then return to the Battalion.
        L.R.B. are covering the crossing by

   (a). Working northwards to W.4.c.3.7. clearing the
        west bank of the CANAL.
   (b) Establishing posts at W.10.a.0.5., W.4.c.2.0.
        and near destroyed railway bridge W.4.c.3.0.

                                                    and assemble
3. **ASSEMBLY.** After crossing the canal Companies will deploy as
   follows relieving all CANADIAN TROOPS in the Battn Area.

   "D" Company on RIGHT   ) On a Two Platoon frontage
   "A"   "   on LEFT   ) on a line W.4.b.9.6. - W.4.a.7.9.

   "C" Company in close support (Southern portion W.4.a)

   "B" Company in reserve (Northern portion W. 4.c.)

   Battn H.Q. with Reserve Company.

   Assembly which will be completed by Zero plus 6 hours will be
   reported to Battn H.Q.

4. **ASSAULT.** Battalion will assault at Zero plus 9 hours under a
   creeping barrage which will advance at the rate of 100 yards in
   8 minutes.

5. **TASKS.**
   (a) FIRST PHASE.
   "D" Company Right Boundary - AGACHE RIVER as far as

- 2 -

POND Q.29.c.
LEFT BOUNDARY. (inclusive) W.4.b.0.8. - Q.34.b.7.0. -
thence along Railway to Q.33.c.0.0. - Q.29.c.2.5.

(b) "A" Company.
LEFT BOUNDARY. CANAL inclusive.

(c) "A" and "D" Companies will clear all WOODS within their
boundaries. "A" Company will also
  (i) Search the bed and both banks of CANAL.
  (ii) Clear CEMETERY Q.34.b.

(d) "C" Company will:-

  (i) Detail 1 Platoon to move along Western Side of WEST
  Bank of CANAL in close touch with "A" Company and 168
  Infantry Brigade. This Platoon will not cross CANAL
  with the Battalion.

  (ii) Move (less 1 Platoon) in close support of "A" and "D"
  Companies which he will assist on demand or on his own
  initiative.
  "B" Company will move in rear of "C" Company and act as
(e) directed by Battalion H.Q.

SECOND PHASE.
  (f) As soon as the leading Companies have advanced through SAUCHY
  CAUCHY, "D" Company will advance through them and occupy
  the line of the road from the CANAL at Q.23.a.6.1. (inclusive)
  - Q.23.central - Crossing of Road and Trench at Q.23.b.8.4.
  with Posts pushed forward to obtain observation, gaining
  touch with Units on the flanks.

  (g) "A" and "D" Companies will reform quickly and consolidate line
  Q.23.c.5.0. along Railway to Q.23.d.0.5. The only routes
  apparently open for these troops are along CANAL BANK and
  along bank of AGACHE RIVER.

  (h) "C" Company will reform and remain in Battalion Reserve near
  Farm Q.29.c.3.2.

6. REPORTS. To Battalion Headquarters, which will move along line of
Railway W.4.a.6.0. - Q.34.d.4.0. - Q.29.c.0.0.

7. ACKNOWLEDGE.

H.S. PRICE.
Capt & Adjt.
1st QUEENS WESTMINSTER RIFLES.

DISTRIBUTION.
(1) Commanding Officer.   (2) H.Q. 169th Inf.Bde.
(3) - (6) Companies.   (7) Transport Officer.
(8) Quartermaster.   (9) "A" ECHELON.
(10) Kensingtons.   (11) 2nd LONDONS.
(12) Lieut PLUNKETT.   (13) R.E.M.
         (14) File.

SECRET.   Copy. No. 9

1st QUEENS WESTMINSTER RIFLES.

Instructions No. 9 in connection with forthcoming
operations.

Ref. Map Sheet. 51.B. S.E.   26th September, 1918.

1. **BATTLE AMMUNITION.**
   Reference Instructions No. 1, Para. 2, the following will be carried:-

   All Other Ranks. 2 No. 23. R.G. and 1 Ground Flare.
   Other Ranks (except Lewis Gunners) 170 Rounds S.A.A.
   Lewis Gunners (except men armed with revolver) 100 rounds S.A.A.

   In addition Companies will each draw:-

   36 Smoke Grenades.

2. **BAGGAGE.**
   Reference Instructions No. 1 Para. 3. Baggage will be stacked at 6 p.m.

3. **EQUIPMENT (Officers).**
   Officers going into action will borrow Binoculars, Compasses and Maps from Nucleus Officers.
   Nucleus will hand over all maps, 51.b. S.E. and S.W. to Corps.

4. **APPROACHES TO BRIDGES.**
   Over Canal will be flagged by R.E. (YELLOW or and PURPLE).

5. **SITUATION REPORTS.**
   All ranks will be warned of the value of frequent reports, whether containing positive or negative information.

6. **PROTECTION (Flanks).**
   Should attack on right fall behind, objectives will still be taken and held. Battalion H.Q. will be at once informed if attack on flank fails and will be the ONLY authority for any necessary partial withdrawal.

7. **BARRAGE.**
   All ranks will be warned of danger of overtaking the barrage or getting too close in the village.

8. **TRANSPORT.**
   Limbers and Cooker foreparts will be unloaded at assembly area and despatched as quickly as possible.

9. **WATER.**
   (a) All ranks will leave present area with full Water bottles and refill them before leaving assembly area.
   (b) Petrol Tins taken up tonight will be dumped WITHOUT guard on departure tomorrow.

                                                    H.S. PRICE.
                                                    Capt & Adjt.
                                              1st QUEENS WESTMINSTER RIFLES.

DISTRIBUTION.

   Same as Instructions No. 1.

VERY SECRET   Copy No. 8

1st QUEENS WESTMINSTER RIFLES.

INSTRUCTIONS No. 3 in connection with forthcoming
operations.

Map Ref. Sheet 51 b.S.E.   26th September 1918

1. GAS PRECAUTIONS

A case has recently occurred in which the enemy used GREEN cross 1 shells to mask a YELLOW Cross bombardment.

As a result our men smelt only the GREEN Cross and knowing its lack of persistency did not take those precautions after the attack that they would have ordinarily done after a YELLOW Cross bombardment. The first indication of the presence of YELLOW Cross was the appearance of burns and a few eye casualties. Rigid precautions were then adopted and further casualties prevented.

All troops should be warned to expect such a mixture of gases and to suspect the presence of YELLOW Cross in concentrations of any nature.

2. SIGNAL ROCKETS

11th Division is arranging to fire Special signal rockets from W.7.c.8.7. as soon as information has been received by aeroplane or other means that the various lines have been captured.

A series of RED rockets will denote   RED Line captured

A series of GREEN   GREEN Line captured

A series of WHITE or YELLOW   BLUE Line captured

3. FLARES

Contact aeroplanes will call for flares at :-

ZERO plus 575 minutes and
ZERO plus 660 minutes

If enemy are seen moving forward for a counter attack, the observer fires a RED parachute flare over the area affected.

4. MOVES.

The hours of advancing from Assembly Areas are confirmed.

5. S.O.S. SIGNAL

The S.O.S.Signal will be a rifle grenade bursting into RED over RED over RED.

6. MEDICAL.

Regimental Aid Post will be :-
(a) (i)(When Battalion is at V.S.c.) at Factory P.34.d.
    (ii)(When Battn is forming up on BLUE Line) near road W.9.a.9.8.
    (iii)(Later in operations) Near Bridge Q.34.b.4.7.

(b) Casualties should be if possible be brought to the nearest point on the CANAL Bank in order to facilitate collection.

7. COMMUNICATIONS

(a) Signallers will not be attached to "A" & "D" Coys.
(b) A report centre will proceed with "C" Coy and endeavour to open visual communication with Battn H.Q.
    All messages will however also be sent to Battn H.Q. by Coy runners. This Report Centre will after capture of SAUCHY CAUCHY proceed with "A" Coy and establish itself at about Q.23.c.8.0.
(c) 4 Signallers will be attached to O.C."B" Coy.

8. AMENDMENTS

Ref. Order No. 73 Part 11 para 3
for ZERO plus 8 hours read, ZERO plus 8 hours and 28 minutes.
Ref Order No. 73 Part 11 para 4.
for ZERO plus 9 hours read, ZERO plus 9 hours and 28 minutes.
Ref. Instructions No. 8 para 4.
YELLOW Flags only will be used and not YELLOW or PURPLE as previously instructed.

Ref. Order No. 73 Part 11 para 4
after the barrage has passed CEMETERY WOOD and SAUCHY CAUCHY it will advance at the rate of 100 yards in every 4 minutes as stated on Map "C" as issued herewith.

9. ACKNOWLEDGE.

H.S.PRICE
Capt & Adjt.
1st QUEENS WESTMINSTER RIFLES.

DISTRIBUTION

1. Commanding Officer
2-5 O.C.Coys.
6. 169th Inf.Bde.
7. Lieut MALTHOUSE
8. "   PLUNKETT
9 File.

SECRET.

1st QUEENS WESTMINSTER RIFLES.

Addition to Instructions No. 3. of today.

SCREENING OF LIGHTS. O.C. Companies will forbid the lighting of any fires or the shewing of any light whatever whilst the Battalion is in the Assembly Area.

26.9.18.

H.S. PRICE.
Capt & Adjt.
1st QUEENS WESTMINSTER RIFLES.

Army Form W.3091.

Cover for Documents.

WAR DIARY

Nature of Enclosures.

Confidential

1/16th London Regiment (Q.W.R.)

for month of

OCTOBER 1918.

Notes, or Letters written.

WAR DIARY

In the Field.		
1918 Oct. 1st.		Clearing Area and Lewis Gun instruction. Total number of M.Gs. and T.Ms salved and claimed as War Trophies - 21 L.M.Gs - 11 H.M.Gs. and 6 T.Ms Casualties - 3 O.R. Sick.
	2nd.	Relieved London Rifle Brigade in Front Line (Right of Canal du Nord) Relief complete 21.30 hours, "D" "C" and "B" Outpost Coys "A" Coy in Reserve. Casualties : Lieut J.A.A. Scott Other Causes, 1 O.R. Reinforcement.
	3rd.	Quiet day. Casualties. Nil.
	4th.	Quiet day. Casualties : 3 O.R. Sick.
	5th.	Relieved by 7th MIDDLESEX REGT. Fair amount of shelling during relief. "B" Coy limber hit, 1 horse killed - Driver and 1 horse wounded. Relief complete 22.30 hours. Moved to area S.W. of RUMAUCOURT. Very poor accommodation Casualties: 20 O.R. Reinforcements.
	6th.	Pay parades, Kit Inspections. Casualties : 2 O.R. Sick, 1 O.R. Other Causes.
	7th.	All men bathed this day. Forty men collecting Salvage. Remainder training &c. Casualties 38 O.R. Reinforcements.
	8th.	Platoon training Casualties 3 O.R. Sick.
	9th.	Training. "Bow Bells" gave performance. Band played at "D" Coy H.Q. Casualties 25 O.R. Sick. Lieut. J.R. Plunkett and 1 O.R. Reinforcement.
	10th.	Commanding Officer reconnoitred new Sector, Coys did training as before. Troops attended performance of "Bow Bells" Casualties : 4 O.R. Sick, Lieut J.R. Plunkett, Other Causes, 5 O.R. Reinforcements.
	11th.	Battalion took over from LONDON SCOTTISH, the Left Sub-Sector of the Right Brigade. RAUMAUCOURT was left at 17.40 hours and relief complete reported to Brigade at 21.00 hours. "A" Coy was on the Right, "C" Coy on Left, "D" in Support and "B" in Reserve. Casualties 2 O.R. Sick, 1 O.R. Other Causes.
	12th	The Commanding Officer with Capt. GRIZELLE, M.C. reconnoitred the Battalion's dispositions. At 10.00 hours the Brigade ordered the Battalion to side-step to the left, taking over from R.8.d.1.5. to R.8.c.5.4 from the 7th MIDDLESEX and handing over from R.6.c.4.3 to R.5.d.1.4. to the

                                                        Lieut-Colonel,
                     Commanding. 1st Queens Westminster Rifles.

WAR DIARY

In the Field.
1918 Oct. 12th Contd: London Rifle Brigade. "B" Coy was accordingly moved up to the Left and the new dispositions were as follows :- "C" Coy on the Right, "B" on the left, "A" in Support and "D" (who took over "B" Coy's previous Disposition) in Reserve.
Casualties 1 O.R. Sick, Lieut. J.J.Westmoreland, Other Causes, 1 O.R. Reinforcement.

13th. On the night of the 12/13th, the Battalion was ordered to cross the CANAL de la SENSEE with the aid of 416th Field Coy R.E. and protect a Company of the 2nd LONDONS, who were ordered to form up on the Northern Bank during the night with a view to seizing AUBIGNY AU BAC at 05.15 hours and form a bridge-head in this area.
The patrol for this purpose was entrusted to 2nd Lt.H.R. SMITH and a platoon on "D" Company.
The construction of the bridge proceeded slowly but with complete success and a passage across the CANAL, which at this point was 70 feet wide and 30 feet deep, was completed by the R.E. by 04.00 hours.
The patrol then pushed forward and formed a protective screen for the 2nd LONDONS, who immediately passed through it and formed up for the attack. The patrol secured two prisoners during this movement. When the 2nd LONDONS had taken up their position a Platoon of "C" Coy Q.W.R. relieved 2nd Lt. Smith's patrol.
The 2nd LONDONS attacked at 05.15 hours with complete sucess securing between 200 and 300 prisoners but were forced to withdraw some hours later under enemy counter-attack supported by very heay Artillery barrages.
A small party remained on the Northern bank of the CANAL and was able to maintain its position covering the bridge.
"A" Coy Q.W.R. which was in SUPPORT during this period in a Railway cutting were held under the enemy barrage from 08.30 to 18.00 hours and at intervals later.
Casualties : 5 O.R. Killed, 2nd Lt. Talling and 14 O.R. Wounded.

14th. A comparatively quiet day. The Battalion was relieved by the 50th Battn. CANADIANS. Marched to SAUCHY CAUCHY. Battalion H.Q. was at the Cemetery.
Fairly heavily shelled on the way out and "C" Coy Billets were shelled after their arrival.
Casualties 3 O.R. Wounded.

15th. A quiet day, The Battalion marched to MARQUION at 22.15 hours to entrain there at 23.10 hours. Men had plenty of accommodation and seemed to be fairly comfortable.
Casualties : Nil

16th. Battalion detrained at AGNEZ LES DUISANS at 08.30 hours (5½ hours late) and marched to HAUTE AVESNES where it was billeted in hutments. The remainder of the day was spent by Coys settling down in new quarters.
Casualties : 2 Reinforcements.

Lieut-Colonel,
Commanding 1st Queens Westminster Rifles

WAR DIARY

In the field.
1918 Oct. 17th. The Battalion started Training.
Lecture to Officers and Sergeants by the Commanding Officer at 11.00 hours followed by demonstration by Platoon drawn from Headquarters Coy under R.S.M.
Afternoon spent playing Football &c.
A Battalion Officers' Mess was started (and proved a complete success despite obvious difficulties) for the first time.

Casualties: 32 O.R. Reinforcements, 5 O.R. Other Causes.

18th. Training continued on same lines as before. Inter-Platoon Football Competitions were started.
Casualties: 2 O.R. Other Causes, 2 O.R. Reinforcements.

19th. The B.G.C. 169th Inf. Bde inspected the Battalion and congratulated it on its turnout, steadiness on parade and fighting qualities in recent operations. He expressed the opinion that the reputation of the Brigade had never been higher than at present, which he considered most creditable after four years of War. The B.G.C. then inspected barrack-rooms &c and found everything entirely satisfactory.
The men bathed in the afternoon and in the evening the Battalion attended a performance of the "Bow Bells"

Casualties 1 O.R. Other Causes.
2 O.R. Reinforcements.

20th. The Battalion attended Church Parade at which B.G.C. was present. In the afternoon a Football match was played between Officers and Sergeants.
Casualties : 2 O.R. Other Causes.

21st. Training on usual lines. In the afternoon Battalion attended a Lecture on "THE PRESENT SITUATION" by the Intelligence Officer 56th Division. The B.G.C. and Staff Captain dined at the Officers' Mess in the evening.
(Training :- "A" Coy on Range, Remainder Close Order Drill
Games, Musketry, Lewis Gun)
Casualties : 1 O.R. Sick 2 O.R. Other Causes,
5 O.R. Reinforcements.

22nd. Battalion carried out an Advanced Guard Scheme. Advance Guard "D" Coy, remainder main body. Very wet afternoon.
Casualties 2 O.R. Sick, 3 O.R. Reinforcements.

23rd. Training "B" Coy Musketry and "C" Coy Lewis Gun on Range. Remainder Musketry, Lewis Gun and open Warfare formations.
In the afternoon a football match between Queens Westminster Rifles and London Rifle Brigade, resulted in a draw, one all.

Casualties: 2nd Lt. G. Delaforce Sick, 4 O.R. Reinforcem[ents]

Lieut-Colonel,
Commanding.1st Queens Westminster Rifles.

WAR DIARY

In the Field. Training by Coys in morning Rifle Grenade Practice
1918. Ocr.24th Lewis Gun, Bayonet Fighting, Gas Drill, Close Order
Drill for Junior N.C.Os.
In the afternoon Lt. Col. James, M.C. Lectured to
Officers, W.Os. and N.C.Os. on "THE WORK OF THE ROYAL
AIR FORCE"
(Since the commencement of the rest the Battalion
had organised various amusements for the men, Football
was a regular feature each afternoon and in the
evening there were Whist Drives for the Companies.
The "Bow Bells" performed each evening, and being close
at hand, were very much appreciated)

Casualties 1 O.R. Reinforcement.

25th. Training in the morning - ("D" Coy on Range for Musketry
and "A" Coy for Lewis Gun. Remainder open Warfare
formations, P.T. and Close Order Drill)
Football in the afternoon.
Casualties :- 2 O.R. Other Causes, Lieut. E.C. HAYES
and 3 O.R. Reinforcements.

26th. Morning. Platoon Competitions in Musketry, Drill,
Bayonet Fighting, and Lewis Gun.
Battalion Parade at noon.
Afternoon Played Football v. 7th MIDDLESEX who
won by 4 - 0
Whist Drive in the evening.
Casualties 1 O.R. Reinforcement.

27th. Voluntary Church Services and Football (Coy and Platoon)
matches.
Casualties 2 O.R. Sick 1 O.R. Reinforcement.

28th. 2 Coys Bathed.
"A" and "B" Coys Lewis Gun practises on Range "C" Coy
Rifle practises on range. "D" Coy Route march.
An N.C.Os. Class was formed and trained during the
morning under the R.S.M.
The Commanding Officer appointed a Committee to arrange
details for a Battalion Dinner on 1st November 1918.
"A" Coy held Whist Drive in the evening.
Casualties 11 O.R. Reinforcements.

29th. 2 Coys and H.Q. Bathed.
2 Coys Route marched.
2 Coys carried out Lewis Gun practises.
Each Coy has now fired Lewis Gun and Rifle Practises
on the Range.
The N.C.Os. Class carried on as before.
The Divisional Commander addressed all Officers
and N.C.Os. of the Brigade on Training in the
afternoon.
"D" Coy held Whist Drive.

Casualties : Nil.

Lieut-Colonel,
Commanding. 1st Queens Westminster Rifles.

WAR DIARY

In the Field.
1918 Oct.30th.   Training Artillery Formations and Fire Discipline
and control.
Warning Order received at 12.00 hours for Brigade
move the following day.
A Dinner had been arranged for 1st Novr. and large
quantities of food and fruit and beer bought. It was
necessary to cancel all orders hurriedly, and
fortunately all the stock was disposed of without loss.

Casualties : Lieut E.C. Hayes and 1 O.R. Sick
4 O.R. Reinforcements.

31st.   Moved at 0820 hours. Embussed near Camp and debussed at
FRETTE AU POIRIER some way past our destination,
(LIEU ST. AMAND) to which we returned arriving at 16.00
hours.
Casualties   Nil.

Strength on 31/10/18 29 Officers, 612 Other Ranks.

Lieut-Colonel,
Commanding, 1st Queens Westminster Rifles

(6392) Wt. W6192/P375 1,500,000 4/18 McA & W Ltd (E 2815) Forms W3091/4. Army Form W.3091.

Cover for Documents.

Nature of Enclosures.

1/16 London Regt
9248

WAR DIARY

QUEENS WESTMINSTER RIFLES

November 1915

Notes, or Letters written.

Army Form ✗2118.

WAR DIARY
or
INTELLIGENCE SUMMARY.
(Erase heading not required.)

Instructions regarding War Diaries and Intelligence Summaries are contained in F.S. Regs., Part II. and the Staff Manual respectively. Title pages will be prepared in manuscript.

Place	Date	Hour	Summary of Events and Information	Remarks and references to Appendices
In the Field.	1/11/1918.		Clearing up billets which were full of debris caused by the British bombardment. Kit Zc. inspections and general preparation to move up to the battle area the next day. The transport which moved from HAUTE AVESNES by road on the 30th October arrived in billets at 1700 hours. Casualties. / 1 O.R. Other Causes. 3 O.Rs. Reinforcements.	✗
	2nd.		Battalion roused at 0430 hours. Stacked packs, blankets, valises and all baggage except essentials. Moved at 0900 hours with transport to a field near MAING, arriving 1230 hours. Dinners were taken here and battle ammunition issued. The Commanding Officer and A/Adjt. rode on from the starting point to arrange details for relief. They found that the Headquarters of the Brigade being relieved were not where it was supposed and a considerable delay ensued in making the arrangements. Finally it was decided that the Battalion would occupy a portion of the front held by the 7th West Riding Regt. The Commanding Officer went up and arranged details for guides at their Headquarters and returned to CAUMONT FARM at 1600 hours. The Battalion had been ordered forward to this place by Brigade and arrived at 1800 hours, having had trouble with the transport - the transport N.C.O. and horses of 1 Cooker were wounded and a Lewis Gun limber ditched. The guides from 7th West Riding Regt. did not arrive untill very late. Two had lost their way and said they were unable to find their way back to their Companies. One guide lost Battalion Headquarters for 2 hours. Finally the whole Battalion arrived in position at 0101 hours, Officers having found their way by Compass and stars. Officers with the Battalion. Commanding Officer. Lieut Colonel. S.R. SAVILL, DSO, MC. A/ 2nd In Command. Capt. J.B. BABER, MC. A/Adjutant. Lieut W.H. GATFIELD, MC.	

Commdg. 1st Battn. QUEENS WESTMINSTER RIFLES.

V.R. Savill
Lieut Colonel.

Army Form C. 2118.

WAR DIARY
or
INTELLIGENCE SUMMARY.
(Erase heading not required.)

Instructions regarding War Diaries and Intelligence Summaries are contained in F. S. Regs., Part II. and the Staff Manual respectively. Title pages will be prepared in manuscript.

Place	Date	Hour	Summary of Events and Information	Remarks and references to Appendices
In the Field.	2nd (Contd).		"A" Company.	
			Lieut. V.G. RAYNOR. in Command.	
			Lieut. I.P. McEWAN.	
			"C" Company.	
			Lieut. O.A.M. EATON. in Command.	
			2nd Lieut. S.F. SIMONDS.	
			"B" Company.	
			Lieut. J.B. MALTHOUSE. in Command.	
			2nd Lieut. E. COAKER.	
			2nd Lieut. I.P. WORTHINGTON.	
			"D" Company.	
			Capt. F.E. WHITBY, MC. In Command.	
			2nd Lieut. F.H.B. MOORE.	
			2nd Lieut. H.R. SMITH, MC.	
			There was very heavy rain after the Battalion arrived in the line. There was no shelter and the Companies got soaked through with rain. They had marched a distance of 13 miles across tracks and open country, the going was very heavy and there were constant checks owing to congested traffic, transport difficulties and to guides who had no idea which way they were going.	
			Rabbits were issued for the third time this year when the Battalion was marching up for a battle. It was of course quite impossible to skin and cook them. The men either ate them half raw or went without their meat ration.	
			Casualties:- 10 O.Rs. Sick.	
	3rd.		During the night 2nd/3rd inst a Brigade order was received for an attack on 4th on SAULTAIN and the country beyond. The Battalion was holding a line between MARLY and PRESEAU. About 0900 hours the 2nd LONDON REGT., on the right noticed the withdrawal of some hostile Machine Gunners and "D" Company sent a patrol forward to ascertain whether the enemy had withdrawn entirely.	
			The Commanding officer proceeded to the front line where he found O.C. 1st KENSINGTON Battn. (on the left) who had received orders for his Battalion to advance. As several parties of 2nd LONDONS were seen moving forward, the Commanding Officer instructed "D" Company with "B" Company in support to push forward and occupy SAULTAIN, keeping touch	

J M [signature]
Lieut Colonel.
Commdg. 1st Battn. QUEENS WESTMINSTER RIFLES.

Army Form C. 2118.

WAR DIARY
or
INTELLIGENCE SUMMARY.

(Erase heading not required.)

Instructions regarding War Diaries and Intelligence Summaries are contained in F. S. Regs., Part II. and the Staff Manual respectively. Title pages will be prepared in manuscript.

-3-

Place	Date	Hour	Summary of Events and Information	Remarks and references to Appendices
In the Field.	3rd (Contd).		with flank Battalions. An advanced Battalion H.Q. and a visual station were established in front line in communication with Battalion H.Q. The "D" Company patrol under Sergt. LAW had advanced through the village in patrol formation. When the civilians saw it they ran out of their houses cheering. The women seized Sergt. LAW's rifle from him and kissed him and brought out coffee for the patrol. Their enthusiasm was tremendous. French and British flags were brought out of the houses and the civilians tried to thrust on the troops all the food and drink they had. The hostile artillery opened on the village but the civilians paid no heed to it or to the damage done by it to their property. At 1140 hours the Commanding Officer was ordered to go back to Battalion H.Q. which were not to move. Orders were also received that the 2nd Londons would advance on the whole Brigade front and that the Q.W.R. would assemble S. of SAULTAIN in support to them. The 2nd Londons advanced without opposition to 4000 yards EAST of SAULTAIN. About 1600 hours Brigade ordered the Battalion to take over from 2nd Londons. By the time the Commanding Officer had gone forward and collected the Company Commanders, it was dusk and the Companies moved forward in the dark, assembling on the ground held by 2nd Londons. The hostile artillery fire was now very heavy and the Companies were shelled throughout the night and were unable to sleep for the second night in succession. Battalion H.Q. moved to SAULTAIN and a Brigade order was received at midnight to attack at 0600 hours.	
	4th.		Casualties:- 2 O.Rs. Killed. 2 O.Rs. Wounded. 8 O.Rs. Sick. 1 O.R. other Causes. Company Commanders assembled at Battalion H.Q. for their orders as this was the only place in which a light could be shewn. The Battalion was to move forward without a barrage as it was possible that the enemy were not holding the ground in front.	

V. R. Sewell
Lieut Colonel.
Commdg. 1st Battn. QUEEN'S WESTMINSTER RIFLES.

Army Form C. 2118.

WAR DIARY
or
INTELLIGENCE SUMMARY.
(Erase heading not required.)

Instructions regarding War Diaries and Intelligence Summaries are contained in F. S. Regs., Part II and the Staff Manual respectively. Title pages will be prepared in manuscript.

Place	Date	Hour	Summary of Events and Information	Remarks and references to Appendices
In the Field.	4th	(Contd).	A cavalry screen was to preceed the Infantry and the 168th Infantry Brigade were attacking on the left and the 11th Division on the right. At 0600 hours the Infantry advanced and immediately came under distant M.G. fire, when the cavalry dismounted. What became of the cavalry later is not known as they were not seen again. The Battalion advanced through SEBOURG under intermittent shell fire and with slight casualties to the first objective (1500 yards beyond the village and 4000yards from assembly area). The troops were met by the civilians in SEBOURG with the greatest enthusiasm and a number of prisoners, estimated at about 50 were captured before arrival at the first objective. The escort became a casualty on the way down and no receipt was obtained for the prisoners. As the rear Companies passed through the village the enemy put down a very heavy barrage on it and on the roads approaching it from the WEST. As the Companies crossed the river AUNELLE the hostile Machine Gun fire became intense. As the average strength of our Platoons was 12, the ground could not be searched and the leading Companies must have passed over hostile Machine Guns during their advance. As "A" Company (on left) and "C" Company (on right) reached the first objective they came under an annihilating Machine Gun fire from the left which forced them into the junction of 2 sunken roads on the right of the Battalion front. The enemy worked up to this junction and enfiladed them badly. As Lewis Gunners got their guns into action on the top of the banks of the road they were almost immediately knocked out. Enemy jumped into the sunken road at the junction and hit the A/C.S.M. of "A" Company, (Sergt. E.W. GILLETTE, DCM-). Sergt. STINCHCOMBE was killed attempting to charge them and 2nd Lieut. F.H.B. MOORE OF "D" Company, who had come up to reinforce, was also killed. Lewis Gunners returned the enemy fire and fired many rounds. Many empty magazines and cartridge cases and two smashed Lewis Guns were found among the dead, at the spot later. "A" Company was forced back to the Both roads, enfiladed by Machine Guns, were untenable. A stand was made at the rear portions of these North and "C" and "B" Companies to the South.	

J R Lewis
Lieut Colonel.
Commdg. 1st Battn. QUEENS WESTMINSTER RIFLES.

WAR DIARY
or
INTELLIGENCE SUMMARY.

(Erase heading not required.)

Army Form C. 2118.

Place	Date	Hour	Summary of Events and Information	Remarks and references to Appendices
In the Field.	4th (Contd)		roads (each on the extreme flanks of the Battalion front). On the left "A" and "D" Companies were relieved by 168 Brigade troops and moved South and established a position in the centre of the Battalion front, protecting the river. "C" and "B" Companies established themselves as a semi circular screen, thrown out from the sunken road, back towards "A" Company. The K.R.B. who were closely supporting the Battalion completed the line across the Battalion front and a portion of the front of the Battalion on the right. The situation was now unpleasant. Word was passed that the Battalion on the right was being counter-attacked. The village was continuously and very heavily shelled. The whole situation was dominated by hostile M.G's. who made any movement practically an impossibility and thus prevented any re-organization taking place. The line ran from 700 to 300 yards in front of the AUNELLE river. In the evening the Battalion was relieved by L.R.B. and reformed just in the rear of SEBOURG. where rations were issued and ammunition completed. Orders were received during the night for a further advance the following day. Company Commanders came to Battalion H.Q. for their instructions. By the time these instructions were issued to the men, it was Zero and for the third night the men had practically no sleep. Casualties:- 1 Officer. 2nd Lieut. F.H.B. MOORE and 20 O.Rs. Killed. 1 Officer. Lieut. I.P. Mc EWAN and 52 O.Rs. Wounded, 2 O.Rs. Sick.	
	5th.		At 0530 hours the Battalion advanced in support to L.R.B. In spite of very heavy shelling the L.R.B. Captured ANGREAUX, an advance of over 3000 yards. The Battalion occupied positions in the sunken road and open ground in rear of the village. The enemy shelled this and all day and night and it rained continuously, the men getting soaked in the wet ground. Casualties:- 1 Officer. 2nd Lieut. H.R. SMITH, MC. and 3 O.Rs. Killed, 3 O.Rs. Wounded. 10 O.Rs. Sick,	

M. Howard
Lieut Colonel

Commdg. 1st Battn. QUEENS WESTMINSTER RIFLES.

WAR DIARY
or
INTELLIGENCE SUMMARY.

(Erase heading not required.)

Army Form — C. 2118.

Place	Date	Hour	Summary of Events and Information	Remarks and references to Appendices
In the Field.	6th.		At 0530 hours the L.R.B. and 2nd Londons again advanced, but were met by strong opposition and were unable to maintain captured ground. They suffered heavy casualties and "C" and "D" Companies went forward to reinforce the L.R.B. and "A" abd "B" Companies to reinforce the 2nd Londons. Only 2 Companies were eventually required and consequently "A" and "D" Companies were withdrawn to their original positions. The rain and shelling continued all day. The officers and men under the Battalion experienced the utmost cheerfulness. It is thought that the Battalion has never before experienced such an unfavourable combination of shelling, rain, mud and the lack of sleep. In the evening the battle area was taken over by 167th Infantry Brigade and the Battalion withdrew to billets in SEBOURG. Casualties:- 2 O.Rs. Killed. 7 O.Rs. Wounded. 16 O.Rs. Sick.	
	7th.		The men dried their clothes by fire as far as possible, washed and shaved and rubbed their feet, which owing to the wet were in very bad condition. The usual returns and indents were compiled. Casualties:- 7 O.Rs. Sick.	
	8th.		Moved from SEBOURG at 1000 hours, arriving ANGREAU, 1100 hours. Transport had great difficulty in operating. The roads were very congested and the transport accommodation is quite inadequate for the baggage which it is essential to carry. Vehicles,therefore, in many cases have to do double journeys. Also there is a deficiency of 6 horses and Brigade H.Q. use officers chargers for Mounted Orderlies. Our limber has now to carry T.M. Ammunition. The whole section is in a state of immobility and if the advance continues will not be able to keep up with the Battalion. Casualties:- 2 Officers. 2nd Lieut. I.P. WORTHINGTON, 2nd Lieut. H.F. SIMONDS and 9 O.Rs. Sick.	
	9th.		Preordered move did not take place and Battalion repaired roads in the afternoon. News from Divisional Commander that German peace delegates had come through Allied Lines and been given untill 1100 hours 11th inst to accept Allied Peace terms. The 167th Brigade which was in the line reported to have gone forward a great distance in pursuit of the enemy. Casualties:- 6 O.Rs. Sick.	

N. Wand
Lieut Colonel.
Commdg. 1st QUEENS WESTMINSTER RIFLES.

Army Form C. 2118.

WAR DIARY
or
INTELLIGENCE SUMMARY.
(Erase heading not required.)

Place	Date	Hour	Summary of Events and Information	Remarks and references to Appendices
In the Field.	10th.		Battalion moved at 1330 hours from ANGREAU to billets in ATHIS. Roads very bad from weather and craters blown by enemy. Village scarcely damaged at all and full of inhabitants, who received us enthusiastically. Sheep and cattle still held by civilians and in good condition. 100 men worked all the morning on the roads and rejoined the Battalion at ATHIS. Casualties:- 4 O.Rs. Sick.	
	11th.		Practically every available man engaged on repairing the roads, aided by willing civilians. Armistice signed at 1100 hours. Complete lack of demonstration on the part of the men, who carried on just as though they were in rest billets. Inhabitants observed in several instances digging up money, clothes &c. out of their gardens. Great difficulty in obtaining rations owing to the state of the roads. They arrived at 0500 hours the next day, I.e. the 12th. Casualties:- 4 O.Rs. Sick.	
	12th.		Battalion continued work on the roads. Congratulatory note received from the Corps Commander on the Division's efforts during the days preceding the Armistice. Our American Medical officer left us and Capt. W.J.O. WATT, RN. replaced him. Casualties:- Lieut. E.B. MUNIER AMRO, to 2/1st L.F.A. Capt. W.J.O. WATT, RN and 3 O.Rs. reinforcements.	
	13th.		No work on roads today. The Battalion spent the day in cleaning clothing, equipment &cM News was received in the evening that the Division was to proceed to the RHINE with the Second Army. The forward movement was to commence on the 17th. Casualties:- 2 O.Rs. Sick. 10 O.Rs. Reinforcements.	
	14th.		Orders received to send 80 men to the Official March Past through Mons on the morning of the 15th. 60 men at work on the roads. Casualties 1 O.R. Sick. 5 O.Rs. Reinforcements.	
	15th.		Capt. F.E. WHITBY, MC, Lieut. G.W. AVENS, MC, MM. Lieut. W.H. GATFIELD, MC. and 80 O.Rs. represented the Battalion at the March Past in MONS. 50 men employed on road repairs. Casualties:- 2 O.Rs. Sick. 2 O.Rs. Reinforcements.	

Commdg. 1st Battn. QUEENS WESTMINSTER RIFLES.

Capt. & Adjt.

Army Form C. 2118.

WAR DIARY
or
INTELLIGENCE SUMMARY.
(Erase heading not required.)

Instructions regarding War Diaries and Intelligence Summaries are contained in F.S. Regs., Part II. and the Staff Manual respectively. Title pages will be prepared in manuscript.

Place	Date	Hour	Summary of Events and Information	Remarks and references to Appendices
In the Field.	16th.		No Change. Work on the roads continued. Casualties:- 8 O.Rs. Reinforcements.	
	17th.		No change. The whole Battalion still engaged on work on the roads in spite of it being the first Sunday after the Armistice. Much of this work was merely tidying up, i.e. scraping mud off cobbles. Casualties:- 1 O.R. Sick. 4 O.Rs. Reinforcements.	
	18th.		100 men required for work on roads. Otherwise no change. Casualties:- 1 O.R. Sick, 1 O.R. Reinforcement.	
	19th.		No change. Casualties. 2 O.Rs. Sick. 4 Officers. 2nd Lts. F.A. HITCHINGS. H. DAVIES, S.H. SMITH, A.P.T. GODLY and 2 O.Rs. Reinforcements.	
	20th.		No change. Casualties:- 1 P.R. Sick.	
	21st.		No change. 21 O.Rs. proceeded to MONS by lorry, with similar parties from the other Units of the Division and were taken over the 1914 Battlefield by General ELKINGTON, B.G.R.A. Casualties:- 2 O.Rs. Sick. 6 Officers. 2nd Lieuts. A.C.C. FRASER, E.S. FOLEY, S.F. DEAN, W.H. ORMISTON, MC. H.J. SIMPSON, D.C. BEADELL, (RAF). *Reinforcements*	
	22nd.		No change. Casualties:- 1 O.R. Sick. 8 Officer. 2nd Lieut. A. EDWARDS and 1 O.R. Reinforcement.	
	23rd.		No work on the roads. Battalion Route march in the morning. Football in the afternoon. Casualties:- 1 O.R. Sick.	
	24th.		Church Parade at ATHIS for L.R.B. and ourselves. A.C.G. First Army (Colonel BLACKBURN) officiated. Football in the afternoon. Casualties:- 3 O.Rs. Sick. 1 O.R. Reinforcement.	
	25th.		Lecture on Venereal Disease by Medical Officer in the morning. Commanding Officer attended conference on Education in the afternoon at Division. Casualties:- 2 O.Rs. Sick. 6 O.Rs. Reinforcements.	

J R Shiel
Lieut Colonel.
Commdg. 1st Battn. QUEENS WESTMINSTER RIFLES.

Army Form C. 2118.

WAR DIARY
or
INTELLIGENCE SUMMARY.
(Erase heading not required.)

Place	Date	Hour	Summary of Events and Information	Remarks and references to Appendices
In the Field.	26th.		Battalion moved to BOUGNIES by march Route. Casualties:- 8 O.R. Sick. 2 Officers. 2nd Lieuts. S.F. SIMONDS, H. WETHERALL and 2 O.Rs. Reinforcements.	
	27th.		No change. Short parades in the morning, sports in the afternoon. Casualties:- 2 O.R.s. Sick.	
	28th.		No change. Casualties:- 1 O.R. Sick. 3 O.Rs. Other Causes. 1 O.R. Reinforcement.	
	29th.		Battalion moved to GENLY, a few miles South of MONS, which is understood to be its winter quarters. The civilians received us most kindly. The billets, on the whole, good, except that the accommodation for "A" Company is cramped on account of a Battery of the 4th Divisional Artillery still being in the village. The men are no longer billeted in barns, but placed 2 or 3 in a house with the civilians. Large Concert Hall and Dining Rooms available in the village square. Casualties:- 17 O.Rs. Reinforcements.	
	30th.		Battalion engaged in cleaning the village. Large quantities of filth and rubbish had been left by the Germans. Casualties:- 5 O.Rs. Reinforcements.	

```
                                    Offrs.    O.Rs.
Strength. 31st October, 1918.        29       612.
                     Less.            5       195
                                     ----    -----
                                     24       417.
                     Add.            14        76.
                                     ----    -----
Strength. 30th November, 1918.       38       493.
                                    =====    =====
```

Lieut Colonel.
Commdg. 1st Battalion QUEENS WESTMINSTER RIFLES.

(6392) Wt. W6192/P875 1,500,000 4/18 McA & W Ltd (E 2815) Forms W3091/4.   Army Form W.3091.

Cover for Documents.

Nature of Enclosures.

War Diary

December 1918.

1/16th London Regiment

Notes, or Letters written.

Army Form C. 2118.

WAR DIARY
or
INTELLIGENCE SUMMARY.
(Erase heading not required.)

Instructions regarding War Diaries and Intelligence Summaries are contained in F. S. Regs., Part II. and the Staff Manual respectively. Title pages will be prepared in manuscript.

Place	Date	Hour	Summary of Events and Information	Remarks and references to Appendices
In the Field.	1/12/18.		Church Parade in the Concert Hall at 1015 hours. Casualties:- NIL.	
	2nd.		Cleaning of village continued. The Divisional Band played in the Concert Hall from 1700 - 1900 hours. Casualties:- NIL.	
	3rd.		No change. Battalion bathed at NOIRRHAIN Coal Mines. Casualties:- 5 Officer Reinforcements:- Lieut. T.H. JENKIN, 2nd Lieut. J.S. GOLDING, 2nd Lieut. S.E. ARBER, 2nd Lieut. R.C. PALMER, 2nd Lieut. A.M. SMITH.	
	4th.		Battalion Parade - a rehearsal for Presentation of Medal Ribbons by G.O.C. on the 11th to all who had received decorations since operations at BULLECOURT in September. Casualties:- NIL.	
	5th.		His Majesty the King visited the Divisional Area. BOURDON-OIPLY-MONS road closed for him between 0930 - 1100 hours. Casualties:- NIL.	
	6th.		Baths at NOIRGHAIN Coal Mines for those not bathed on 3rd inst. Work on square for 2 Platoons. Remainder of Battalion cleaning own areas. Address at HARVENG to Officers by Rev. W.E.S. HOLLAND who had been sent by Archbishop of Canterbury to address troops in France on work of Church after the war. Casualties:- NIL.	
	7th.		Work on village square continued. Casualties:- 1 O.R. Reinforcements.	
	8th.		Church Parade 1000 hours in Concert Hall. Casualties:- NIL.	
	9th.		Company Training. Casualties:- NIL.	
	10th.		Battalion Parade - Rehearsal for Presentation of Medal Ribbons by G.O.C. 16 O.Rs. Reinforcements. Casualties:-	

Major.
Commanding 1st Battn. QUEENS WESTMINSTER RIFLES.

Army Form C. 2118.

WAR DIARY
or
INTELLIGENCE SUMMARY.
(Erase heading not required.)

Instructions regarding War Diaries and Intelligence Summaries are contained in F. S. Regs. Part II. and the Staff Manual respectively. Title pages will be prepared in manuscript.

Place	Date	Hour	Summary of Events and Information	Remarks and references to Appendices
In the Field. (Contd).	11th.		Battalion started at 0900 hours in column of route for Presentation of Medal Ribbons Parade at MOUVELLES. Heavy rain. Order received on reaching BOUGNIES cancelling the parade owing to the weather. Casualties:- 9 O.Rs. Reinforcements.	
	12th.		First men in the Battalion (7 Coalminers) demobilized and sent home. Casualties:- 7 O.Rs. Other Causes.	
	13th.		Company Training. Casualties:- NIL.	
	14th.		Lecture on Exploration by Colonel Swayne in Concert Hall at 1150 hours. Casualties:- 1 Officer Reinforcement. 2nd Lieut. G.F. WESTWOOD.	
	15th.		Church Parade 0945 hours in Concert Hall. The Colonel left for England on a months leave. Casualties:- NIL.	
	16th.		Company Training. Casualties:- NIL.	
	17th.		Battalion parade in preparation for Brigade Parade tomorrow. Casualties:- NIL.	
	18th.		Battalion started by march route for Presentation of Medal Ribbons by G.O.C. originally fixed for the 11th. Heavy rain again and orders received soon after leaving GEMLY, cancelling the parade. Casualties:- NIL.	
	19th.		Battalion bathed at NOTROHAIN Coal Mines. Casualties:- NIL.	
	20th.		Battalion engaged in scrubbing and cleaning the Recreation Rooms, Dining Halls and Institutes. Casualties:- NIL.	
	21st.		B.G.C. presented Medal Ribbons in the village square to all ranks who had earned decorations at BULLECOURT (September 1918) and subsequently. This took the place of the parade for G.O.C., originally ordered for the 11th near MOUVELLES. B.G.C. inspected Recreation Rooms, Dining Halls and Battalion Institutes after the parade. Casualties:- NIL.	

[signature] Major.

Commanding 1st Battn. QUEENS WESTMINSTER RIFLES.

Army Form C. 2118.

WAR DIARY
or
INTELLIGENCE SUMMARY.
(Erase heading not required.)

-3-

Instructions regarding War Diaries and Intelligence Summaries are contained in F.S. Regs., Part II. and the Staff Manual respectively. Title pages will be prepared in manuscript.

Place	Date	Hour	Summary of Events and Information	Remarks and references to Appendices
In the Field. (Contd).	22nd.		Voluntary Service in Chapel at 0945 hours. Rugby Match v 282nd. A.F.A. Bde. R.F.A. at BOUGNIES. Lost by Two tries to Nil. Association Match v 513th Field Coy. R.E. at GENLY at 1430 hours. Lost 1 goal to Nil. Casualties:- 1 O.R. Other Causes.	
	23rd.		Company Training and working parties. Casualties:- 9 O.R.s. Reinforcements.	
	24th.		All the Institutes were fully decorated for Christmas with materials obtained from MONS and ETAPLES. Casualties:- 8 O.Rs. Other Causes.	
	25th.		Short Service in Concert Hall at 0930 hours. Christmas Festivities a great success. Programme :- Dinners - 1300 hours. Menu :- (ROAST TURKEY (2-lbs. per man). SAUSAGES, POTATOES, BRUSSEL SPROUTS, CAULIFLOWER, PLUM PUDDING, WALNUTS, APPLES, BEER, COFFEE. ~~Officers and Sergeants waited on the men and assisted further etc~~ 1500 Hours. - CHILDRENS PARTY AND CHRISTMAS TREE in CONCERT HALL and DINING ROOMS. Every child in the village received a personal invitation. The Mayor and 20 civilians helped to organise the party. Address presented to the Battalion after the presentation of toys (more than one per child) which was read out by small child aged 12. (copy of address attached). *Appendix A.* Teas (cakes, biscuits, fruit, coffee etc.) provided for each child at 1600 hours. 1900 hours. DANCE in CONCERT HALL. Light refreshments, coffee, lemonade, cakes, biscuits, fruit, beer - on sale in Canteen. Casualties:- 1 O.R. Other Causes.	
	26th.		League Match v 169th Infantry Brigade H.Q. and T.M.B. at 1415 hours. Result. WON. 3 - 1. Battalion Concert in Hall at 1930 hours. Casualties:- 1 O.R. Sick.	

H. Shuttle Major.
Commanding 1st Battn. QUEENS WESTMINSTER RIFLES.

Army Form C. 2118.

WAR DIARY
of
INTELLIGENCE SUMMARY.
(Erase heading not required.)

Instructions regarding War Diaries and Intelligence Summaries are contained in F.S. Regs., Part II. and the Staff Manual respectively. Title pages will be prepared in manuscript.

Place	Date	Hour	Summary of Events and Information	Remarks and references to Appendices
In the Field. (contd).	27th.		Battalion Whist Drive in Concert Hall at 1730 hours. Casualties:- 2 O.Rs. Other Causes.	
	28th.		Company Training. Casualties:- 8 officers cross posted to own Unit. Lieut. T.J. HUDSON. 2nd Lieutenants A.P.T. GODLY, S.H. SMITH, H. DAVIES, F.A.A. HITCHINGS, A. EDWARDS, H.J. WETHERALL, G.F. WESTWOOD. 1 O.R. Other Causes.	
	29th.		Voluntary Service in Chapel at 0930 hours. Casualties:- NIL.	
	30th.		Education Scheme started. Classes in Arithmetic, English, Spanish, Shorthand, Bookkeeping opened for all volunteers. Casualties:- 8.O.Rs. Other Causes.	
	31st.		Company Training. League Match v 1st LONDON RIFLE BRIGADE at HARMIGNIES. at 1415 hours. Result. Won. 3 - 2. Casualties. NIL.	

	Officers.	O.Rs.
Strength on 30/11/18.	38	493
Less.	8	30
	30	463
Add.	6	34
Strength on 31/12/18.	36	497

H. Kinzle. Major.

Commanding 1st Battn. QUEEN'S WESTMINSTER RIFLES.

Copy Appendix A

Monsieur le Commandant,
    Messieurs les Officiers,
        Messieurs,
————————————

    Au déclin de cette belle journée à jamais inoubliable pour la population de GEMLY, je serai certainement l'interprète de tous les habitants de la commune, et en particulier des enfants ici réunis, pour vous remercier de tout coeur de la bienveillante générosité avec laquelle vous avez organisé, en notre faveur, cette fête magnifique. Merci pour la gracieuse réception que vous nous avez réservée, merci pour les beaux objets que vous nous avez offerts. Nous y attachons le plus grand prix et nous les conserverons soigneusement dans la famille, comme un précieux souvenir de votre heureux passage à GEMLY.

Messieurs,

    Vous avez acquis tous les droits à la gratitude éternelle de la Nation Belge; vous avez largement contribué à délivrer notre chère patrie des troupes ennemies qui l'avaient injustement envahie. Votre glorieuse intervention restera gravée en lettres d'or dans les annales de la Belgique. Soyez remerciés à jamais pour cet insigne bienfait. Qu'en retour, la Providence daigne exaucer les voeux que nous formons pour le bonheur et la prospérité de la grande Nation Anglaise.

    Et à vous Messieurs reconnaissance inaltérable pour la joie que vous nous avez procurée en ce beau jour de fête.

    Vive la Nation Britannique! Vive l'armée! Vive le Roi!

Army Form C. 2118.

WAR DIARY
or
INTELLIGENCE SUMMARY.
(Erase heading not required.)

Instructions regarding War Diaries and Intelligence Summaries are contained in F. S. Regs., Part II. and the Staff Manual respectively. Title pages will be prepared in manuscript.

Place	Date	Hour	Summary of Events and Information	Remarks and references to Appendices
In the Field	1.1.19.		Battalion still stationed at GENLY, South of Mons.	
	2.1.19.		ASSOCIATION FOOTBALL "B" Coy beat "A" Coy by 2 goals to 1 goal in Brigade inter Company Competition. Casualties :- 8 O.R. To Dispersal Stn. 2 O.R. Reinforcements. ASSOCIATION FOOTBALL. "D" Coy v "C" Coy in Brigade inter Coy Competition - Result - No score. Casualties :- 4 O.R. To Dispersal Stn. for Demob.	
	3.1.19.		FOOTBALL "D" Coy beat "C" Coy in re-play by 1 goal to nil. Casualties :- 2 O.R. to Dispersal Stn. for Demob.	
	4.1.19.		Casualties 2 O.R. to Dispersal Stn. for Debom.	
	5.1.19.		Church Parade C. of E. and other Services. Casualties :- 4 O.R. to Dispersal Stn. for Demob.	
	6.1.19.		RUGBY FOOTBALL. Battalion drew with 282 A.F.A. Bde SCORE 3 Points each. Casualties :- 4 O.R. to Dispersal Stn. for Demob.	
	6.1.19.		Casualties :- 5 O.R. To Dispersal Stn. for Demob.	
	7.1.19.		FOOTBALL Brigade inter-Battalion League Match v. 2nd London. RESULT. 2nd LONDONS. 4 Goals Q.W.R. 3 goals. Casualties :- 3 Other Ranks To Dispersal Stn. for Demob.	
	8.1.19.		Casualties :- 6 O.R. To Dispersal Stn. for Demob. 10 O.R. Reinforcements.	

Army Form C. 2118.

WAR DIARY
or
INTELLIGENCE SUMMARY.
(Erase heading not required.)

Instructions regarding War Diaries and Intelligence Summaries are contained in F. S. Regs. Part II. and the Staff Manual respectively. Title pages will be prepared in manuscript.

Place	Date	Hour	Summary of Events and Information	Remarks and references to Appendices
In the Field	9th Jany 1919		Casualties 5 O.R. To Dispersal Stn. for Demob.	
	10th.		Casualties :- 2 offrs. Lt. A.E.Clapham Demobilized. Rev. Christford Despatched to England for duty. 8 O.R. To Dispersal Stn. for Demob.	
	11th.		ASSOCIATION FOOTBALL Divisional Association Cup Match v. 168th Inf. Bde.H.Q. RESULT. 168th Inf. Bde. 3 Goals. Q.W.R. 1. Five of the Battalion Team were not present, owing to the Motor Transport proceeding from GENLY without them. Casualties :- 11 O.R. To Dispersal Stn. for Demob.	
	12th.		DIVISIONAL RUGBY FOOTBALL CUP. L.R.B. Scratch Match. ASSOCIATION FOOTBALL "D" Coy drew with "B"Coy in Brigade inter-Company Competition There was no score. Casualties :- 7 O.R. Demob.	
	13th.		ASSOCIATION FOOTBALL. "D" Coy beat "B" Coy in re-play by 3 goals to 1 goal. Casualties :- 6 O.R. To Demob. Camp. 1 Officer, Rev A.C.C. Lewis & 1 O.R. Reinforcements.	
	14th.		ASSOCIATION FOOTBALL Battalion drew with 169th Inf. Bde in Brigade League. There was no score. Casualties :- 1 O.R. Sick 1 Officer Capt. B.L. Miles to Dispersal Stn. for Demob.	
	15th.		TUG OF WAR v. 282 A.F.A. Brigade. Latter scratched. Casualties :- 1 Officer, Lt. S.L. Mann, Medical Board ordered 1 O.R. to Dispersal Stn. for Demob. 2 O.R. Reinforcements.	

Lieut Colonel
2/ Queens' Westminster Rifles

Army Form C. 2118.

WAR DIARY
or
INTELLIGENCE SUMMARY.
(Erase heading not required.)

Instructions regarding War Diaries and Intelligence Summaries are contained in F. S. Regs., Part II. and the Staff Manual respectively. Title pages will be prepared in manuscript.

Place	Date	Hour	Summary of Events and Information	Remarks and references to Appendices
In the Field	16th Jany 1919.		ASSOCIATION FOOTBALL "D" Coy v. 2nd LONDONS in Brigade inter-Coy SemiFinal - Latter scratched. Casualties :- 1 O.R. Demobilized.	
	17th.		ASSOCIATION FOOTBALL Battalion beat L.R.B. in Brigade inter Battn. League by 8 goals to nil. Casualties 2 O.R. To Dispersal Stn. for Demob.	
	18th.		Final of Brigade inter-Battn. TUG o' WAR v. L.R.B. Results :- Won catch weights Lost 100 stone team. Casualties :- 2nd Lt. R.C. HURST, struck off strength as Education Instructor A.O. XVIII 1918	
	19th.		Casualties :- 5 O.R. To Dispersal Stn. for Demob.	
	20th.		RUGBY FOOTBALL. Final of Brigade Rugby Football Competition. Result No score. Casualties :- 10 O.R. To Dispersal Stn. for Demob.	
	21st.		ASSOCIATION FOOTBALL "D" Coy beat Brigade H.Q. in inter-Company Competition by 2 goals to nil. Casualties :- 16 O.R. To Dispersal Stn. for Demob.	
	22nd.		BRIGADE BOXING COMPETITION Cpl. MASLIN scored a walk over in the heavy weights. Cpl. COLLINS won the Welter Weights. Rfn. Kramer won the Feather Weight. Casualties :- 2 O.R. Demobilized.	
	23rd.		Casualties :- 4 O.R. To Dispersal Stn. for Demob.	
	24th.		Casualties :- 2 O.R. To Dispersal Stn. for Demob.	
	25th.		Casualties :- 6 O.R. To Dispersal Stn. for Demob.	

Army Form C. 2118.

WAR DIARY
or
INTELLIGENCE SUMMARY.
(Erase heading not required.)

Instructions regarding War Diaries and Intelligence Summaries are contained in F. S. Regs., Part II. and the Staff Manual respectively. Title pages will be prepared in manuscript.

Place	Date	Hour	Summary of Events and Information	Remarks and references to Appendices
In the Field.	Jany 26th 1919.		Casualties 10 O.R. to Dispersal Stn. for Demob.	
	27th.		Casualties 7 O.R. To Dispersal Stn. for Demob.	
	28th.		Casualties 1 Officer, Lieut W.F.D. Young struck off Strength as Educational Instructor. A.O. XVIII 1918. 2 O.R. Despatched to Base for clerical Duties. 2 O.R. To Disp. Stn. for Demob.	
	29th.		Casualties. 1 Officer, Lt. W.H. GATFIELD, M.C. and 9 O.R. to Dispersal Stn. for Demob.	
	30th.		Casualties :- Nil.	
	31st.		Casualties :- 1 Officer, 2nd Lt. D Delaforce, Reinforcement	
			N.B. Throughout the month 2 days a week were allotted to Military Training when the weather permitted. On remaining week days the 1st hour was devoted to Military training. The rest of the morning was spent in Education classes for those who took the various subjects, while the non educationalists carried on fatigues.	
			Strength on 31.12.18. — — OFFICERS. O.R.	
			36 497	
			Less 7 165	
			29. 332	
			Add 2 13.	
			30. 345.	
			STRENGTH ON 31st January 1919.	

WAR DIARY
or
INTELLIGENCE SUMMARY.

(Erase heading not required.)

Army Form C. 2118.

1/16 London

Place	Date	Hour	Summary of Events and Information	Remarks and references to Appendices
Genly, Belgium.	1st Feby 19.		Demobilization continues at a good rate, many men being demobilised on leave. The Education scheme continues. Ground frozen and too hard for training or sports.	
	2nd "		Casualties :- 1 Offr (Lt. E. Coaker attchd 169th T.M.B.) and 1 O.R.Demobilized.	
			-- do --	
			Casualties :- 18 O.R. Demobilized	
	3rd "		-- do --	
			Casualties :- 2 O.R. Demobilized.	
	4th "		-- do --	
			Casualties :- N I L.	
	5th "		-- do --	
			Casualties :- 1 O.R. Demobilised.	
	6th "		Anniversary of formation of 56th Division. G.O.C. gave a Dinner to C.O's who were serving in Division at time of formation. Orders received to detail a draft of 10 Officers and all O.R. retainable in Army of occupation under A.O. XIV.	
			Casualties :- 1 Offr (2/Lt A.M.Smith) and 7 O.R. Demobilized, 1 O.R. Sick.	
	7th "		Battalion dinner and dance arranged in the evening.	
			Casualties 13 O.R. Demobilised, 1 O.R. Sick.	
	8th "		Preparation of draft.	
			Casualties :- 12 O.R. Demobilised 2 O.R. Sick.	

Army Form C. 2118.

WAR DIARY
or
INTELLIGENCE SUMMARY.
(Erase heading not required.)

Instructions regarding War Diaries and Intelligence Summaries are contained in F. S. Regs., Part II. and the Staff Manual respectively. Title pages will be prepared in manuscript.

1st QUEEN'S WESTMINSTER RIFLES

Place	Date	Hour	Summary of Events and Information	Remarks and references to Appendices
Genly, Belgium	9th Feby 19		Church Parades.	
			Casualties 2 Offrs, (Major H.F.Grizelle M.C. & Capt N.T.Thurston M.C. & 1 O.R. Demobilized. 1 O.R. Re-inforcements.	
	10th	"	Draft does not leave, and informed that it will probably not go for a fortnight.	
			Casualties :- 13 O.R. Demobilized 2 O.R. Reinforcements.	
	11th	"	Battalion reorganised in 2 Companies No 1(Draft) Capt. F.E.Whitby M.C. in charge. No 2 Coy. men eligible for demobilization, Lt V.G.Rayner M.C. in charge.	
			Casualties :- N I L.	
	12th	"	Roll forwarded of Officers and O.R. volunteering for Army of Occupation - 12 Officers 2 O.R.	
			Casualties :- 1 O.R. Sick, 1 O.R. Reinforcement.	
	13th	"	N I L.	
			Casualties :- 1 Offr (Lt J.B.Malthouse M.C.) and 3 O.R. Demobilized 1 O.R. sick.	
	14th	"	N I L.	
			Casualties 1 Offr (2/Lt S.E.Arber) and 14 O.R. Demobilized.	
	15th	"	N I L.	
			Casualties :- 1 O.R. Demobilized.	
	16th	"	Voluntary Church Service.	
			Casualties 2 O.R. Demobilized.	

Army Form C. 2118.

WAR DIARY
or
INTELLIGENCE SUMMARY.
(Erase heading not required.)

Instructions regarding War Diaries and Intelligence Summaries are contained in F. S. Regs., Part II. and the Staff Manual respectively. Title pages will be prepared in manuscript.

Place	Date	Hour	Summary of Events and Information	Remarks and references to Appendices
Genly, Belgium.	17th Feby 19		2 Officers and 50 O.R. proceeded to Mons Station as Guard and fatigue party, found from men for Army of Occupation	
	18th	"	Casualties :- 1 O.R. Sick, 1 O.R. other causes. 1 Officer (Lt.W.F.D.Young retaken on strength from 169 Inf.Bde.) & 1 O.R. Reinforcement.	
	19th	"	Casualties :- N I L.	
	20th	"	Casualties :- 9 O.R. other causes.	
	21st	"	Casualties :- 10 O.R. Demobilized.	
	22nd	"	Casualties :- 1 O.R. Demobilized 1 O.R. Reinforcement.	
	23rd	"	Casualties :- 2 O.R. Demobilized. No Church Service, all O.R. being employed.	
	24th	"	Casualties :- 3 O.R. Demobilized (including R.S.M.)	
		"	Casualties 2 O.R. Demobilized.	

Army Form C. 2118.

WAR DIARY
or
INTELLIGENCE SUMMARY.
(Erase heading not required.)

Instructions regarding War Diaries and Intelligence Summaries are contained in F. S. Regs., Part II. and the Staff Manual respectively. Title pages will be prepared in manuscript.

Place	Date	Hour	Summary of Events and Information	Remarks and references to Appendices
Genly, Belgium	25th Feby 19		N I L. Casualties :- N I L.	
"	26th "		N I L. Casualties :- 1 O.R. Demobilized.	
"	27th "		N I L. Casualties :- 8 O.R. Demobilized.	
"	28th "		N I L. Casualties :- 2 O.R. Demobilized.	
			Offrs. O.R.	
			Strength on 31/1/1919. 30 345	
			ADD 1 6	
			31 351	
			Less. 6 134	
			Strength on 28/2/1919. 25 217	

S. R. Davies
Lieut-Colonel
Commanding 1st QUEENS WESTMINSTER RIFLES.

WAR DIARY
or
INTELLIGENCE SUMMARY.

(Erase heading not required).

Army Form C. 2118.

Instructions regarding War Diaries and Intelligence Summaries are contained in F. S. Regs. Part II. and the Staff Manual respectively. Title pages will be prepared in manuscript.

Place	Date	Hour	Summary of Events and Information	Remarks and references to Appendices
Genly, Belgium.	1919. March 1st.		There is nothing to report in the doings of the Battalion. The rate of demobilization rather slows down. 4 Officers and 60 O.Rs. are found at MONS for a Guard at the station. This leaves very few men with the Battalion at GENLY. It is only just possible to find the necessary duties and fatigues by allowing only one batmen to two subaltern officers. The transport is gradually getting rid of its horses, this making demobilization of the personnel possible. Casualties 12 Other Ranks Demobilized.	
	2nd.	NIL.	Casualties 7 O.R. Demobilized.	
	3rd.	NIL.		
	4th.	NIL.	Casualties - 2nd Lieut R.C.PALMER sent for duty with 183rd Prisoner of War COMPANY.	
	5th.	NIL.	Casualties 2 O.R. Sick. 2 O.R. taken on strength of 189th Bde H.Q., 2 O.R. retaken on strength of Battalion from 189th Bde H.Q.	
	6th.	NIL.	Casualties 3 O.R. taken on strength of Division.	
	7th.	NIL.	Casualties 1 O.R. Demobilized, 1 O.R. sent to Base for duty as clerk.	
	8th.	NIL.	Casualties 1 O.R. Sick, 20 O.R. Demobilized.	
	9th.	NIL.		
	10th.	NIL.	Casualties, 1 O.R. sent to HELFAUT for duty with Special Bde R.E.	
	11th.		Guard at MONS STATION returned to Battalion. Warning order received for despatch of Draft to 20th Battalion K.R.R.C. Casualties, NIL.	
	12th & 13th	NIL.		

Army Form C. 2118.

WAR DIARY
or
INTELLIGENCE SUMMARY.
(Erase heading not required.)

Instructions regarding War Diaries and Intelligence Summaries are contained in F.S. Regs., Part II. and the Staff Manual respectively. Title pages will be prepared in manuscript.

Place	Date	Hour	Summary of Events and Information	Remarks and references to Appendices
Genly, Belgium.	1919. March. 14th		Draft of 10 Officers and 64 Other Ranks despatched to 20th Battalion K.R.R.C. with Army of Occupation (Officers:- Capt F.E.WHITBY, M.C., Capt G.W.AVONS, M.C., M.M., Lieut T.H.JENKIN, Lieut O.A.M.EATON, M.C., Lieut W.F.D.YOUNG, Lieut E.C.HAYES, Lieut W.H.ORMISTON M.C., 2nd Lieut A.C.G.FRASER, 2nd Lieut H.J.SIMPSON, 2nd Lieut S.F.DEAN) 1 O.R. Demobilized.	
	15th		NIL. Casualties 1 O.R. Taken on strength of 56th Division.	
	16th		NIL. 1 Officer (2nd Lieut J.A.N. WEBB, M.C.) Demobilized.	
	17th		NIL.	
	18th		NIL. Casualties 1 O.R. Sick.	
	19th		Warning Order received to move to JEMAPPES AREA on the 22nd. Casualties 3 Officers (Capt J.B. BABER, M.C., Lieuts J.E.S.GOLDING & D.C. BEADELL) and 4 O.R. Demobilized.	
	20th		Warning received to be prepared to move tomorrow.	
	21st		Billeting Party took over new area at QUAREGNON. News received that Battalion would move to QUAREGNON on the 23rd. Casualties 1 O.R. Sick.	
	22nd		NIL.	
	23rd		Battalion moved to QUAREGNON in the afternoon. 5 Lorries allotted to the Battalion to move stores. Thus ended a very enjoyable stay of nearly 4 months at GENLY.	
	24th		NIL. Billets fairly comfortable in new area. Draft of 31 O.R. left to join 2nd Battalion QUEENS WESTMINSTER RIFLES at CALAIS.	

Army Form C. 2118.

WAR DIARY
or
INTELLIGENCE SUMMARY.
(Erase heading not required.)

Instructions regarding War Diaries and Intelligence Summaries are contained in F. S. Regs., Part II. and the Staff Manual respectively. Title pages will be prepared in manuscript.

Place	Date	Hour	Summary of Events and Information	Remarks and references to Appendices
Quaregnon, Belgium.	1919. March 25th.	NIL.	Lieut P.I.WORTHINGTON proceeded to join 2nd Battn QUEENS WESTMINSTER RIFLES.	
	26th.		Owing to a case of smallpox being reported in JEMAPPES, all ranks were vaccinated today.	
	27th. 28th. 29th. 30th.	NIL.		
	31st.	NIL.	Casualties. Casualties. 2nd Lieut S.F.SIMONDS and 3 O.R. proceeded to HALTE REPAS MONS for duty and were transferred as from this date to 2nd Battn QUEENS WESTMINSTER RIFLES.	

```
                              Offrs    O.R.
STRENGTH on 28/2/19.           25      217.
ADD.                            -        2.
                               25      219.
LESS                           17      155.
                                8       64.
ADD, attached from 169th T.M.B. 1        3
TOTAL strength on 31/3/19.      9       67.
```

P. R. Lawrie
Lieut-Colonel.
Commanding 1/16th Battn THE LONDON REGIMENT
(1st QUEENS WESTMINSTER RIFLES).

Army Form C. 2118.

WAR DIARY
or
INTELLIGENCE SUMMARY.
(Erase heading not required.)

Instructions regarding War Diaries and Intelligence Summaries are contained in F.S. Regs., Part II. and the Staff Manual respectively. Title pages will be prepared in manuscript.

Place	Date	Hour	Summary of Events and Information	Remarks and references to Appendices
QUAREGNON, BELGIUM.	April 1919.		This month was spent in QUAREGNON. It was originally understood that the Cadre would go to the United Kingdom on the 12th. This was not, however, so. No information as to our date of departure could be obtained. There were practically no facilities for Sports or Recreation. This fact, coupled with the uncertainty of our stay, inevitably caused great boredom for all ranks.	
			All remaining "retainable" Other Ranks were either despatched or transferred (on paper) to 2/16th Battn. LONDON REGIMENT, and all remaining demobilizable Officers proceeded for dispersal.	
			Battalion reduced to Cadre strength.	
			Lieut-Colonel E.R. SAVILL, D.S.O., M.C. proceeded to United Kingdom on short leave on the 26th inst. and Capt & Adjt. H.S. PRICE, M.C. assumed command of the Battalion.	

STRENGTH on 31st March 1919.

	Officers.	Other Ranks.
	9	67.
ADD	-	5.
	9	72.
LESS	4	31.
STRENGTH on 30th April 1919.	5	41.

1st QUEEN'S WESTMINSTER RIFLES.

30th April 1919.

H.S. Price Captain.
Commanding 1/16th Battn LONDON REGIMENT.
(1st QUEENS WESTMINSTER RIFLES).

Army Form C. 2118.

WAR DIARY
or
INTELLIGENCE SUMMARY.
(Erase heading not required.)

Instructions regarding War Diaries and Intelligence Summaries are contained in F.S. Regs. Part II. and the Staff Manual respectively. Title pages will be prepared in manuscript.

Place	Date	Hour	Summary of Events and Information	Remarks and references to Appendices
Quaregnon, Belgium.	1919. March 25th.	NIL.	Lieut P.I.WORTHINGTON proceeded to join 2nd Battn QUEENS WESTMINSTER RIFLES.	
	26th		Owing to a case of smallpox being reported in JEMAPPES, all ranks were vaccinated today.	
	27th) 28th) 29th) 30th)	NIL.		
	31st.	NIL.	Casualties. Casualties. 2nd Lieut S.F.SIMONDS and 3 O.R. proceeded to HALTE REPAS MONS for duty and were transferred as from this date to 2nd Battn QUEENS WESTMINSTER RIFLES.	

```
                                    Offrs    O.R.
STRENGTH on 28/2/19.                  25      217.
ADD.                                   1        2.
                                      25      219.
LESS                                  17      155.
                                       8       64.
ADD, attached from 189th T.M.B.        1        3
TOTAL strength on 31/3/19.             9       67.
```

P. R. Lewis
Lieut-Colonel.
Commanding 1/16th Battn THE LONDON REGIMENT.
(1st QUEENS WESTMINSTER RIFLES).

Army Form C. 2118.

WAR DIARY
or
INTELLIGENCE SUMMARY.

(Erase heading not required.)

Unit:- 1/16th. LONDON REGIMENT
QUEENS WESTMINSTER RIFLES.

MAY

Instructions regarding War Diaries and Intelligence Summaries are contained in F.S. Regs., Part II. and the Staff Manual respectively. Title pages will be prepared in manuscript.

Place	Date	Hour	Summary of Events and Information	Remarks and references to Appendices
	1st.		2nd. Lieut. G.DELAFORCE now administered by the 9th. LONDON REGIMENT to which he was posted.	
			1. O.R. despatched to Dispersal Station for demobilization.	
			2 O.Rs. despatched to 2/16th. LONDON REGIMENT to which they were posted as from 7/4/19.	
			15 O.Rs. taken on strength as from 15/5/19 from No I Area H.Q. where they will remain employed.	
			1 O.R. not accepted as interpreter on H.Q. Rhine Army. Now on strength of this Unit.	
	11th.		Lieut-Colonel S.R.SAVILL D.S.O. M.C. returned from leave and re-assumed command.	
	12th.		I.O.R. on strength of 2/16th LONDON REGIMENT despatched for duty with the 56th. Divisional Pool of animals.	
	17th.		4 O.Rs. despatched to Dispersal Station for Demobilization. The Cadre entrained at JEMAPPES in the morning for ANTWERP. Train due to arrive at 1900 hours but did not do so till-	
	18th.		0400 hrs. Detrained 0700 hrs. Left vehicles on quay under a guard and marched to Embarkation Camp.	
	19-23rd.		At Embarkation Camp. Men allowed passes to ANTWERP till midnight nightly.	
	22nd		Cadre dinner at Cafe Verlaert.	
	24th.		Personnel embarked on S.S.ABKATH for United Kingdom. Axles on barge P.D. 13.	

Strength on 26/4/19.
```
              Offrs.   O.Rs.
                5      41
Add             -      16
                5      57
less            1       5
                4      52
```

Nominal Roll of Cadre of 4 Officers and 35 O.Rs. attached.
17 O.Rs. still employed overseas.

Commanding 1/16th. LONDON REGIMENT
Lieut-Colonel.
26.5.19